Love, Truth
&
CommunIslamic
Sociopaths

A Love Letter to the Lost

CLIFFORD JAMES

This Book is Dedicated to My Wonderful Wife Angie

I love her more than life itself.

Special Thanks to Kris "Moto" Cover Art

&

Design and Nick Redwood, Editor

Foreword

When I saw Glenn Beck for the first time I was moved. I saw somebody doing something that needed to be done. He really was the inspiration for this book. I just thought about who was listening. I knew that most of his audience was people like him and that left out a whole segment of our population. I am older than Glenn but relate to people much younger than either of us. Then there are people of my generation, baby boomers, ex-hippies and ex-drug addicts. But this book is really written for the young people now. Not everybody that has followed rock bands is unsalvageable- nor anyone brought up in a single parent home. Our new Tea Party patriots of the 2010's are aging and we need young people to rise up. This is why I am writing this book.

This book is written for people like me. This book's brevity and simplicity is just a way to make this mountain of information as easy to digest as possible for the people I want to speak to. Most grew up in single parent homes. I'm attempting to speak to them and hopefully enlighten them as to what can be. In other words, Glenn Beck has his audience; I have mine. Glenn Beck's father and grandfather gave him good role models; mine did not. Every ounce of maturity has been strained out of me by one disappointment after another, one crisis after another. I have cried more than I have smiled. The last twenty years have been nothing but hardship and I'm sure that I'm not alone.

The fact that I think I'm not alone is what prompted me to write this book. There are other people out there that have lived much as I have lived and for me to have found the way out and not share it with them is unthinkable. You see them everywhere. The guys have skinheads or long hair. The girls dress kinda slutty. They have tattoos. They are decent people but have not found a forum to express their genuine love for others. There's simply too much hatred in their world. These people are generally a bit independent and when they hear the voice of reason they usually resist but are open enough to relate to someone like me- one of them. I am here, I understand.

I am starting this book with a treatise on sociopathy because it is the foundation for the whole work. People living in a pampered society do not realize that there are profoundly evil people around them and they need to know how to recognize them. The whole of this book will deal with sociopaths, in their many cultures and types- and how they affect our lives and world. It will also deal with how to identify them- and what to do about it.

I love you and I have put my heart in this book for you to see. Read it and know you are loved

CONTENTS

Foreword

Introduction: The Sociopaths among us and Why they're Here   VIII

I.   ON LOVE & INTROSPECTION

II.   ON COMMUNISLAMIC LEADERSHIP

III. ON GOVERNMENT & MEDIA

IV. ON THE TRUTH SETTING YOU FREE

Introduction

The Sociopaths Among us and Why They're Here

What is a sociopath?

Sociopaths are predators. They have no empathy, for anyone. They have no conscience. They have no bonding ability. They can take on a "running partner" or even a wife but this is only a temporary measure to use the other. Sociopaths are usually, but not exclusively, of the masculine gender. There are exceptions; I have a close relative who is a female sociopath and I have met others. They are usually attractive, educated enough to move in many circles, and are tireless opportunists. Sociopaths do not speak frequently. They listen for opportunities. When they do speak it is usually with some content. They have a sense of humor that is witty and funny and can even be self-depreciating. Nonetheless, the sociopath will display childishness in the things they want and do. At the furthest extreme, child rape can be common and an expression of their hatred for humans. They also seem to feed on strife and conflict. This is used in a 'divide and conquer' kind of approach, using friendship to gain control over people and situations resulting in some monetary or social benefit. Sociopaths, oddly, given their hatred for people in general, seem to desire high standing in social settings. This is undoubtedly because they believe this will help them meet their desire for control. This is why they seek position and privilege. Sociopaths can be charming and engaging. They are often fun to be around- even sexy and clever.

They can mimic empathy and caring often much more convincingly than those who actually feel these things. They grew up aware that the other children received things they did not. And they learned why that was; the other children could give and receive love. They studied them. That is how they learn how to mimic these kinds of emotions.

One thing I have noticed is that sociopaths are cowards. Most everyone I have met (with the exception of one) is afraid of physical confrontation. This is evidenced in the way the communist sociopaths abhor confrontation. They don't want to be called out for the things they do. This is because they are WRONG.

For some years now we have been raising sociopaths by the things we have been teaching our children. Most of this has come in through the psychiatric community. Teaching children not to feel guilt is telling them that they can feel good about themselves regardless of their behavior. This is raising a sociopath. If your children have been taught these things, you bought the lie. That's what Eve did. It wasn't an apple; it was, "my opinion is as valid as this God's opinion", the fruit or outgrowth of the other tree- the tree of your own opinion.

There are two kinds of sociopaths.

The non-circumstantial (or, organic) and the created. The organic sociopath is seemingly born that way. There is no external reason why. The reason I call them organic, even though this may be unfair, is the fact that I have never seen a repentant or a rehabilitated sociopath and have studied them since I was fifteen. The created sociopaths are living in a milieu that supports and necessitates their self centeredness. There is hope for the created sociopath because they started out with some semblance of humanity. The organic sociopath will always be that way. If anyone has met an organic sociopath they might notice that they all have exactly the same personality. They have the same patronizing sense of compassion, phony sense of humor and the same opportunistic self interest.

Do they organize and how do you know their organizations?

Yes- they do organize and their organizations can be seen because they always bear bad fruit. The only beneficiaries are themselves. One must look at anything the sociopaths do for its development, where it is going, not just where it is now. Sociopaths are master manipulators. They will prepare their plans at great length. The political world is full of sociopaths. This is natural, given their lust for power and control. They are pretty much the only people that can lie while maintaining perfect eye contact. I have watched many politicians from President Obama and his wife on down do this. Yes, I'm saying that many of our current leaders and lawmakers in Washington are sociopaths and pathological liars!

We have choices and sociopath instated communism relieves them.

In a communistic society all action and behavior is dictated by a government that restricts choices and financial activity. Children are taken and indoctrinated and even the number of them is monitored. The United States has been slowly incorporating this into our natural mindset for many years, i.e. the government program of HEADSTART. It started out with a pre-kindergarten program to assist less educated families in preparing their children for school, and was very soon broadened to include ALL children. In Christian belief and true democracy, choices are what we are supposed to make and have. The choices separate the "wheat from the chaff." In a democracy people govern themselves. The choices you make prove who you are. Either you choose to love people (and Jesus Christ) or not. Under communism these choices are removed and the people simply follow the demands of the state, and their necessities are provided for their compliance. Sociopaths think people are stupid.

Most communist leaders are organic sociopaths. Not all of their followers are sociopathic. Many are simply buying the lie- carefully crafted to deceive them. During the sixties, our music and culture became totally communist. Communists are right; people are sheep. The sheep will not be beneficiaries of the communist environment, even though they were used to implement it. They will simply be worker bees or put to death, but are duped into believing they will be in "the King's court." President Barack Obama is one of these. I have known one black sociopath and I'm sure he is far from alone but many sociopaths who are white like to believe that they are part of a master race and that when they come into power they will impose a racist agenda and cleanse the world of, what they believe to be, inferior races. Hitler tried to do this in his own lifetime. Satan often overplays his hand. This is where most black communists are short sighted. They, in their acquired, defensive superiority complex, fail to notice, that in the upper echelon of this socialist/communist/fascist society, blacks are conspicuously absent. This is a heartbreaking, but obvious fact. So many black people- the very ones that have been duped into promoting communism- will be eliminated.

Sociopaths and communists answer only to themselves.

This is why sociopaths and communists hate the concept of God, because the concept of a God decrees that we not only love one and another but that we serve God alone and not man. God in many ways demands we practice rigorous honesty- something the sociopath cannot do. They are all pathologic liars.

They want world domination

This is when they organize. They want this so they can fully use humans for their own pleasures. They have a utopia in mind and that utopia will look much like the Rome of Caligula.

They are cruel.

The idea of torturing, beating and raping is exciting to many of them. Che' Guevara is an example of this. He loved the idea of becoming a "killing machine".

Sociopaths have a deep seated hatred for all that is human. They believe humans are here for their use. They will use people for whatever they want and then quickly discard them. If you have ever encountered a sociopath you will notice that they are angered and frustrated with anyone they have already used that continues to try to maintain friendship with them. Sociopaths will try to ignore and marginalize them until they just go away.

They want to deify themselves.

This is sociopathy at its furthest extreme and the most satanic. A few sociopaths are concerned with things like world domination but more are focused on gratifying their immediate desires (childish). The former are megalomaniacal. This extreme sociopath wants the world to worship him. The Russian composer/pianist Alexander Scriabin displayed this kind of megalomaniacal behavior when he decided he was greater than Christ and insisted on getting into a boat and then walking on the water outside it as he had convinced himself of his miraculous powers. After being rescued he began preaching to the fishermen. He also said that Jesus was communist. This is all motivated by disdain and anger towards other people in general and the desire to be worshiped. This was evidenced in 2009 when several schools began reporting a little sing-along for the schoolchildren that went, "Mmm mmm mmm Barack Hussien Obama, equal work for equal pay," along with many other lyrics. If carried out, those little kids' admiration would eventually become adult worship. Saddam Hussein, Mao Tse Tung, Joseph Stalin and many other communist leaders have put up giant statues and pictures of themselves all over their country in praise of themselves. Currently Vladimir Putin is circulating videos of himself wrestling on the mat, shirtless (ick!) horseback riding and in public places with some of the most beautiful women.

Islam and Sociopathy:

How Muslim men are raised.

In most Muslim countries and/or families the boys have very little feminine contact besides their mothers and sisters, as women are not supposed to communicate with men outside their immediate family. This helps surround them with a "boys club" impenetrable by anyone- especially anyone who could second guess them on any decision they want to make.

In some countries/cultures Muslim men even go so far as to remove the clitoris of their girls so they do not feel any pressure to pleasure their mates. They know they would desire someone else if given the opportunity because the girls are purchased, meaning there is no real love in their existence. They make women wear stifling face covers in the heat of the desert so they do not have to worry about other men desiring their women. They restrict and control the women in the family at every turn. Their wives, mothers and daughters are slaves. In many Muslim countries women have sought peace through suicide.

In the Bible, God gave Adam his woman because "it is not good for man to be alone." Why is this? Man needed someone to provide balance in the decision-making since God did not indicate at that time that it was for procreation. He decreed that later after man committed sin, when God said, "Be fruitful and multiply." Women, obviously, are to be a companion not a servant.

Why do they hate women and Jews?

The root of why they hate women with such venom is grounded in the spiritual fact that they are descendant sons of Ishmael, the son of the bondwoman Hagar. They hate the bondwoman for, well, being the bondwoman. This has been handed down, for generations, in the form of an attitude. In western culture (which has been traditionally Judeo-Christian), a man is the spiritual leader of his family. A man is to serve his family and guide them to spiritual fulfillment. Handling the responsibility of doing this is part of what matures him. In Islam a man is served by his family. His wife is his servant. His boys are to be trained. His girls are to be sold. You should be able to see, now, how growing up this way makes the Muslim man a created sociopath. Because of this, he never becomes an adult. In psychology we call this stunted growth and development.

This is also the root of their intense hatred for the Jews. Jews are the sons of Isaac, considered the first born of Abraham. Ishmael was Abraham's true firstborn- the bondwoman Hagar's son. Muslim origins believe they should have inherited all God's promises to Abraham, as firstborn "of the law". They are taught from birth that Jews are pigs and not to be trusted. I'm not saying Muslim men look at a Jew and think, "I hate you because you think you're Abraham's firstborn." But since 1948, when the Jews returned to their homeland and it began to prosper, when it had previously been all but desolate, the Arabs inhabiting nearby Palestine were angered. How did prosperity come to the region- and even it had begun to blossom? It didn't just randomly happen...this was predicted by Isaiah in the Hebrew Scriptures. Their hatred, again, is handed down in the form of an attitude that is inherited from generation to generation.

Why they hate freedom.

They hate freedom because freedom provides choices and choices are exactly what both communism and Islam remove. Choices force one to fully disclose what your motives are, because they can be seen in the decisions you make. Freedom is the enemy. Sociopaths want total control.

They hate God for denying them what they think they deserve. They instead want a man-centered world with man-inspired gifts. Just look at what they see as their paradise: the Muslim man who dies in battle will get seventy-two virgins, although their short sighted followers don't connect this with their leaders teaching that they should not look at a woman lustfully. This is obviously a 'man-centered' final resting ground for them. In the Jewish and Christian scriptures our Heaven is not disclosed, it just says, "Man has not seen nor heard what the Lord has prepared for you."

Why Islam is not a religion.

Islamists decree that apostates from their religion be put to death and the same with anyone who dares to insult or blaspheme the prophet Mohammed. This in and of itself indicates that the founder of Islam did not think that the religion would hold up under scrutiny. Islam uses the Quran as its main guidebook, and the Hadith- the latter being a book containing sayings of Mohammed collected by his wives and friends. Between them they have come away with the ideas that they must conquer the world and make Shariah the law of the world. It is also the only supposed religion that mandates the extermination of a group of people. These people obviously are the Jews and other "people of the book", which are the Christians. Islam is also an autocratic philosophy dictating all behaviors and removing choices. Simply put, people control. Does that sound like sociopathy and communism enough? People under Shariah law answer only to Islamic dictates, as it is a man-made god and a man-made law.

Scripture states, "The thief (referring to the devil) comes but for to steal, kill and destroy", and Jesus says, "I have come to give *life,* and that more abundantly." The difference between the two deities described is painfully obvious. They are to die for their god, while the Christian God died for His people.

Why they're here

If one reads the Old Testament, they will notice on multiple occasions that God's people "rose up to play" and harsh things subsequently happened to them. This is not to indicate that "playing" was a problem, but that when they did, they would forget their God and start to worship false idols (ie. the 'golden calf'). At this point, they were slain in the wilderness or taken into captivity into Babylon. No fewer than three times the Israelites were taken into harsh slavery, according to the Hebrew Scriptures. *These were God's beloved Israelites!* Each time, they would start adapting themselves to the ways of the heathen people and their gods. Scripture states that people become like the god/gods they worship. Time and time again, the Israelites were lured into idol worship, and subsequently into slavery.

Throughout history, nations and peoples whom have received the God of the Bible into their hearts have prospered. If you follow them further into their cycle of belief into apostasy you will see that as they begin to seek other "gods" they would begin to lose prosperity. You can see this in Rome, as it was once the world's superpower, and now just another state. France and Germany, ditto.

England, once the nation who boasted that "the sun never sets on its shores," also had fallen into abject poverty by the end of the nineteenth century. It was just earlier in that century that British people began to become spiritually dead and very decadent, churches were empty and the people going were older and just going through the motions. This is referenced in Christ's letter to the Church of Sardis in the seven Churches in Revelation. A dead church to Christ is as repulsive as the decadence of Weimar

Germany in the 1930's (we all know how that turned out). As they all lost faith, they also lost blessings.

Just look at the 1950's in America and how prosperous we were. And then came the 'falling away' 1960's and 1970's, where poverty began to rise. With the 1980's came a revival of Christianity and a bit of a prosperous renaissance. Then came the 1990's and certainly the 2000 decade, where our rejection of God came to the forefront. So now look at us! I'm just waiting for the day when "In God We Trust" is taken off of our currency. Economically we are falling fast.

The current Islamic takeover of Europe is not God's judgment; it's actually His providence. In slavery people will, by necessity, learn obedience. Undisciplined people are not ready to steward their inheritance. Europe has not been following God's teaching for some time now. Post-enlightenment Europe was too smart for that. Not only secularism, but also the anti-God socialism is now the state of affairs in almost all of Europe. They are, just now, noticing how Islamic they have become.

The current state of America seems to reflect the plight of Israel centuries ago and Europe in the 1800's and 1900's. Americans began as a God-worshipping people and prospered more than any nation in history. For most of the twentieth century Americans have slowly been taken in by the enemy's philosophies and values. Often this starts as something innocuous as celebrity worship (yes this is worship), sports fanaticism or life revolving around a supped-up car, but develops into other man- centered and Godless focuses, which are all materialistic in nature. Idol worship metamorphosizes into habitual indulgences like pornography and infidelity. And of course, money (which is the root of all evil) becomes their god. People who have many pets and spend most of their time catering to them, while neglecting attention to their family/close friends, are doing what the scriptures refer to as "worshiping the creation rather than the creator". In our media-driven society we now have the ability to entertain ourselves with almost anything we want. This leads to decadent behavior, and becomes what we worship. Television itself can not only distract us from following God but can be a form of worship. Where there's dependence, there's dominance; just look at S&M culture. Decadence is not freedom; it's the opposite: its slavery! A people enslaved in their minds will go into slavery in the flesh. We follow what we worship, period.

People in Europe and the United States are slowly migrating into slavery. What starts out as protective helmet and seatbelt laws soon become food and speech monitoring. Remember: watch anything the sociopaths do for where it is going.

The fact is that sociopaths are living among us and we must combat them with truth because they are profoundly evil. But we must realize at the same time, through their manipulative behavior, we learn more about who God *doesn't* want His children to be. Through these peoples' control, He teaches us obedience. God lets the sun shine on both the good and the evil because the evil have a reason to be here too. You are being molded- into something beautiful. These are but the tools used to mold you. Fight the good fight. Jesus told us, "When you see these things" (ie. sociopathic takeover), "do not be troubled as these things must take place".

Clifford James

I. ON LOVE & INTROSPECTION

Chapter 1 Where Have all the Cowboys Gone?

A friend of mine, Sandra, said she once went to see Eddie Murphy live and said he walked onstage, stood in the very front and simply said "White men". She said the entire audience roared. I would too. This is all it takes.

In the eighties, I couldn't help but notice that most of the really pretty girls went for the black guys and asked my girlfriend why and she said it was because they were more masculine than white guys. I agreed. I was a bodybuilder training in Oxnard, CA, and most of my training buddies were black, Hispanic or Oxnard Police dept. I just couldn't stomach making friends with most other white guys because I had nothing in common with them. All they talked about was sports. I mean I am well aware that men differ and one man's fun is another man's torture. I'm good with that.

Since then I have noticed that black men have joined the ranks of emasculate know nothings and there is a real void in any search for a real man in America. I would hate to be a girl in the present climate.

Just look at the present state of the Republican party. What is this "Mama Grizzly's" stuff Sarah Palin is expounding? Sarah Palin, Ann Coulter, Michelle Malkin, Sharron Angle and Michele Bachmann are now the men in our forest and these have to cut the trees while the men are......watching football. Even Megyn Kelly has joined the ranks and proven herself a real stud.

Look at how the average male in America expresses himself. If he isn't acting just plain goofy (see: "The Office"), he is putting on his pseudo-masculine "tough guy" mask and talking about feminine conquests or ball games. Neither of these things really speak to anyone but other males that this guy is a real man. Mmmm, other males. Y'know I made the observation a long time ago that guys who love women with big breasts and have blond hair, really just want arm pieces. For, well...other guys to see. And why do they care what other guys see? I don't really know. I guess this makes me an unusual kind of guy. I don't really care if the guys over there think I'm the cool guy with the hot girl or if they think I'm a real nerd. I think this is healthy. I'm free.

So what is it that determines what a real man is? I'm sure the answer to this varies, but to most men it would be measured in the form of sexual prowess or combat ability. I strongly disagree with this but just for playing 'develular' advocacy let's say this is it. Does the normal American man even live up to this short-sighted measure? I think not. Most men, as I have found from talking to many girls, simply pounce and chase their own gratification. There are exceptions; I am one. I am a pleaser. I often neglect my own gratification for the girl's. So let's take combat. Sorry, my observations tell me that almost all men when confronted with a hostile person are immediately petrified and seek any way out of the situation. This is not to say that picking a fight is good, but when confronted with someone who has already expressed a desire to do you or your friend(s) harm, a real man must be prepared to defend their loved ones and protect them. Today's man is a swaggering bullshitter afraid of his own shadow. This is going to hurt...but a man that can't be faithful to commitments is a coward.

Another thing pushing real manliness into the shadows is the current state of unemployment and entitlements handed those not working. The modern man can sit on unemployment for as long as 99 weeks and frequently manage to get Social Security benefits with a simple backache. A new report says that one in seven

Americans are receiving food stamps. The man who doesn't provide for himself cannot be much of a father (or much of a man).

Just how much crime in America do you think is directly a result of crappy fathering? Think about that! If fathers were mature enough to parent the way that it works (which always takes genuine heartfelt involvement), crime would shrink to unnoticeable levels.

I've already stated that I do not believe that sexual prowess or combat ability are the true measure of manliness, so what is? Let me throw this at you. The measure of a man is his ability to be faithful to his commitments. How many men do you know that can do this? How many men these days can even be honest? If a man can live up to a commitment to protect, provide for his family and to be faithful to his wife, isn't he living up to his "manliness" requirements in all these areas?

So what is it that causes so many men in modern America to fall short of living up to the expectations that women (and even other men) have of them? Let's start with his addiction to television watching. What is manly about being glued to a TV screen most of the day, even if it is watching other boys playing ball games? A man that reads the sports page for an hour in the morning, then goes to work and discusses new recruits and draft picks with his buddies, then goes home and turns on the TV and takes in a three hour ball game is good for his family in what way? His wife is in the kitchen talking on the phone with her friends; his kids are in their room or outside playing.

Don't get me wrong- I'm not trying to say that ball games are bad or that someone who has discovered they have a talent playing them is bad for pursuing a career in sports. I was a competitive bodybuilder for ten years. I also boxed for fourteen years and studied Thai boxing in Hollywood off and on for six years. When I boxed, I read Ring Magazine cover to cover and watched as many fights as I could. When I stopped boxing I stopped reading Ring Magazine. When I was a competitive bodybuilder I read Muscle and Fitness and Flex magazine and even was in those magazines myself. When I stopped competing, I stopped reading muscle magazines. I think sports are good for kids, as they teach them how to interact with each other within the boundaries of the rules of the game being played. Good...for kids.

For dad however, I do have a problem with it. A man is supposed to be the spiritual leader of his family. He, in Judeo-Christian culture, is to bring his family into spiritual fullness. What if he raises his son to be a pro basketball player, but has not instilled in him the things to make him independent, honest, loving and trustworthy? Has he done his job?

The problem really is that so many kids these days are brought up in single parent homes and do not have a reliable father figure. They get into sports simply for the fame and money (and occasionally an escape from 'hell') and are not true lovers of the game for the games' sakes. It is all about the wrong kind of conquests. Girls, money and personal fame are not going to make someone reliable, trustworthy and honest. This is not the goal of most young men. Just look at how every time there is a 'shoving match' on the baseball field the whole stadium goes bananas. I say 'shoving match,' because this is all it ever is. They're wanna-be tough guys. Sissies.

There are many things in our culture that distract us from realizing our role in our families and our friendships. Yes...I said in our friendships. If you truly care for someone, be it a family member or a good friend, do you not want the best for them? Of course you do. Then why sit idly by while they piss their life away?

The reason I singled out sports fanaticism so quickly (given the multitude of other things I could have used) is that I see this as one of the most destructive forces currently distracting American men from their responsibilities. Anybody hear of "football widows?" These are women whose husbands are all but deceased in front of their beloved televised games. I already know; I'm going to make a lot of enemies here. Somebody has to say it. A grown man that sits and watches other boys play ball games during all his free time is a man that has something kinda unhealthy going on! I'm just sayin.'

How do you suppose a man would respond to a friend coming to him and saying 'Hey buddy, do you know your family is largely estranged from you and watching sports consumes all your time? Do you know that your family knows nothing of the Bible and your kids are not being equipped with the things they will need as adults because you have stopped growing yourself?" He would probably be quite angered- and maybe cease to be your friend. I would like to know if you agree with me. If so, what do you think makes a grown man so fanatically absorbed in something that is just a game?

In ancient Rome after its decline had started, according to Gibbon, author of "The Decline and Fall of the Roman Empire", there were two teams, one the blues, and the other the greens. All of Rome followed these teams and would get in fights in their drinking places over the superiority of their chosen team. The entire country was enthralled by this game and its participants. Does this sound familiar? So this was a civilization in decline. Guess what?...So is this.

Why are sports a part of every news broadcast? I want to know the news- dammit! I don't care what the Jets are doing. It's obvious someone does, and they are numerous. I think Superbowl Sunday is a good day to read the Bible to your family.

However, given my distain for males, a lovely black haired beauty named Nancy I lived with in Seattle briefly (who is a Christian and I was totally in love with) kept trying to convince me to go to men's church meetings; I resisted. Also, I met a wonderful guy named Nick at the coffee shop I go to who I saw reading his Bible and started talking to. He took an interest in this book as I was writing it and has been helping me by editing it. As a matter a fact he has gotten so involved with this book that his contributions became essential! This book would not be the same without his input! Nick is a football coach. I think someone is trying to tell me something.

Baseball is, I know, the all-american sport but is following it, instead of playing it, good for anyone except the players? Who benefits from this? Not your wife. Not your kids. Not even you. I really think trying to get a man to stop following sports would be just like trying to get him to stop smoking. He would be caught in the basement with the sports page or outside on his cell phone talking to his buddies, catching up on all the events he had missed.

We all must remember the saying by Edmund Burke: "All it takes for evil to triumph is for good men to do nothing." While we have been laughing, being silly and "entertaining ourselves to death," we have given strength to evil.

And we must know that not voting IS voting. You have voted by omission.

It's no wonder that Cass Sunstein and other communist sociopaths refer to the modern American males as 'Homer Simpsons.' Goofy-acting, wanna-be tough guys. Look- I really think they're right. You want to know what else I think? I'll bet not at this point, but you're getting it anyway.

It is my firm belief that these pampered, over-confident, under-educated know nothings and even-do-lesses are going to go into slavery. You don't think that's where this kind of people are going? Look around you at the political climate. These guys won't. You see socialism creeping in at every turn. Where do you think this is progressing? Trust me: it *is* progressing. The sociopaths that have *accuratly* identified these simpering wanna-be men, know exactly what they want and how to get there. And have you seen and heard these guys? Cass Sunstein, John Holdren or Eric Holder? Sissies all! I think Homer Simpson actually might be part of the problem. Look at how men are portrayed on television: silly-acting goofballs with handy one-liners at every turn! I have never watched this kind of stupid entertainment. I have never owned a television until recently; I watch the news.

Please don't get me wrong: I'm not trying to say I've always been some noble super male. No way, baby! When I was getting ready before bodybuilding contests, was I approachable by anyone? No. I played in bands for many years. Was I anyone's friend before going onstage in Hollywood? No. And believe me: there's a lot more than this I'm going to disclose later. I've been a bad man---and I know it. I've woken up. I see now what it takes to be a real man. I still need some growing up. I am trying.

I can't have children and I'm kinda happy about that. Given today's political nightmare, I don't know what might happen to them if I had kids. If you do, you've got a tougher battle than I have. If these monsters ever got to the point that they could go into any household and confiscate property and people, I definitely would not just give them what they wanted. They assuredly would have to take me on. I really wonder if most men would just say "okay, take them, let me get back to the game, it's not halftime yet."

I think I've hammered the sports fans enough. There's a lot more than this that is keeping Americans from being aware of what is going on around them and acting on it. Can you imagine how different our elections would turn out if we could just get to the potheads watching the Osbornes? The jerkoffs staring at reality TV shows? The numbskulls out working on their hot car? NASCAR. There's another one for you. Jeeeesus!

Y'know...I can't be too hard on these people, because I know where people are. We are a society that has simply grown complacent. I understand. I think men have just gotten so comfortable that they fear the possible failure that could come from engaging. There's a responsibility that comes with going out into foreign territory and evaluating things they know nothing about and then being in a position that requires action. They might cease to appear to be real knowledgeable men. People don't want to learn new things. They want to use the things they already know- but still appear strong and knowledgeable.

When I was playing in my home studio writing songs about who cares what, or boxing with my Dad, or when I was competing for bodybuilding titles I wasn't seeking to learn either. But right now the United States is in maybe the worst and certainly most insidious circumstance I've seen in all my years. So what's it gonna take? Somebody's gotta stand up and shout "Turn off the T V! Get out and stand for something! Wake up!"

But will anybody listen? Do you think America is in denial? You do know all this is worship. You will become like the gods you worship. Is it really time for most Americans to go into slavery? Maybe it is. Jesus said, "When you see these things, do not be troubled, as they must take place." So just give up?

I can't. Why? Well...I'm just not that quick to give up on these guys. If they care that much about something as silly as a ball game, then maybe they can be enlightened enough to see what is going on around them and start caring. . . maybe. At least I don't have to teach them how to care! They're not sociopaths...they're just lost in a daily do-nothing abyss of entertainment.

It is really uncomfortable to approach a grown man and talk to him about something you know ahead of time is just going to irritate him. Maybe guys like you and I need to grow a pair and learn to talk "man to man" with the guys closest to us that are lost.

Jesus said to go into the world and give them the Good News. He also told his followers to go into the city and preach the Gospel, and if they choose to ignore you, to "shake the dust from your feet" and continue elsewhere. Notice this: if we ignore the command and keep our feet 'clean' all time, what impact does that have on anything? We have a mandate- to at least tell them the truth- before shaking off the dust.

I'm not saying to get all "Jesus" on them right away. But they NEED TO BE AWARE! Just what I said earlier, "Hey buddy, do you know what is going on right under most peoples' noses?" and proceed from there. Some guys might feel privy to some secret knowledge that might make them feel special. Look: I'm just as dumb about these things as any of us. I just think there are some cowboys out there just waitin' to put their boots on. Hell, they played competitive sports in high school. If you once could tackle someone on the field or knock out a home run, I think you can vote. Start with taking out the trash...then get your own beer...and then Voila! Absentee voting! Oh, and watching the news once in a while would help.

Chapter 2 Why I Love Women

I have always loved women and prefer to be around them. When entering any party or social gathering, there is usually some kind of separation between the sexes and I always beeline right for the girls. Why, you ask? Because maybe I might get laid? Might get at least a number?

No, I like the way they smell. Ok...that's part of it, but really it's because I know I will get more intelligent conversation. I love the things that women choose to talk about. I love the way they think. I can enjoy being around them doing anything; I just like hearing their voices. Things that don't matter to girls usually don't to me either. Girls usually think and talk about things that *do* matter to me. They talk about people. They talk about relationships. They read romance novels. They love the idea of being in love, and I love them for that. Because I love the idea of being in love too. Girls are precious to me. I even tried to become one, but we'll get to that...later.

Sometimes they talk...and talk... It can get irritating but I love this about them too. I just like to watch while they live...I love women so much.

I really would love it if I were surrounded by them and all the men would just evaporate. No, I mean it; all guys seem to want to talk about is some sexual conquest or sports. Some like to talk about fighting, but none of them can. To me, this is ugly. Always has been.

Hey, maybe Christian guys would be better, right? Not. They may be better in that they don't talk so much about having sex with anything that is available, but they're just as bad about money. To me, that is the ugliest part of it.

When my parents split up, my mother saw that I was not like other boys in that I would sit in my room, write books and bind them. This, to her, was not what a young man should be doing. She quickly entered me in Little League. After a whole summer of the coach telling her that all I did was stand in right field and save the world from space invaders, she succumbed and pulled me. Thank you Mom! She should have known I'd become a musician and never be a ballplayer; my dad wrote poetry as did my mother. For whatever reason, the only athletic endeavors I ever competed in were "solo" acts- just like Neil Diamond: a "Solitary Man."

But, seriously, one thing I did learn from my mother was how to treat a lady. I liked the idea of pulling out a girl's chair and opening the door for her. Standing when a woman comes to the table always made me feel good. I like making a girl feel special. I'm even diligent about returning the toilet seat to the down position.

There have been hundreds of books written about how one or the other sexes has the upper hand in relationships, but I still maintain it is the man who controls most everything. There are many exceptions, but I think men are a lot more savvy than they let on when it comes to getting their way. I mean, who is it that sits in front of football games and who is it that does the housework and the bills?

So I'm not a normal guy, we've established that. I just think it's healthier to have come up the way I did than to be an adult and spend my time following boys' ball games. Sorry. It's certainly better for relationships.

An interesting thing I've noticed is that the more hedonistic a society becomes, the more inflammatory it becomes towards women. This is the state of affairs I find America in right now. In the fifties, a guy who slept with someone other than his wife had some shame to deal with. Not now. Now as many conquests a man can have makes him more of a stud.

In America now, so many people are single. Women have such a hard time finding someone who will be reliable and love them, that they are turning to sex sites and finding men simply to sleep with, despite the proliferation of sexually transmitted diseases. This is because the communist free love mindset has so ingrained itself into our society that men (and even women sometimes) just don't care anymore. There are even adultery "search" websites now.

Just look at former Presidential candidate John Edwards' scandalous affair in which he fathered a child with his mistress. His wife was cancer-stricken and he was a public figure! She has since died. Look at South Carolina Governor Mark Sanford and his Argentine mistress. He and his wife Jenny have four young sons. What does this say- not only to his sons- but to the rest of the country? When public people like this do these kinds of things, how are common men, who (sadly) admire them, supposed to behave?

In this new American society, men are increasingly aware of their options and want it all for themselves right now. This means they don't have to stay with one woman for any length of time. Women, in response to this, have become suspicious of men and are very guarded when encountering men they do not know. They may dress provocative but are guarded around their counterparts. Women have become a commodity now: use them and move on.

Women have so much to contribute. Their insights are so much more emotionally driven than men's. That's why they are such a beautiful counterbalance to men, and were given to us in the first place. God gave Adam woman before she was meant for procreation. She was obviously meant to be a companion. A companion means an equal. Men tend to be the pragmatists. Women are more emotionally driven and can add a new perspective to decision making. Emotions can be good. Some decisions need this. Emotion=passion. A woman's viewpoint is always beneficial. A man might pragmatically think a career move is necessary while his wife may see all the necessary emotional reasons not to uproot. Look, men, when just surrounded by men, tend towards violence. Just look at Muslim nations, where women are left at home. Thank the Lord that we have them; they're here to bring out the love in us.

Women in America follow the fashions of the day, which are often provocative, whether or not they desire any contact with a new man. They fuss over their hair; how their clothes fit and spend so much time on their makeup they seem to have lost sight of where they really fit into society. Women in America find possessions such as nice cars or clothes that make them feel stronger about themselves, complimenting their self-worth. The reason for this, I think, is because the men in their life are largely absent. Men use them for gratification and then go away.

Other women today are able to pursue a career, which also helps them find high standing, into what was previously a man's world. Procreation is now less important, as women and men must work. It's just not economically feasible as it once was. It's just another way the covenant of marriage has gone under attack.

Women don't evaluate men these days on the right things. This is because these things are all they have to evaluate men on. I have always said that the measure of a man is his ability to be faithful to his commitments. Women don't even seem to expect that anymore. They've begun to look for the same "surfacey" things in men that men have looked for in women for centuries. The proliferation of breast implants and dyed blond hair is a testament to this. The men I have known that swoon over girls with big breasts and blond hair have always struck me as insecure and superficial. Are these really the kind of men these girls want? I think not. But what have they to choose from? Men only pursue their own desires today- whether it is watching sports, having a hot car or even pornography, married or not. What's a woman to do?

Well, one thing is waiting for a man to come along that likes her for who and what she is. I assess women on who they are, inside and out. On the surface, I absolutely love small-breasted girls and know many men who feel the same way. Blond hair means little to me. I, personally, do not swoon when I see a tall (especially dyed) blonde girl because I think they all look like Stepford Wives. Dyed blond hair tells me the girl is insecure. Insecure often means competitive and prideful. Competitive for what? An insecure guy who wants an armpiece? Great!

Also just look at *how many* men are gay. Notice how many of them have girls hanging around them. Girls like being with gay dudes because they giggle with them and are playful. The girls even sometimes fall in love with them! These are the men girls in their twenties and thirties are hanging around with because men are talking sports or playing with computerized video games. This is shameful.

A great many women have even sought out other women for a kind of surrogate male in the absence of men who will give them the emotional support they need. This is not to say that there aren't lesbian women, but that's another story. I'm referring to women who desperately crave support from *human* beings, and in this case they don't care that they're women.

Women need men to be sensitive *and* strong. And when they're not, they will look elsewhere, whether it be in a career, in other men or sometimes other women.

Christian men can be all these things. Unfortunately, many Christian men can be strong in most ways women need, but also can be so pandering as to appear effeminate. Many times my wife and I have seen a man acting effeminate. We would wonder if he was gay and she would then say, "Maybe he's a Christian." I knew exactly what she meant. Men of all stripes these days can display the passive-aggressive type behavior I once saw only in children and very manipulative women.

Sarah Palin began to describe the virtue of the new female Senatorial, Congressional candidates and media figures in early 2009 as "crusaders for the family and the American dream." What I do not like about this is simply that she needed to do this. Why did she need to do this? It's because Sarah Palin, Michele Bachman, Jan Brewer, Michelle Malkin, Pamela Geller, Ann Colter and Sharon Angle are standing in for absent men. I mean, who among men is standing up against the outright evil coming against our country? Well, there's Glenn Beck. And well, Glenn Beck. Wow! I'm so happy to see these girls standing up and fighting this behemoth that wants to turn us little "stupid" people into genderless, drugged robots serving the oh-so-intelligent elite. These girls want to be mothers and wives, and are tired of the far left thinking that is trying to make us an "anything goes as long as we can live off the government" society.

These girls believe in an America where girls become wives and have beautiful children and care for them, as their husbands work to earn enough to pay the mortgage on their home sweet home. As their kids become men and women and leave home to start their own families, their parents have saved enough to retire and enjoy their children's children. This is America. These are American women. I don't care what The Guess Who and Lenny Kravitz sing about. Black, white, brown, red or Asian, these are American girls and they are beautiful.

The role of the woman- American or not- has been the same in society for over 2000 years. Who are we, in just the last 50, to try and manipulate that? Women are beautiful, and we should love and respect them for WHO THEY ARE- just the way that God intended.

Chapter 3 Why I Love Black People

and What I Want for Them

My family moved to Auburn, California, forty miles northeast of Sacramento in the low Sierra Nevadas, in 1961, when I was five years old. Its population at the time: 7,001. I remember two black families: the Kennedys and the Robinsons. I don't remember seeing their kids in school at all- although I did see them playing in front of their houses down by the railroad tracks. They were always a source of intrigue for me because they looked different.

When I was 15, I moved with my father to Camarillo in southern California, where there were many black people. It was a state mental hospital and many of the employees were black. My father was a psychiatric technician, as I became much later, and after two years he had befriended a lovely black girl named Irma. Later, they moved in together and I stayed with them frequently. After a while, I just happened to notice that most of my friends were black people. My boss at work was a beautiful black girl named Ann. Downstairs was a party girl named Cassandra and my friend James Hughes; all were black. The drug program spawned a lot of black people I got to know- I loved these people very much.

After a few years Irma had loaned me her guitar, as she was a music therapist, and I quickly learned to play it. In a couple of years, I started playing in bands. Some of the musicians I met were black guys. I still remember the good times we had at Irma's listening to Al Green and Isaac Hayes. In the late seventies I had grown a bit fat and joined a gym. I soon became enamored with bodybuilding. It was in this endeavor that I was surrounded by black guys as black people, in general, have a natural predisposition for beautiful physiques.

In short, I have grown to love black people and their culture. I like black men because they seem more masculine than most white guys these days. I also think black women are absolutely beautiful. My wife will stiffen up when we're having lunch and a pretty black girl walks by. She'll say "Aaa haa, little brown yummy!" A girlfriend of mine in the early eighties told me that I seemed like I should be with a black girl (if I wasn't with her). That never materialized. I have always wanted so much for my black friends and often they have not only let me down- but themselves. Look- I know I am an assertive, goal-oriented, type-A personality and I don't expect everyone to mimic my behavior. I just see so much talent in some people that goes untapped. If someone possesses natural God-given abilities for something, there is no requirement that they use this- but at least apply yourself in some way to something!

America has always been a nation of people willing to seek opportunities and take advantage of them. Many black people do this, but so many more learn to be comfortable in just lounging around on entitlements and getting into trouble, or just turning into uneducated do-nothings. The black people I got to know were fun-loving and applied themselves whenever they could. We all got along very well, and there was no evidence of racial tension anywhere. Black, White, Latino or Asian, we were musicians, athletes and psych workers.

What happened? All of a sudden in my wife's workplace, the black people are undermining the white folks. This is not reciprocated though. On the street, I see black guys giving me the 'evil eye.' I hear conversations about people racial profiling, and police brutality against blacks. Black people say they are being marginalized. Often times blacks will pull the 'race card' anytime things do not go their way. People like Al Sharpton do this all the time. Look, since the sixties, white people all over America LOVE their black friends. This "shit" is just that: "shit" people use to their advantage. This is evil and anyone who buys into this kind of stupidity is just lost.

Calling conservatives racist whenever they are being effective in their arguments has been a tool of the left all along. The fact that President Obama was elected by WHITE PEOPLE shows that America is a fair and non judgmental place and everyone can excel if they want to.

Look I don't believe this! I won't. Something has happened and I don't like it. I really believe that in the eighties, people had forgotten all about the old racial prejudices and were getting along just fine. I was living in my van in 1992 when Los Angeles lit up with the Rodney King situation and because I had trained in Oxnard with police, I knew how my cop friends were 'clannish' and could get real ugly with people who they disliked. But that tape really set me off- and, obviously, I was not alone. But even this didn't seem to affect normal race relations that much in the regular working population.

Something has happened in the last decade that has intensified in the last two years. I really miss being able to approach black people and spark up friendships quickly and get along without some race-related topic springing up. It adds tension to what should be a pleasant time. I would not say this difficulty in relations between the races just came in with the Obama administration, but I will definitely say it has grown more noticeable. I think the reasons for this are obvious. Communists (yes Obama's policies are communist) have always been the ones to pit people against one another for their own inevitable gain. Always seeking the proletariat, they find a people susceptible to anger. They help promote this anger towards a group that seems more privileged. Then, the communists divide and conquer. Unfortunately, my beloved black people were sitting ducks for this evilness.

Another thing I see that is driving my loved ones to the wrong side of the fence is the fact that they have now learned how to make a lot of money by simply expounding stupidity, i.e. today's rap music. They now can see the possibility of gaining wealth by just rapping about any dumb thing going through their heads. And then the people worship the artists. Listen to how much hatred you hear in some rap music. So when the people begin to worship this hatred and stupidity then their society begins to decline. And it has, as a result of this. I find this saddening for their culture. My friend Sandra speaks out very adamantly against this part of black culture and is a black girl herself and remembers when black music was just that...music. I was in the gym recently and heard some new hip hop music that sounded like somebody actually composed something in it. This was encouraging.

I'm sure that African Americans have been wishing to be represented by one of their own for some decades now. I wanted this too. I am so glad to see this happen for them, but I am so grieved that it turned out to be someone with a desire to break down the very nation that gave them such opportunity in the first place. Just look at how far these beautiful people have come in the last few decades. Look at any high rise office building and count how many black people are coming and going. Look at the entertainment industry. Black people are now at the forefront of everything you see. I truly believe that pretty much all the racism in America is manufactured by the far left and is just a ploy to divide to conquer. The United States today is very tolerant and open to all races! Look at how many interracial couples you see today. Look, WHITE PEOPLE LOVE BLACK PEOPLE! It is the sociopaths that want YOU to think otherwise. If you can't see this you are being stupid.

Look, stupid people are always among us, and are often the racist ones. Black people can be as racist as anyone. Just listen to Al Sharpton, Reverend Jeremiah Wright or Louis Farrakhan. Spike Lee recently said that the United States is the most violent country in the world. You've got to be kidding. Pakistan? Iran? Half the countries in North Africa? These people act like children- shame on them! None of them are standing up for (or representing) black people at all. They are most of the problem!

Latinos can be very racist. What is 'La Raza?' Why do we even pay attention to these idiots' rantings? Do people harbor such hatred in their hearts that they willingly give way to stupid brain death, talking about some race being somehow superior to another? This is a travesty. It's an infringement on the love that we all can express for one another. Cultures are cultures; people are just people. If anyone moves their dwelling place to another country and lives amongst other peoples, they are expected to assimilate to the other's culture. Hopefully they can prosper there. Black people have assimilated- and quite a few have prospered- in what *was* primarily a white European culture. There are poor people; unfortunately, a lot of these are black people. But a lot of them are white people too. Poor people will always be envious of wealthy people. Most of the time this is simply due to the fact that people who are poor are less educated than their country mates. If one doesn't go to school, one cannot expect to prosper unless they have mastered some art form or a skill that allows them to find a place in the workforce or art community that rewards them. Or they can become good at some athletic endeavor that can bring them to prosperity.

Obama's policies make blacks less independent. As a leader, he is as divisive and destructive a force as has been seen in as long as I can remember. Super hottie Deneen Borelli, a black Republican activist, and others call Obama's policies 'plantation' politics, because he is returning black people to a state of dependency. He is consciously teaching them to resent white entrepreneurs that are successful, rather than encouraging them to be entrepreneurial themselves.

Do you know that the Dayton OH police department in March 2011 decided to lower the test score requirements for their police officers because there weren't enough black officers on the force? Tell me, what would this do to the existing black police officers? What would this do for the safety of their citizens? How is this helping black people? Tell me... how is this hurting black people?

It is very important that we NOT let people become comfortable in poverty! They must be UNCOMFORTABLE enough to want to get up and do something. Allen West is a retired black Lieutenant Colonel of the United States Army and he knows this. I really believe he would be the best man in the White House we could find, if he would only decide to run! Herman Cain is another black man that knows everything and he IS running and IS NOT a politician and DOES know what to do to fix our country and is my pick! If they would run as president and vice president this country would be on the right track in no time.

Mr. Obama appears to me to be a textbook sociopath in that he is attractive, charismatic and knows how to 'play' people. He knows how to work people up into a frenzy. He knows how to stimulate them and make them worship him. Just count, during any of his speeches, how many times he says "Me," "I," and "my." You tell me, is he helping black people? Or is he returning them to a state of dependency and idol worship? Believe me this will become slavery.

Well, let's take a look: A Sept. 8, 2010 Politico story says the black unemployment rate rose from 15.6 in July to 16.3 percent in August; this was more than whites or Hispanics. Obama also dumped billions into welfare programs, making them beholden to the Democratic Party. 4.4 million people are on welfare as of early 2011; half of them black. 50 million are on Medicaid, many of them are black. 40 million are on food stamps.

Having 99 paid weeks on unemployment discourages job hunting. These programs will be difficult to simply do away with, even if the recession ends. Many will lose their ability to seek employment as this grows more difficult with the absence of seeking (or even knowing how to seek) and the relative comfort of being able to relax and still have food on the table. Trying to get young blacks to behave or speak like the cultural norm is being hampered by multiculturalists.

The sixties were, ironically, a horrible time for black people. The communists had already gotten into most of our campuses and had found their proletariat (our black people), and were stirring up hatred for white people. The Black Panthers formed, thanks to the 'Students for a Democratic Society' and race wars began in Oakland and Los Angeles.

During the 2008 elections, members of the New Black Panther party were standing outside a voting place, wielding a big stick and intimidating voters. Attorney General Eric Holder, who is black, refused to indict the men because they were black and admitted as much. Just what would have happened if the situation were racially reversed? And just how does this help black people? Isn't this just as bad as the Ku Klux Klan?

'Get back is a mutha.' Stir up the hatred, progressives.

They don't want people to get along, they want to be superior. Remember what I said in the foreword to this book about sociopaths and their racial agenda? Black people, I love you, but you will never have this. Why? The Bilderbergs don't want it; they're the privileged ones (and they're all white except for one and he thinks he's going to rule the rest!).

As I said earlier, I'm seeing more racial tension than ever. I feel strained to freely communicate with the people I so want to love. Interesting, multiculturalists are the ones that seem to be causing this division. Multiculturalism implies cultures cohabitating freely in love. But they seem to desire that cultures not adapt to the predominant culture of a nation in which they live, but that they live under their own laws within a body of people that have already developed their own set of rules. This cannot work. Any body of people must have laws that they live under. Otherwise there is chaos.

It seems to me that chaos is exactly what is desired by the people on the far left right now. Chaos works for them because they want to walk into a chaotic situation with the solution. That solution will be a society under government rule and a leader that is nothing short of a king. This, as mentioned earlier, is by finding the proletariat (in this case the black people), identifying the overlords (white people), reminding the proletariat of past misdeeds, and then exploiting their anger. My dear black friends: some peoples' hatred is making you turn on yourselves. Be smarter than this.

The reason for this is obvious. Many years ago, evil white people took for themselves slaves from Africa to sell here on the mainland. People here bought these slaves and put them to work on their farms. Then, as good people saw this injustice and rose up to fight for these peoples' freedom, they became free because they were taught things they had not previously known- things like the Good News of Christ's redemption for all people. Had these things not taken place, the Africans would all still be wearing plates in their lips (some still do) and would not know Jesus' gift of redemption. God uses the evil to bring the good people to Himself. I understand: simple missionary work would have done this. But don't you think that maybe God wanted these people to prosper too? Right now it is my opinion that the black churches are by far the most spirit-filled of any. Whatever misdeeds white people have done from generations ago have not only been corrected- but overcompensated for.

Look, what is Affirmative Action? OVERCOMENSATION!! What did it do? Created lazy black Americans that feel entitled. Why are almost all city, county, and federal government jobs almost exclusively manned by black people? Affirmative Action. They become the managers and only hire black people. Understandable, but the result is people that feel they have a RIGHT to be employed there and as a result are lazy. Why is it always so hard to get things done in county offices? Yeah.

I under stand, the racial prejudice that was present even in the early sixties necessitated a program like this. But after the overcompensation was fully entrenched (and it was) the program needed to stop. Black Americans, like everybody else, need to learn to be responsible and respectful.

White people are now the ones maligned at every turn for, well, being white. Anything a white conservative says or does that a liberal doesn't like is called 'racism.'

Just look at any Africans in Rwanda (or most countries in that area), and then look at the black couple next to you at the Cheesecake factory. Then tell me that these peoples' good life was not paid for by their ancestors. This is the way God's world works- like it or not. If a people were brought to the Lord through the sweat of their fathers do you think God does not acknowledge this? God says that the sins of the fathers are passed to the sons up to the third generation. Don't you think the blessings are too? Trust me- those slaves (and obviously that couple at the Cheesecake Factory) are happy people now. And they are likely overjoyed for their offspring, too. God loves us all.

What I want for my beloved black people is for them to retain their own culture and for them to be loved, as I love them. I want them to enjoy all the benefits of our culture and love their own. We white Americans have enjoyed the black peoples' music and art for decades now. I want us to continue to respect them and to stop seeing them as anything other than Americans. I wish more black Americans would seek an education that propelled them into a prosperous life. I would really love it if more black Americans would stop seeing political candidates for their skin color and be educated enough to listen to what a candidate had to say and follow their politics. I want them to know a way of life that inspires a willingness to work, prosper, and see differences in philosophies- not one that inspires dependency. Look: if you make people uncomfortable enough in their poverty, then they will rise to the occasion and get busy. Make them comfortable, and then what are they naturally going to do?

A dependency on the state will only lead people into slavery. Black people should be the first in this country to want to do away with anything that would lead into slavery. But instead they are often duped into believing that voting for another black man will free them. Black people: you are already free! Please do not return to slavery. Do not listen to the voice of hatred. Listen instead to the voice of love and reason. Let's return to the time when we were all getting along.

Chapter 4 Why I Love Mexi-Cans

Because they can. When you can't. These people are hard-working and love their families (and their cerveza!). You tell me they don't eat some really good food? When I'm out and see a white or a black guy that gives me the evil eye (this actually happens to me), I just try to ignore them and think, "Don't you do anything buddy, or...." But when it is a Latin guy (and it rarely is), I actually think twice. Why? Because they're usually *real* men. Real men usually don't look for a fight but will finish one if necessary. I like Latin guys. I like Latin girls too. Aren't they just lovely? Little raven-haired yummies!

I grew up around Oxnard, CA. This city has always been about seventy percent Hispanic. In 1973, I joined a band with a guy that had previously been my pot dealer. His name was Willie; he was a Mexican and a decent musician. It was the second band I played with (the first was a bluegrass band). Then some friends of mine from the hospital I worked at had their son from Fresno over. He was such a great guitar player that we just had to ask him to stay and join our group. His name was Mark Rodriguez. We were "Kwik Flo," named after Willie's water heater. Then Steve, a friend of mine from the drug program at the hospital joined and we began to play out. We played at Mexican company parties and biker parties filled with heroin addicts and, well...my kind of people.

I still remember the time Willie's neighbors, mexi-gang people, that didn't like his white friends, jumped over his fence and beat his ass so bad that he was bleeding from his nose and had two swollen eyes. This happened right as we were packing our gear to go play out. Willie had to play and sing looking like that! We couldn't stop busting up.

I eventually got booted from that band for being too much of a drunk (imagine that!), and being a bit violent. Also, some of the guys had started moving toward jazz and I hadn't learned that yet. I just wanted to rock and roll all night, and party every day. Well I showed them! I eventually became a classical composer.

Anyways, my guitar style is pretty much what I call "bad Santana," meaning: I copied Carlos' style for so many years I began to sound exactly like him. I've even gotten complaints from one band member that "We don't need another Santana." I loved the way Santana was not dependant on 'licks' to get a guitar solo across, but instead would let the notes sing, using long sustaining feedback notes to play so much more melodic than most rock guitar players. I really am a melody guy. I love beautiful music (and beautiful girls).

I had gotten fat from years of drinking and joined a gym in Camarillo then another one in Oxnard. I approached this new endeavor with the usual aplomb accorded anything I pursued and in a couple of years I was competitive. I eventually won a California championship and a Western America trophy before I injured myself training too heavily and had to change course.

Training in Oxnard, pretty much all my training buddies were Hispanic. A few were black or Oxnard PD. I noticed my Mexican friends were such hard workers in the gym, at making music and at work, and I loved it. Hard work can really make you feel good about yourself and makes you a valuable asset to anyone. I loved it when we would all pack up and go wherever the contest was that month and cheer on our friends. The Chevera's that owned Oxnard Fitness Center gave me the key to the gym after I won the Ventura County Championship and placed in the Pacific Coast Championship in the same night.

We Anglo-Americans (especially in California) have gotten so pampered and lazy as to think we should not have to work at anything and still be able to eat and live. California- the land of entitlements.

Just look at how many Anglo guys work at their jobs, and then, quite frankly, do a terrible job at it. I remember one time when I was having cell phone problems; I called the company to discuss my issues. When I would get a girl, she would be able to help me quickly or know where to go for help. When I would get a guy, he would stutter and stumble around trying to just get me off his back. It was clear to me that he didn't want to be bothered by me- even though he was at work! I really hate having to deal with men in the workplace. They're often so lazy and incompetent!

It seems that our Latinos are the only people that help each other even when they don't have much. They're still fair- minded people and are willing to do what it takes to support their families. Aside from the Christian population, where race doesn't matter, Hispanics are pretty much the only people that hold dear the strong family unit and take care of their elderly. They are, by and large, honest and trustworthy. Mexican men really are some of the nicest guys I have ever met. And THESE PEOPLE REALLY DO LOVE THEIR MUSIC! If they're working nearby you will hear it. I'm talking about working Latino people; not gang members. They can be as bad as anyone. I really think California should be handed back to these hard workers. They should be living in those houses in the Hollywood Hills. There might be cars on the lawn...but people would be living there that deserved it!

Latinos deserve credit for this, but instead are being used as pawns for the Democratic party. They usually vote democratic and typically are used for votes. I mean, look at how Los Angeles County spent $600 million on illegal immigrants' welfare last year. This is not fair to the Mexican people who came over here legally and have found a way to work and support their families. The illegal immigrants are being welcomed in by the far left by policies like President Obama's proposed 'DREAM' Act. Look: I have nothing against Latinos that want to work at jobs Americans don't want to-even illegally. Or the child of an immigrant getting to go to college. The liberals really want anybody to be able to come in, even illegally, because they will claim responsibility for it and garner their votes. Then they will be cast aside as just more useful idiots.

The communist sociopaths are doing this with our Hispanic people, just to divide and conquer. I don't think anybody has anything against Mexicans coming across our border and slaving at jobs that, really, most Americans are not interested in doing. Now drug cartels are coming in and assassinating our citizens; that's another story. The communists don't mind this because they love the chaos.

People without a solid family structure usually end up relying on government for everything and become dependents. You know, it's only a matter of time until human nature kicks in and Latinos become like everyone else. This hurts. When Latinos become like post-Christian, postmodern Americans, all will be really lost.

Chapter 5 Are People Really Stupid?

First, let's define "stupid." My online dictionary says: "lacking ordinary quickness and keenness of mind. Dull." Now let's define 'people,' as we are referencing them. I would say any reference to people in general would likely mean, more than 50 percent, or, 'most people.' So going with this, would you say most people are dull? Do they lack keenness of mind? Bill Maher seems to think most Americans are stupid. I think not. Uneducated: yes. This simply means they are capable but choose not to think about things they need to. This is not stupid; this is a choice. I think this is universal, not necessarily American.

People generally choose the path of least resistance when deciding what to spend their time thinking about. That's right- I said thinking. People are generally lazy thinkers. Why do we have car keys that open the car from yards away with the push of a button? Elevators? You get it. There's nothing wrong with this technology, but to have the same laziness with your mind? Now this is downright dangerous. This means people vote without knowing all the facts. It's been said that people deserve the government they elect. I agree. Very often people vote in a candidate and are sorely disappointed. Is this really because the candidates lied during their bid for office? Maybe, but anyone who is interested enough can look up candidates and explore their background and policies. When they choose not to look for these things, whose fault is this?

People do not want to watch the news because it's so depressing. But what makes the news so depressing? Take Senator Gabrielle Gifford's gunman in Tucson. *That* became news because nobody around him was aware enough to help guide his deranged mind from returning to the proper healthy path. If you are aware of what's happening in your community- even with the people directly around you, there's always some preventative action one can take to make things safer. The news IS depressing, life is hard, boo hoo!

Most people, when not toiling at whatever they do for work, seek the reward for their toil, usually in some form of pleasure or entertainment. All good. Now, what if there is an important decision to make about something that is uncomfortable to do? Well, as a rule, people will just shirk the responsibility and continue with whatever they were enjoying at the time. You can call this procrastination, laziness, a diversion or whatever, but this is what most people do. This can have dire consequences for themselves and even others.

Different societies have been more, or less, prone to this laziness. In history, ancient Greece, ancient Rome and many other societies have lapsed into this kind of 'apathy,' so to speak. This always happens when that society begins its decline. Throughout history, all great civilizations have risen, usually due to a high point in their nationalistic pride and their willingness to produce. To produce means to work. When that society becomes rich, and it has enough wealthy citizens that have the leisure time to be creative with the arts, the rest of the population will begin to seek this entertainment as well. Unfortunately, this is the beginning of a civilization's decline.

This almost sounds like all we are supposed to do is work. I don't believe this to be true. It's just that when people begin to get involved in any kind of recreational activity, they seem to want to immerse themselves in it to the point of excluding everything else. People are creatures of habit, and when the habit becomes leisure, it becomes a problem. Out go the important things, in come the superficial ones. Values are the first thing to be distorted. This is very natural for a people whose sole purpose becomes recreation.

A lot of great artistic and athletic achievements come out of these societies. I am a classical composer. Classical composition came out of post-enlightenment Europe. I was a competitive bodybuilder. Bodybuilding came from post-Christian America. Am I a bad man for my indulging in either of these activities? No. I do believe I used to be. That was when I was asleep. I have woken up. I am older and have many weight training injuries. This is a blessing, I've realized. Otherwise I might still be tempted to compete and I have already decided this was a waste of time even though I was more successful at it than anything else. My compositional spirit is still alive but I have become aware of the crisis happening in my country and I simply must act. Songwriting can wait.

So how do you help a people to see what is happening around them when they are busy entertaining themselves? Good question. It is my feeling that a lot of people in this country, and many others, are being fed a philosophy that is meant to eventually enslave them. The people professing this worldview are spending their time with the pursuit of attaining the utopia they have in mind. A people enslaved in their minds will go into slavery in the flesh. So what are Americans enslaved with in their minds? Well just look around you. This will become obvious. There are the aforementioned ball games and sports cars among the men and fashions and celebrity worship among the women. Many other things are consuming the minds of Americans, thanks to our media.

In psychology and physiology it has been established that people have a left, or analytical side of the brain and a right, or creative side. When one watches television, the analytical side, that one would use if they were reading a book, is usually bypassed. Information just comes in and lodges itself into memory and the viewer is unconscious of what has happened. This is called 'programming.' Americans have been programmed to think like dependents and servants. It's sad how willingly they walk into this, like "lambs to the slaughter." The programmers behind the scenes don't care if you write an expose' on what they're doing; they want to control the population that doesn't read- and that'll be more than enough.

So what's with the ADD epidemic? It stems from chronic television watching. Really, that's all it is. Also Twitter, Facebook, video games, e-mail and all this other instant stuff. Information comes across so fast, then disappears, and is replaced by new information. After a while, one expects life to be like this and their attention span cannot tolerate the pace that the real world happens at anymore. They're unable to concentrate on anything for a protracted period of time.

Comedian Jon Stewart just held a counter rally to Glenn Beck's restoring honor rally, called "Restoring sanity." Stewart and Bill Maher are both proponents of a worldview that supports a dependent class of people and an elite who sits above them and dictates their every move whether they know it or not. They think Americans are stupid. Are they right? No, as I said before, Americans are asleep. They care only about their pastimes. Why? It's because the establishment has slowly implemented a lifestyle that is totally hedonistic. This has been brought in carefully, and one step at a time. Easy to do, when people are self indulgent- bring in more indulgences. Pornography, S&M culture, ball games, fashion culture, whatever- it all leads to a frivolous culture. People are dependent on these kinds of things for their emotional survival. What they don't know is they make themselves that way. A frivolous culture will be enslaved because they are already dependent.

When you have a population that prefers servitude what can you do? You can try to open their eyes but you will be met with resistance. These people are comfortable. They will not change because you want them to. They have to need change for survival. What will cause this? Well, they will have to see where their chosen lifestyle is going. It is not obvious slavery yet. How will you get it across to them that servitude is where they are headed? You can teach them about the past and how civilizations have gone this way before. But do they want to know this? I think not, because what they are currently doing is working for them. That would be irritating to them. Are they beyond reach? I don't know. I don't want to think so but I have more evidence to support the notion that they are. I might have a solution, however. Read on.

What has happened in America is a group of sociopaths from another country has come in and convinced our people that pleasure is more important than responsibility. They have done this elsewhere and have found success. It was easier elsewhere than here because of our constitution, which was drafted with the knowledge of totalitarian life and meant to prevent it. But will our constitution prevent a subservient society that desires it? Trust me- people lounging on welfare and SSI will not give this up easily.

Freedom is our inheritance. It was fought for and is not to be taken for granted. Freedom is granted by God to a disciplined people. An undisciplined people will be poor stewards of their inheritance. They will lose it because they will squander it. Just like what? Children. Americans have been reduced to the status of children. Remember when you were a child? It was nice. Everything was decided for you and your sustenance was provided for you. This is what communism looks like. This is what they want: a bunch of simpletons incapable of making their own decisions serving the oh-so-intelligent elite. They sell it as a way of life, where all peoples are equal and have equal rights, but that is just to implement it. When they have their way, it will look more like serfs just obeying their kings. It is the oldest trick in human history. They are sociopaths. They will eventually desire worship- and will get it.

Civilizations always decline, and all I'm pointing out is how ours is declining right now. And it's the communists that have taken our hard-working, proud (not prideful) people and reduced them to mere children. Don't you love it when Dick Morris, Karl Rove or Charles Krauthammer (Fox news analysts) survey the political climate and talk as if our problems are due to mismanagement? You're kidding! Communist sociopaths have an agenda! Nobody is mismanaging anything; in fact, it's all going according to plan.

I'm going to give you some examples of what I'm talking about: Look around you at people in general and how they only think of themselves. See how rude people are. Look at the way they drive! You really need to drive defensively these days. Almost everybody lacks common courtesy. They don't care, because everything is about 'me.'

In front of the coffee shop I go to, a woman pulled up to the stop sign and hit another woman in a wheelchair. She backed up drove around and sped off. This was in Beverly Hills! Another driver hit a stroller and did the same.

Some people whom are atheists deplore Christmas but instead of letting people who do enjoy it celebrate it, they object and the courts step in and cancel a good time for all because of just one objection. Politicians don't even say the word 'Christian' anymore. They've even attempted to put 4 other Holidays (including one that means nothing to anybody but Jerry Seinfeld: "Festivus") at the same level of importance on our calendars as Christmas. Tell me- can wishing you a "Merry Christmas" ever be as important as a "joyous Kwaanzaa?" And then there's Ramadan...don't get me started!

I saw on the news recently how some small partnership had arranged a betting scheme on old people and their life insurance policies and how the earlier the old person died, the more money one would win. Do you see how easily this could lead to murder?

Response time was so slow in the Christmastime 2010 NYC blizzard, it became responsible for two deaths. NYC had dealt with similar blizzards before and had done much better. But the sanitation workers' union was instructed to sabotage the snow removal. This was in protest over budget cuts.

A Rutgers University student killed himself after his roommate filmed him and a male student having some kind of sexual encounter- and now his parents are suing the school.

In November 2010, a Toys for Tots bin was vandalized, and the thieves made off with several hundred dollars worth of toys.

This lunacy has also come into my life. I went to the gym one morning a little later than usual. I always work out before eating breakfast to burn more fat and this works, as long as you are fully hydrated and haven't starved yourself so long that you have gone hypoglycemic. Well...this one time I did wait too long and before you knew it, I was doing leg presses with 1200 pounds and 'snap'...there went a beautiful 20 inch arm. My bicep folded up under my shoulder and my wife took me to the emergency room. There I was shuffled over to a very knowledgeable doctor who told me he was going on vacation the next day. So he told me to find another doctor and make sure to have the surgery within one week. The next doctor I found was a short black man, who told me he had done these surgeries three months after the initial injury- and the patients were fine. This didn't make sense to me, as I know muscles atrophy when not in use (this is why older people have hip surgeries so often, no muscle around to support the bone.) but I trusted him (he was the expert). Something bothered me when I first walked into his office. He looked at me like someone who wished I wasn't there. At the time I weighed about 240 lbs and was pretty ripped. I also saw him rubbing the ass on one of the girls working in his office. Later others told me he felt insecure with me there. To complete a long story, two months later, he performed the surgery on me and when I came out of the anesthesia I was told the surgery had failed. Big surprise!

So I decided to sue him because of his negligence and found that I would need another surgeon to testify. Surgeons do not do that to each other. Kinda like police officers. What I regret is that I decided to sue in the first place. Jesus told us that He alone will vindicate our losses; He is the judge. I just wish I had my arm back. Now I have a big rose tattoo on my arm to cover the scar from the ineffective surgery. Damn!

Also look at how lazy people are anymore. Ever since the Civil Rights movement of the sixties, look at black workers and how they perform at their jobs. Do you see hard-working, reliable people or do you see the 'diva' of the Post Office? The 'grind-it-out' janitor or the lazy do-nothing? How many guys spend their time at work just hitting on the girls that come in and have not even learned their jobs well enough to really serve people in the way they are expected to? The work ethic in America is sickening. My Bible says, "If one won't work, neither shall he eat."

Back to the communists and the stupids, but first, an important Biblical question. What is the last thing Jesus said to Peter? "Feed my sheep." Hmmm, sheep. The communists see people as sheep. Jesus called them "sheep" because He is the good Shepherd. Sociopaths call them sheep because they think they are stupid. Well, if they *are* sheep how are we to lead them? The first way is by example. The example we want to give them is our adherence to truth. If you are always honest about everything you do you will stand out. This is not the way the world works. Say what you mean and mean what you say. Do not cower before evil; it cannot hurt you. If you walk in truth no one can sway you. The truth does not have an agenda. It is the truth. It is love.

We can also lead them through love. Love your brothers and sisters with an unconditional love. Love them when they are mean. Do not return evil for evil. Again, you will stand out. If you stand out for these things, people will start to listen to you. You can't twist their arms; you can only be different. When people see that you love them whether or not they are being nice to you, they will respect you. With respect comes a willing ear. With that willing ear, you can tell them just where their chosen way of life will lead. This simply takes patience.

Do you see now what you are called to do? This really is all it takes. In 2010, I saw a Republican supporter kicking a liberal from 'moveon.org,' the hateful communist organization, in the head. Do you think that made *anybody* 'on the fence' change to the Republican side? Of course not. That behavior looks too much like the stupids that want servitude in the first place. What if he had given her a space, expressed some warmth to her, and asked her if they could have lunch and talk? Which one, in your experience (head-kicking or lunch) has worked better to open somebody up to a point of view? Stupids!

That's right I said stupids. Who is really stupid but one that hates his fellow man and wants them to serve him. This is really a stupid person. They can't see past their own desires. Isn't this just like the people that they have singled out as so stupid?... The irony of it all.

Chapter 6 Once a Man, Twice a Child

Have you ever heard this saying? What does that mean to you? It's an old saying my father used to say. He was born in 1925, so I'm going to assume it's pretty old. And it is...see Act II, Scene II of William Shakespeare's "Hamlet." Okay...I'm going to tell you what it means for those of you who don't know. A man comes into this world a child, becomes a man, and then returns to childlike behavior in his old age. What surprises me about this is that in most societies that have been very patriarchal, the elders are reverently treated and respected. They are the ones that have been through life and are the ones that teach the younger ones wisdom and how to prosper. It seems to me that until the 1950's, America was one of those societies. It's not anymore- I'll tell you why.

A lot of things changed with the World War II generation. It is commonly dubbed "the greatest generation." I think so, but at the same time, I think not. These great men fought and helped defeat Hitler and the Japanese, winning World War II. That's what made them great. The women also had to rise up and work in our factories. Many also served in the armed forces. This generation was truly great, but something happened. Something went terribly wrong. Their children seemed to go crazy. In a single generation America and indeed, the world, was turned upside down. Why?

Well, for starters, in 1963 the birth control pill became available on the market. Most historians, I think, have not given this its due. All of a sudden sex did not mean procreation. Believe it or not, this changed everything. The WW II generation really had it all.

Then the other thing was the television. Television was invented in 1948, introduced to the American household in the early fifties and became a standard fixture in almost every household within a decade. The greatest generation was also the first generation in human history that was able to neglect raising their children. They could just place them in front of the TV for hours while they did as they pleased. I have heard much about how the sixties generation was pampered, spoiled and resorted to radicalism, much like neglected rich kids who tend to get into trouble. I think this is only partly true.

My father was a WW ll veteran. I was glued to the TV most of my childhood. My parents parted ways when I was eleven. I needed to stay with my disciplinarian mom until I was fourteen. At that point I went to live with my father, because he let me smoke and let my hair grow- things my mother would have never tolerated. He had gone to school to become a psychiatric nurse, as I also did later on. The psych community was and is a very liberal left wing bunch partly because of its origins, which is another dissertation altogether. They all smoked grass in the late sixties. Because my Dad and his friends smoked pot, I followed suit. By the time I was fifteen I was dropping acid and using methamphetamines. I was definitely a 'baby boomer' despite being only thirteen at the time of Woodstock. Damn...I barely missed out on all the fun!

I want you to notice something. Whatever kind of personality disorder one has, it always goes back to the way they were parented. Classic excuses: "It's because my dad was a drunk and abusive" and "My mom used to not care about me." How many psychiatric patients talk about their parents? So tell me: how important is parenting? Food for thought.

My father had not a clue how to raise children. He instilled in me some very good things. He was a reader and led me to a love of it. Literacy was a big deal in our family and was the primary way I entertained myself. He hated football, as do I. He was a poet; I became a musician. He taught me how to box. This was a great help after I had been bullied for years by athletic tough guys in school. He also bowed to my every will. This made me a real tyrant of a teenager. I demanded and I got. This led to a very irresponsible adult. I think I have only started growing up in the last ten years or so. Most of my life I have not cared at all about money, but instead have just pursued my dreams. I have been homeless in Venice, Hollywood and Seattle. Just look at the age of most homeless people. I'm 54. I think most of them are in my age bracket. Do you think this is for a reason?

So many homeless people I meet and talk to are lost, drug addicted and appear to be talking to individual oxygen atoms. A lot of this talking to oneself I think is simply their anger. They are living on the street and feel cheated. I met a woman recently that was homeless, an alcoholic and a drug addict- like so many of my old friends. She told me she had five children and they had been taken away because of her frequent trips to rehab. She was about my age. I met a very good guitar player about my age the morning I wrote this and he played some of his songs for me because I told him I was a composer. The lyrics to his songs contained references to 'monsters in my brain' and things that just told me how lost he was. His songs were well crafted. He too had close calls with record deals but just never took root.

The sixties have really taken their toll on Americans. So many of us are still living as if it's still 1969 and we are just wandering minstrels. Finding people to stay with until we get back on our feet, like rolling stones. The problem is....we keep rolling. Sometimes working, often not. Love is absent except in memory (or lack thereof); affection happens- but just fleeting. Drifting from one relationship to another. Lost. And (the worst part) getting older every day.

Can you imagine being sixty-four years old, white haired, rickety-boned and homeless? No modern skills, almost devoid of possessions. This is where so many of my old friends that I loved so much are. Boy, we were the really cool ones in high school. Long haired, bitchin' clothes and drug connections. But there was no foundation to build upon. Dropping acid and listening to Blind Faith did not prepare us for adult life. We never learned how to meet responsibilities. Mmmm, blind faith...

So now we're older and I hope I'm wrong... but I can only name one that has had an awakening and turned around and that is myself. And that would have probably not happened if my mother had not been en route to a believer's convention in 1995.

An ex-drummer of mine I recently connected with said to me, "I have examined the aging process from every angle and have decided there's nothing good about it." Now let's back up a bit and look at biology for a minute. Let's examine the aging process. My favorite topic....not. Look, babies really do look alike. Sorry you may think this one is cute or that one is not but really! Little genderless rolly-pollys that make lots'a poop. We grow up and our gender becomes more evident. We mature and have rolly-pollys of our own. Later we notice changes in our bodies. Our hair starts becoming more brittle and begins to change color and sometimes just go away. To an interesting color? Nope...for every one of us it goes grey...then white. Our eyelids begin to sag. We start getting jowls. Hormonal changes in women alter their menses and their vocal tone. Male erectile ability begins to decline. What once were round pleasing looking buttocks become flat, sagging cracker butts.

One thing you must know is that most of the way you see older Americans walking with walkers and barely making their way across a room is avoidable. People grow older in front of their television sets, and this leads to atrophied muscles in the hips, gluteals, abdominal areas and thighs. Atrophied muscles means the bones, which are becoming brittle because of aging, are not supported by the muscles needed to move them. Therefore the brittle bones are the only thing supporting their entire structure. This is why we're seeing all the hip replacement surgeries. But...I thought watching TV makes you smart?!!

I truly believe that modern medicine is not really helping our elderly. I have read that forty-five years old was the average lifespan in the nineteenth century. I don't know if that is true, but I do know that our pension plans were designed when the average lifespan was sixty-five to seventy. Now, thanks to modern medicine, more people are living to ninety plus if they stay healthy. This is part of why states are going bankrupt: they can't afford the exorbitant pensions of these elderly. Retirement age was lower but people were only on the plans for three to five years. Social Security only had to pay out for a couple of years to each person.

My point is that I don't think this is good for our economy. It's shitty to say that, but really, for our seniors to be living until they can no longer talk seems to me to be immoral. Think about it. I mean I'm not for pulling the plug on grandma, but why do we want to stay alive until opening our eyelids is a great ordeal? Remembering our children's names is next to impossible? Listen to most seniors' conversations and how much of them are centered around doctors. Do you relish the thought of walking around with a walker and not being able to go to a restaurant without holding up the customers? I see older people every day walking into the coffee shop and standing there in everybody's way looking around like, "I think I'm in a place, I see people around so it must be a place." I know I sound terrible, but someone has to say it. I just think it was better when we died when we still could hold a conversation and walk around. I have absolutely no intention of staying around until I no longer can function. I have options! Sorry but I won't be humiliated like that! I've humiliated myself quite enough, thank you!

Seriously, though, I have prayed the Lord, "Let me be strong and confident all the days of my life." Then let me go.

If it isn't obvious to you yet, here's another fact: the brain ages too. It becomes feeble and response time is longer. When I saw Jimmy Carter recently on TV talking about how President Obama's detractors were racist, you could see he was barely able to even manage saying what he was saying and keeping track of what he had just said. I thought, "Jeeeese...he defiantly needs his didie changed.

How about another octogenarian (Pat Robertson), saying that the Haitians had made a pact with the devil and that was what was responsible for their earthquake. He needed to be taken back to his room and given a sedative as he was acting out. And what about every Pope? Nasty old codgers; all of them. And they always have something really useful to say, like, "I'm denouncing all the bad people in the world and abortion is bad." They all talk the same way.

An eighty something year old man a couple of years ago in Santa Monica ran into the Farmer's Market and killed ten vibrant younger people because he refused to acknowledge that his driving ability had diminished. I see the potential for this everywhere. Isn't it time that people over seventy be tested every year for driving competency, just for our safety alone- if nothing else? Look, I have used public transportation for years at a time; so can our seniors.

This is about the time a lot of men seem to think they are ripe for a younger, prettier companion. (Yuck!) I'm even guilty of thinking like this but I'm not that old yet (or at least don't look it). When I am I will make it a point to stop. I have very long brown hair and because I was a competitive bodybuilder, I am in very good shape. Younger women still flirt with me. However, I think my days are numbered. I'm seeing most of these signs creeping in. The center section of my beard is now grey...at least in one way I'm not going to be twice a child!

So as we age, we seem to return to a state where we all look alike and our gender becomes blurred. Old women can look and sound like men. Old men can look like women. Tell me old rock stars with long hair don't look like old girls...great!

I remember when I was very young, visiting some of my relatives and noticing how happy they were. They were grandparents and great grandparents. They were fun-loving older Americans, planted gardens and were somewhat active. Is it just me...or do older people now just seem bitter? They often look as if they are scowling all the time. I mean...this could be the sagging eyelids. I just see disenchantment with life in their eyes. I really hope I do not become one of these but I strongly suspect I will have to work for happiness during my 'golden years.' I *really* hope I never see them...and why the HELL are they called 'golden?' When are your "silver" years? Platinum years? Why haven't elderly members of "La Raza" complained about the lack of "anos oros" as a common term?

Everything I've done with my life has been so youth and beauty-oriented. I am a musician and have been an actor, competitive bodybuilder, male exotic dancer and erotic art model. All my life I have been in front of microphones and cameras. Selling myself on my physical appearance is second nature to me. What on earth am I going to do when I start going grey and my face starts sagging. Dyed hair and botox? At least I'm writing this book in Beverly Hills!

One thing that disturbs me is that the only people that actually know what's going on in this country are the Tea Party people. These people remember what the country was like and want what they had back again. The problem is that if you look at any Tea Party gathering, you see an ocean of white. Hair, that is (modern day Whigs). My problem with this is that old people are not the ones who usually change things; it's the young. Look at any revolution and see who brings it about- good or bad. Older people are on the way out. Our youth have been so indoctrinated, they're subconsciously privy to the communist agenda. We really need- desperately- for young people to wake up and see what is going on because they are the ones that are going to live in this world in the coming years. We need a youthful Tea Party!

I think the only thing to do about this is to become what older people used to be: the wise ones. Talk to older people today and listen to the content of their dialogue. I do- and I am usually disappointed. They are either complaining about how things are not the way they remember them or are talking television drivel. From brave WW II fighter pilot to babbling incoherent...great.

Look, one of the biggest things that mature us is the handling of responsibilities. You don't get older, necessarily, and then find yourself capable of dealing with life's situations. But dealing with these things *is* what matures you. This is where our older people are at a deficit. Because they have grown up in front of television, and many have even gone on to living off of entitlements, they have not grown up themselves and aren't people of wisdom. But because they grew up in a time when older people were respected, they expect to inherit it. When they do not receive this, it will naturally lead to a bitterness and disenchantment with life. Thus...twice a child!

So, as I referenced earlier, the only way to combat this is to make the effort and become a person of wisdom so you will be able to earn the respect you so rightfully deserve. How is this done? Well the first thing is to become well-informed. This is not done by watching American Idol. This is not done by watching baseball. Anyone who grows older sitting in front of television will become a babbler. Read. Watch a news program you trust to be accurate and fair. There are a lot of bad books out there. There are many news programs that are so biased as to misinform you. Look, with the state of the world right now, you must be very discerning- more than anyone ever had to be years ago. You have to be able to discern character. Look for smugness. Trust me, real knowledge does not come out of a haughty countenance. Listen for a loving spirit. A mature person loves much. Knowledge that smacks of television psychology is just babble.

Imagine yourself older, but hostile and angry. Do you think anybody wants to know you? One big mistake that a lot of people make is once they have a little bit of knowledge is to talk too much. Learn about the real world first. Have a humble heart. If you are constantly talking, not only are you not learning, but you will appear naïve. You'll be perceived as youthful- in all the wrong ways. Listen to people- not always to learn from them but simply to find out *who* they are. Speak infrequently but always have some content when you do speak. If you do not have something to contribute to a conversation, shut up! Wait until you do. Don't be searching for something either; let your dialogue flow with your good intentions. Then you will be seen as wise- wise is good. Especially when you have little else to offer.

Today's youth have been indoctrinated to believe they can follow any passion they feel, neglect any responsibility, and be fine. Do you know who has taught them these things? Older people who themselves are people of no wisdom. They see themselves as more intelligent and worthy of others' servitude. They are themselves led by their own passions and emotionally are children. Our country (and indeed the world) is due for a catastrophe of the largest dimensions. There will be chaos. Rioting and bloodshed. If you don't believe me then you need to start educating yourself.

When these things happen, who do you want to be? Another crushed individual huddled in a corner? If you want to matter, you need to be the wise ones. You need to learn to serve, not be served. To serve you need knowledge. This is *true* maturity and wisdom. One of the things we have lost is our ability to love enough to serve. Love your neighbors- even when they are mean. Stand out. Be truthful in all things. Our youth need you desperately. Be well informed, patient and willing to be a guide to those who are lost. Know your God. Love much. Then you will matter.

Chapter 7

Is the Whole World Going Crazy?

If you have been watching the news you have seen what is happening all over our country and indeed the world. It kind of looks like the 70's on steroids. Women and men killing their children, women being murdered, Islamic terrorists blowing up innocents and drug cartels slaughtering people and even killing their own lawmakers. There is rioting in many countries around the world and a lot of this is due to entitlement reductions. The world really is more dangerous than it was twenty years ago. Even entertainment is more violent than it was. Gangsta rap and violent reality shows make hatred more acceptable.

And the hatred is now widespread. Our family units are disintegrated. People do not stay together and raise their children anymore. They, instead, seek their own desires and leave their children to fend for themselves in this cruel world. Is it any wonder that our children are killing themselves (and each other) when what they see on television and Sony Playstation is disrespect and violence? All this has been going on since the sixties, when our country was invaded by people that want to see America disassembled. We really were the last bastion of freedom and that is why they want to tear us down.

See what happened since the sixties. Charles Manson. Ted Bundy. The Zodiac Killer. The Hillside Strangler. So many more. Things like this were rare in the decades prior to the sixties. Well what was unique about the sixties? Communists began to teach in our schools, telling our children that America was bad and that they should rebel and cause mayhem. Violence was now acceptable. All of a sudden pop or rock bands were not named Buddy Holly and the Crickets or Frankie Valli and the Four Seasons but Megadeth and Judas Priest. A new popular band is Death Cab for Cutie. Real cool. And no one wants to think this, but the result of this mindset is the following: The shootings at Columbine High School.

Seung-Hui Cho went on a rampage at Virginia Tech University leaving thirty three dead, including himself in 2007. In 2001 a scientist, Robert Schwartz was brutally murdered using ritualistic, occult and wiccan symbols carved onto his neck. In early 2011, a very disturbed young man shot Congresswoman Gabrielle Giffords and many others including a nine year old girl. Michael Hall tortured and killed a mentally challenged teenager named Amy Robinson in Texas in 1998. In 2010 Joshua Komisarjevsky and Steven Hayes broke into the home of a Connecticut endocrinologist at 3:00 AM, bludgeoned him, raped his wife Jennifer and their two daughters, and then burned the house down, killing all three.

These things that were rare in the past are now becoming frequent occurrences. Why is this? People are not loving anymore. We don't love others, but instead, envy them and want whatever they can bring to us- whether they want to or not. We want and we want. I WANT FOR ME is the way children think and the way people think nowadays. Adults have not only become children- but hateful monsters.

Two things are in short supply these days: truth and love. People are not truthful anymore. Lies are expected. Movies aren't even written anymore unless lies are involved. Love is fleeting- when it is even present. People talk love when it is only lust. Think about the last song you heard that said something like, "Oooh baby I want to love you all night long," and tell me, do you think they were talking about love? Of course not. Most entertainment today supports the thought that love=desire and violence is always an option and works for solving any problem. If I desire you, I love you. If you don't like something, abandon or smash it. If your mother won't give you money, abuse her. All this sounds very childish; doesn't it? This is what Americans have been reduced to: children. What do children need? Supervision. From who? Obviously the government. Is this how you want to live?

Women today are raising their children alone while they have to work. They have to work because the men in their lives are absent. Sports and entertainment have gotten a vice grip on our men and the sorry fact is that they have grown up this way and know nothing else. They couldn't care less if their country is becoming communist or Islamic, they just want to keep entertaining themselves. So children grow up without parental supervision. Without a strong father figure, children become adolescent monsters. They are educated by their television sets. All kinds of decadence is available on the internet. Pedophiles cruise the internet for your children.

Children are the targets. When the communists began to come into our country ,the first thing they did was to target our children. Khrushchev said to Ezra Taft Benson, "You Americans are so gullible. No, you won't accept communism outright but we'll keep feeding you small doses of socialism until you will finally wake up and find out that you already have communism. We won't have to fight you; we'll so weaken your economy, until you fall like overripe fruit in our hands." And we have.

The first place the communists went was to our "older children," ie. our colleges. That's why college students were the first to begin protesting in favor of communist ideology. The people who are the real haters always go after the most vulnerable among us: Women and children. Both of these seem to be targeted for assassination in this time. Children are turning up dead all the time.

Desperate women are lured into working in pornography. What a humiliating way to seek a survival! Desperate people do desperate things. Sometimes they hurt their loved ones. Sometimes they hurt themselves. Sometimes they find no other way but to drink themselves into oblivion or use drugs to cope with this crazy world. Do not be desperate.

Most all the killing we are seeing is done by cowards- pitiful, weak, frightened little cowards. Anger is usually caused by fear. People angry enough to kill others are afraid of something...losing something. If they do not kill someone, they will lose something in their deranged minds.

Communists, when they take power through their revolutions, usually kill off a portion of their populations. It's easier to manage a smaller number. Death is now the order of the day....why does someone want to see death? Who is it that is inspiring all this hatred? Who wants to see so many dead? What is needed is for us to look beyond the physical plane and to seek the spiritual. This is the only way we will find out why the world has gone crazy.

There are only two spirits influencing us on this earth: one of hatred and death. One of love and peace. Who are these spirits? What do they want? I've just said what they want. So who are they? Real spirituality seems to be so out of fashion these days that bringing up Jesus or God immediately gets a shrug or a sneer. Who has brought things to this point? Who do you think? If you believe in God at all, you must believe there is a Lucifer as this is clearly stated in the Christian scriptures. If you ignore these things, you are at the mercy of the enemy that is making the world crazy. Is this where you want to be? You need something to believe in or else you will be (or become) one of the hateful people that might succumb to the impulse to commit murder. If you do not want this then, damn it; believe in something greater than yourself. Do not be a coward- believe in Jesus Christ; for your own peace of mind and for the sake of your family.

Isn't it obvious that something profoundly evil is influencing people today? Well, why does it seem it has gotten so much worse in recent years? Our scriptures say in the latter days Lucifer "comes down with great wrath, as he knows he has but a short time."

Jesus is truly the only place to look for comfort in this crazy world today and any day. Our world is spinning out of control, and there's only one place of refuge. That is in your Creator.

If nothing else convinces you that there is a Lucifer, just look at the world today. If you don't think the scripture I just mentioned is true, maybe you are as crazy as others are. Ask most people what they believe in, and listen to what they say. If they do not believe there is a God, they do not believe there is a Lucifer. Then look at their behavior; not for a few minutes, but over a period of time. Look for arrogance. Look for smugness. These qualities are not love. Our God is going to separate the "wheat from the chaff," whether you believe it or not. Please believe in love. Not the counterfeit kind that only yearns for self-satisfaction, but real love. Love is unconditional.

God loves you so much he sent his only Son (Jesus) to pay the price for your sinfulness- your faults. How much love is that! Christ loved the ones that tortured and killed Him even when they were doing it. Be wheat, not chaff. You have a place given to you after this life is over that you can't even imagine. All you have to do is believe and accept it. This world really has gone crazy. Be sane. Love one another. Be honest. Find Jesus Christ. He loves you.

II. On CommunIslamic Leadership

Chapter 8

By the Sweat of Your Brow, You Shall Eat of It

Isn't it a shame that we have to work? Work is laborious, makes you tired, and often, you need a shower afterwards. It's usually is not something you like to do in your spare time and overall, it's just a curse. That's it- a curse. The title of this article is what God decreed after man had committed his first sin. Ever since then almost everyone has had to work at *something*. Quite a lot of people over the centuries have tried to come up with ways to avoid this- and some have even met with success. Their methods vary. Here are some examples:

Absolutely the best way to avoid toil is to work very hard for a time so you can avoid it later. The way to do this is to start your own business. Just use your imagination and dream up an idea and involve like-minded colleagues- be it your bank or some friends. Work your butt off for six years, manage your business for a couple more, hire a manager, and then....relax and enjoy.

Another way is to play at a sport of some kind, keep at it until you are very good and join a team. Or if it's something like boxing, a solo sport, compete, win (this helps) and then you will have made enough money to retire early.

Music or acting is another option. Either train your voice (vocal coaches are good) or learn an instrument. Beware though, in these things there's absolutely no guarantee of success. I know firsthand that you can become good enough to be at the top of your craft and still go unnoticed. You need to become a good marketer-especially in music. Promotional ability is a must. I can write any kind of music just by listening to a piece in its style and then write my own original piece of music in that style using whatever instrumentation used. I have written and recorded country, rock, dance and classical pieces- but I have no idea how to market anything. Don't do this. Be smarter than me!

Another way is to live off of other people. This requires not only sharp social skills, but also an ability to separate yourself from your conscience. Some people are capable of doing this (ie. sociopaths!). It also helps if you are very attractive. If you are not, then you will have to be much more manipulative.

The last (and least desirable) is to live on the street. In this case, it helps to foster some kind of drug or alcohol dependency, as the shame involved can be quite a burden to bear. You also need to get used to sleeping during the day, as nights can be dangerous. Also relieving bodily waste in semi-public places and getting used to your own smell will have to be tolerated. I have lived homeless off and on but always in a car or van. I kept a gym membership, so I was clean.

Okay...we've examined four ways of avoiding 'the sweat of your brow,' two of which involve some hard work in the beginning and two that are a bit difficult and have a short lifespan. But wait, there's still another way...

This other way has been around for a little more than a century and a half. It certainly did not originate then, but definitely became the most well-known in history with: Karl Marx and Friedrich Engel's Communist Manifesto. You should know that Marx was a man who detested physical labor. Using Marxist philosophy, one must be 'people savvy' enough to be able to manipulate others. You must be able to 'read' people in terms of where they are politically and emotionally, along with being able to gauge their assertive abilities.

To do this, you need to avoid the assertive people and go towards the weak, feeble and downtrodden. In short- find what they call the proletariat: the people living at the bottom of the social ladder. These are the people that are the most susceptible to your influence. This will involve the use of propaganda. You will need to undermine those at the top and cater to the egos of those at the bottom. It is very good if those at the bottom are one unified race, as their bond will be stronger. Using leaflets (or in modern times, websites), just spread your hatred for the upper class and attack individuals with half truths and outright lies. It also helps if you can divide those at the top also, weakening them. Just place people (or a person) in the other camp, altering their message enough to cause division. A house divided will naturally fall.

Now, to do any of this, you must give the proletariat a picture of a better society. Those at the bottom in any society are the ones who bear the burden of labor. You must be able to give them a vision of a society that will give them leisure and place them in 'the king's court' following the revolution. Any proletariat working class will be extremely numerous, and you will be unable to live up to your promises, so you will have to be convincing. When you can manage to accomplish your revolution and overthrow the current *bourgeoisie* (or upper class), you can simply exterminate most of whom you used to bring you to the top.

At this point, you are in a position that does not necessitate labor of any kind on your part. You can even use people for whatever kind of pleasures you want. What a life! A few years of stirring up trouble and now you are a king.

There are people in the world right now that are trying to do this very thing and finally, after many years of building their framework, are meeting some success. This time it is not Nazi Germany trying to conquer Europe; this time it is on a global scale. These people have pretty much taken over all of Europe and are occupying China, North Korea, North Vietnam, and Venezuela. Most of Europe is already socialist. Brazil is giving way as well. Russia, although not officially communist anymore, is still being led by the same people that managed the old USSR. The United States is now controlled by a totalitarian regime, and are wrestling for complete control of your life.

In fact, the last obstacle for these people has been, and is, the United States. Our Constitution was drafted with an inherent antipathy towards totalitarianism. Our founders believed in the God of the Holy Bible. The God of Abraham. Ours is the first truly free Christian society on earth! Never before has Christianity been able to live on its own without having to first bow in allegiance to a king. Worldly kingship is an anti-Christian principle. We are to serve God alone and not man. We need to be free so we can choose. A king can instruct you to do something contrary to your belief, and impose a penalty of imprisonment or even death- if not met with compliance.

Paul, the man who wrote most of our New Testament, lived in occupied Israel. The Romans had conquered most of the known world, and already led the Israelites in most of their decision making. Paul spent much of the final years of his life in prison, in chains. He wrote what turned out to be most of the New Testament scriptures from there.

Jesus was beaten, tortured and then hung on a cross to pay our debts for our transgressions. Paul sat in chains in the name of Jesus. If they can do this for us, then we must be prepared to do the same, if need be, for our brothers and sisters.

The people that are trying to impose a communist life on us are, first and foremost, *lying*. They are godless. They have no intention of creating an 'equal work for equal pay' system. This is how they sell their philosophy. They really want to be kings. They think people, in general, are stupid bumbling fools that do not know what is best for them. They want us to be their servants. They are (obviously) sociopaths. They have no empathy for anyone and will even 'eat their own' if they need to. If you live in the city, chances are you communicate with these people daily. They can be quite engaging. They can be funny, clever and intelligent. They love playing with people's hearts and minds and using them to get the things they want.

So they already have much of the world in their grasp and now the last bastion of hope is the only nation truly free and founded on a belief in Christ's redemption. We are in their way. They will, at some point, try to exterminate us. They may or may not be successful. We are not to be concerned for our lives but for the lives of our families, brothers and sisters. We will inherit the Kingdom of Heaven after this life. We are to walk in ever-present truth with an unconditional love for all- even these sociopaths. This is what will be the distinction between us and them. Trust me: if you are always honest in all things and you do not return evil for evil you will stand out. Some will realize their ways are evil, will feel ashamed and will cry out to your God. This is your mission accomplished, and what you are called to do.

You are not called to twist anybody's arm, but to be an example. Share the truth by being the truth, and use words if necessary. Do not fear for your life; you will be taken care of. Be a beacon of light in this dark world.

So, naturally, you will be willing to accept the fact that you need to work for a living and you will make the best of it.

Learn to enjoy your work. Know that your toil is providing for both you and your loved ones. Repairing railroad cars can be burdensome- but at the end of the day others will be thankful for what you have done for them. Telling them you love them helps, but your sweat proves it. Where your heart is, there lies your treasure. Love conquers all.

Chapter 9

Homo-Communist Rebellion

From the beginning, man has wanted to tell God he knows a better way of making His world work. However, mankind has never found a way to create a peaceful harmonic society apart from clinging to his maker. In the United States today most people that envision a truly peaceful society refer to the American Indian. But this isn't true. Indian tribes were at war with one another at the time of our European ancestors' arrival.

Some look to the Buddhists. But they have been at war with the Hindus for decades. Sorry it hasn't been done! It cannot. It will not. Mankind flails and rails against God and tries to form society after *his* own fantasies, always envisioning something that appeals to *his* wants as *his* perfect world. That's just it- *his* wants.

So just what is it that man wants? Well...for one thing, God gave us the sexual ability and the good sensations that come with it for procreation. One thing man has always wanted is to have this gratification without the responsibility of the children that come with it. It finally came about, without the painful 'coat hanger procedure' or the falling down the stairs method, with the birth control pill in 1963. Previous ways of doing this were always extreme perversions, like homosexuality, child molestation or rape. Wherever you find a society running from God, you will find at least one of these things prevalent. Child rape is prevalent in many Muslim countries, as men sell their daughters, at ages starting around six, to men for wives. Homosexuality was prevalent in ancient Sodom, in Greece and again surfaced in Rome even before Christ. It became more mainstream in the late nineteenth century in Paris, and it's big in America right now.

God gave Adam a mate, Eve, because "it is not good for man to be alone." He clearly gave her as a companion, as God did this before man had fallen. She was cursed with the pains of childbirth after man had fallen. The Hebrew Scriptures dictate that a man who engages in homosexual behavior be put to death. Our Christian Scriptures say that homosexuals (along with thieves and murderers) will not enter the Kingdom of Heaven. Gay activists claim that the reference to 'homosexuals' in the New Testament refers to pedophiles. If you look this up in the Greek, the language the New Testament was written in, this reference to homosexuals referred to a 'man who lies with a man as a woman.'... Sorry.

Look I don't want to seem like some gay basher here so I'm going to come clean about something here. I was a psychiatric nurse in the eighties, a songwriter, band member and bodybuilder and was very successful at it. An injury in 1985 left me with a good physique but no longer a competitive one. I desperately wanted out of the hospital I had been working at for 20 years and started working as a male exotic dancer in Ventura, California. Soon I joined DG'S Hollywood Hunks and started doing private parties. I also started going up to a nude beach by Santa Barbara during the day. My mother came down from Washington to visit and caught me fresh back from the beach, getting ready to go work at the club in Ventura and told me, "If you continue in this lifestyle you will get AIDS."

I scoffed, "you don't get AIDS from dancing for girls." She just warned me about the direction it was going.

She was right.

In 1989, as the year was drawing to an end, I decided to quit the hospital and to move down to Los Angeles. I played in a band in Santa Monica that was formed in the gym in Venice. I always wanted to move to L.A., and this was as good of a time as ever. My plan was to work as a stripper. I rented a living room sofa bed from a girl in West Hollywood. But there was a problem: male exotic dancing had suddenly gone out of fashion and I noticed a lot of the guys I had been working with had been going to gay clubs and finding work there. Since I didn't find work, I succumbed and began working as a stripper in some places and a go-go boy in these gay clubs. I was later propositioned by two agents and some photographers and did some acting parts and worked as an erotic art model.

As the pay was not as good anymore, I was frequently propositioned by club goers for quite a lot of money. I soon found myself entertaining male clients, dancing at their parties and working as an escort- in other words, a prostitute. Ironically, here I met some people who had an influential effect on me. One, an art dealer with a museum in Oakland, who exposed me to modern classical music. Another was a classical pianist and an artist. I became their friend. I really didn't mind my new life, as I was finally living in Hollywood. I just did what I felt I had to and simply kept my dealings secret to my band mates.

I still had girlfriends from time to time and finally put together a personal training business. So I was free of entertaining gay clients...or so I thought. At Gold's Gym in Hollywood, the bulk of the members are gay, and I soon found myself training many gay clients- most of whom became my friends. All of my clients were television producers and actors or screenwriters who were gay or gay-friendly.

So I don't want to be one that beats up on smokers once I quit; I just have been enlightened. I now realize that homosexuality is, at its core, rebellion against what God has given us. Sorry- it is. I love my gay friends, but can very clearly see their rebellion when I listen to them talk. They can be really petty and talk about women as "leaky twats" when their 'fag hags' backs are turned. They are very backbiting. If you have any gay friends, you'll see that I'm right about this. Look- I have too many gay friends to not see that they run at the first sign of discomfort in relationships.

If you read some gay literature, you will find many references to gay men (or women) attempting to pick up on straight men (or women). There's even a popular cable TV sitcom called, "Queer eye for the straight guy." I have a problem with this! If their lifestyle was as pure as they would have us believe, they wouldn't need to convert straight guys. Notice that straight guys never try to convert homos!

I rented a room in a condo in West Hollywood with a gay guy that was very overweight. He had friends, but when he would throw parties for them we would invariably end up alone. He would be so disappointed. Gay men can be very superficial, flitting around West Hollywood and talking about all the 'stars' they have been working with. Such name droppers! This makes them feel special. And have you ever noticed that 80 percent of gay peoples' conversation is centered around their sexuality? Why? This is what happens when peoples' existence revolves only around the "here and now." This life is all gay people have!

When I was in nursing school, we were reading from a book called "Normal Growth and Development," and I read a passage that said homosexuals displayed "childishness in the way they behaved and the desires they have." This was 1980, and I was appalled! I had to look up the publishing date and it was 1963. I KNOW that this book would have never been published in the era I was reading it. I don't remember the author. But I definitely see these things in my gay friends. I also see their love, which is real, but am very aware of their stunted growth and development.

During my time in the gay community I made many good friends- some whom remain. Neil and Alan, two personal training clients of mine, bought a CD player and a bicycle for me. So even though I see the gay lifestyle as basically a superficial life, these people were very good and caring. It should be obvious to anybody that men were meant to be with women for the sexual experience that naturally leads to procreation. Why is this obvious? Because the parts are there to facilitate this! It's all in the parts, baby! Anybody that claims they were born gay is justifying their decision. Nothing wrong, but call it like it is. They might have felt this way for as long as they can remember, but that's just the nature of the beast. The first step: being gay is presented as an option. Then, appealing to the self-serving nature of man, a logical alternative. Once entertained long enough, it becomes an identity.

I'm not protected from hate speech, so why should you be? This is true and not just with gay people. Tell me: why can progressives slander anyone in any way but if it's a conservative opinion then their view becomes hate speech? Listen to the hateful vitriol coming from the left at anyone who disagrees with them. This, my friends, is hate speech. I think they should be able to do that; it's called 'freedom of speech.'

Last fall, Apple computer banned the "Manhattan Declaration" app on their Iphones. The "Declaration" is composed of a group of prominent Christian clergy, ministry leaders and scholars. The ban occurred after gay rights groups protested it. Now another similar app has been shut down: Exodus International, a Christian ministry that helps people who want to leave the homosexual lifestyle. What this is doing is curbing freedom of speech. These people want freedom when it applies to their desires, but when it doesn't, they want to quash it. They are trying to marginalize, intimidate and silence anyone who opposes their viewpoint. What this is called is hypocrisy!

I have even been to one gay church. The gay church I went to was definitely full of love, but short on accountability. I'm not here to judge them. This is between each one of them and God.

My main point is that the homosexual lifestyle is one that naturally leads to a degradation of the family structure that we were designed for. In this lifestyle, relationships are fleeting, and the kind of love that is needed for bringing up children is not present. At the coffee shop I go to, (you will hear about this place constantly, sorry this is the place where I'm writing this book) there are two gay men that have 'acquired' the cutest little girl I have ever seen in my life! She is just adorable! I'm praying for this girl as we speak because I already know what she is in for. The things they will teach her make me weep.

In ancient Rome and Greece, people were ruled by kings. In both of these countries, homosexuality became prevalent. Listen to any of the sociopaths trying to implement a dependent lifestyle for Americans. If you notice, most of them are or seem to be of homosexual persuasion. So what's the catch? Why is homosexuality tied in with communism? Because they want genderless servants for themselves to use in any depraved way they want. A strong family unit will be, naturally, anathema to their desires. They want complete control. Capitalism is also their enemy. A free enterprise system gives control to the people over their welfare and their way of life.

Even Bohemian Grove, the 2500-acre resort in Northern California where the 'uber rich' and powerful go to 'play' was addressed by President Nixon, when he made a trip there, as being too 'faggy.' Read up on this place and you'll see the sickening kind of depravity these men do. You will read about infant rape and hunting naked women out on the grounds with rifles! And these are supposed to be the "leaders" of the free world, our supposedly "straight-edged" political figures!

So homosexuality is a natural evolution from communism. And communism from homosexuality. And, believe it or not, homosexuality from Islam...for that matter. Shariah law and its hatred of women is definitely a form of homosexuality in that the men do not put women in a place of importance at all and instead prefer to keep the company of males. These men don't recognize that other men really don't provide the kind of emotional balance that women will. I see hints of this in sports enthusiasts as well.

Boys just enjoying being with and watching other boys. I have a problem with this. It neglects everything a girl has to offer. Your girl should be a companion in most things in your life. If your pastimes take you away from her, something's wrong.

Communism loves depravity. Homosexuality loves depravity. Just look at the sex clubs in gay neighborhoods. Communism, Islam and homosexuality all involve the worship of men, or man.

When America was a country that loved our Lord, were there any of these things present? No. The sociopaths want God out of the way. They obviously want a society that looks like the Rome of the emperors. People you know, are buying into this madness totally unaware that it's what they're buying into. We have been force-fed a way of thinking that does not require love as its foundation. Children require love. None of these approaches demand love as a necessity because the family unit and children are not necessary. That which is not grounded in love will hurt you. Love conquers all. Our God loves us. We love God, our families, and children, which are a gift from God. We also loved our country before it became overrun with this hedonistic 'pretend love' and, in reality, hatred of all that is good. These people are perishing. We must, out of our love for them, try to save them from themselves. We need to show them the love we have, even when they are cruel. Trust me: if you love your fellow man when he is intentionally harming your way of life, he will listen. He might not admit it right away but your work is done. Remember, love conquers all.

Chapter 10 Suicidal Tendencies

Can someone tell me why almost all the revolutionaries of the past two hundred years seem to be Jewish? Karl Marx, Abbie Hoffman, Allen Ginsberg and George Soros are all Jews. Even Adolph Hitler was repudiated to be Jewish. Don't they know if their communist utopia is instated, they might be exterminated? Well, if the conspiracy theorists are right and there is a group of world leaders known as the Bilderbergs that want world domination and you research this group, you will also find a good part of them are Jewish as well. Maybe a Jewish conspiracy? I don't think so, because of all the hatred towards Jewish people is from both the Muslims and the far left. Remember the flotilla in May 2010? That was perpetrated by Bill Ayres, his wife Bernadine Dohrn, and the anti-war women's rights group Code Pink, who has Hamas protecting them. They're communist sociopaths who all want Israel to fail. Why? Because they hate God's people, and gentile Christians. These people must go if they are to attain their utopia. And *that's* why you stage a flotilla!

Not once...but twice in the book of Revelation there is a reference to "those that say they are Jews and are not." This clearly was important. Who do you suppose these people are?

One theory over the years against the Israelites being actually Jewish has been that the Khazarian conversion of the eighth-century spawned Jewish people who were not actually Jewish. The Khazars occupied Eastern Europe and Turkey and wanted a religious identity that fit in with the other peoples around them. So they decided to convert to Judaism. In the twentieth century, people that foster Jewish hatred have identified the Israelites being the Khazarians.

I personally would, given this theory, think it would be the other way around. I would think it would be the secular Jews. There are just too many Jewish people out there that seem to want the extermination of their fellow Jews.

I think that leftist revolutionary ideology, with its requisite godlessness, is just too powerful a force for those wanting to police themselves and create a world after their own desires. I think they want anyone out of the way that lives under the rule of God, be it Jews or Christians. The fact that so many of these revolutionaries are Jewish is puzzling. Who would wish the subordination or extermination of their own peoples? Answer: godless revolutionaries. Jews have always been known to be ultra-intelligent and very driven. Somewhere in history, at sometime, there *must* have been a major cloggage of bloodlines. Who are the "chosen ones" in 2011? Who are the trueblooded Jews? It's certain that some Jews love God while some truly hate Him!

The "Chicago seven," which included some Jews, were all communists. Tom Hayden took people from the Students for a Democratic Society to Cuba to show them what a wonderful thing Castro had done in Cuba. Abbie Hoffman studied under famed psychologist Abraham Maslow who taught Humanistic psychology.

Jacob Frank, a polish Jew in the late seventeenth century, led Jewish people to believe more in the Kabbalah than the Hebrew scriptures. Later, the Rothschilds, also Jewish, began a banking system in France and a shadow government in Britain.

If these people are indeed Jewish, then it seems that they are so married to their revolutionary purposes and can only see this at the exclusion of faith. Seems kind of suicidal to me.

I live in West Hollywood, surrounded on all sides by Russian Jewish immigrants. I go to a coffee shop in Beverly Hills where I'm surrounded by Hasidic and secular Jews. Just talking to these folks or looking at their bumper stickers, you can see that pretty much

ALL the secular Jews voted for Obama even though he is openly hostile towards Israel.

Margaret Sanger also was an early Jewish feminist/eugenicist who tried to implement eugenics (the concept of population control by ethnicity) into American life. Her eugenic theme figured prominently in the Birth Control Review, which she founded in 1917. She published articles such as: "Some Moral Aspects of Eugenics" (1920), "The Eugenics Conscience" (1921), "The Purpose of Eugenics" (1924), Birth Control and Positive Eugenics" (1925) and Birth Control: The True Eugenics" (1928).

Sanger spoke of sterilizing those she designated as unfit- a plan she said would be the salvation of American civilization. She also spoke of those who were "irresponsible and reckless." She included, in her sterilization plan, those whose religious scruples prevented their exercising of control over their numbers.

Now let's look at the women's liberation movement, which definitely has its origins in the communist movement. Betty Friedan's "The Feminine Mystique (1963)," which sold more than five million copies, is considered the manifesto of the modern feminist movement. Incidentally, this was the same year the birth control pill was released for public consumption. Friedan and French existentialist philosopher Simone de Beauvoir are the pioneers of modern feminism. In "The Feminine Mystique," Friedan describes herself as a typical suburban housewife and mother who had a revelation. She concluded that women like herself are being exploited and dehumanized. She went as far as to compare their plight with that of Nazi concentration camp inmates. She pointed to career as a woman's only path to identity and self-fulfillment.

What Friedan didn't say is that she wasn't a typical housewife. Rather, she had been a Marxist activist since her undergraduate years at Smith College (1938-1942) where she wrote for the college newspaper. She dropped out of grad school to become a reporter for a radical left wing news service. From 1946 -1952, she was a reporter for the union newspaper of the United Electrical, Radio and Machine Workers of America, (UE) "the largest communist-led institution of any kind in the United States." She was born "Bettye Naomi Goldstein."

The sixties brought forth a populist women's liberation movement that remains to this day. The feminist movement has become much more outwardly communist in the last few years. They now are supporting almost any movement that is anti-capitalist and anti-American. Example: "Code Pink: Women for Peace." Karl Rove, a senior advisor to George W. Bush, in March 2010 was doing a book signing event in Beverly Hills when Code Pink members showed up and ambushed him. They forced him to leave the event. A Code Pink co-founder walked towards Rove with handcuffs, saying she was making a citizens' arrest.

"Code Pink," who has a history of working with enemies of the Egyptian government, Hamas and the Muslim Brotherhood, said on Feb. 3, 2011, they wanted to raise $5,000 to fund the next big uprising. Code Pink co-founder Madea Benjamin posted on Twitter later that day that $10,000 had been raised. They have reportedly marched in the past, with a huge banner that read, "We support the murder of American troops."

Code Pink recently took an ad out on a popular Muslim website, saying, "Help us *cleanse* our *country.*" Tell me, what does this say to you? Cleanse our country? Sound like Hitler enough? That right there should speak volumes to you. The very fact that Code Pink (Women for Peace) would support Islam, the most repressive environment for women in the world, should tell you there's something wrong with the whole women's liberation movement. It IS communist.

At present the feminist movement, ironically, is for a dependent, communist world. Example: Sarah Palin, Michelle

Bachman and Christine O'Donnell have all been treated egregiously, but no feminist groups came to their defense. All are conservative women in political circles. The feminist groups, who one would expect to be the most supportive, are actually the most vicious in their attacks. Why would this be the case? It's because these organizations are really promoting the communist worldview. What's puzzling about the new feminist movement is their blind adherence to Muslim culture, or, more accurately, their tolerance of Muslim Shariah law. They are defending it all the time. Islam is well known as the most repressive culture for women in the world. Women are second-rate citizens and are basically slaves to their men. Female genital mutilation and honor killing are hardly promoting freedom for women. The feminist movement was initially a movement for the emancipation of women and now it has been revealed as the monster it was from its inception.

The feminist movement never was about emancipating women, but actually about enslaving more people. Women have been lied to by sociopaths. Feminism, Islam and communism are totalitarian forces that want to bring people under their rule. They are all liars. They hate human life and pretend to be working for freedom. Supposedly, Argentinian militant Che' Guevara, the 'killing machine', was a freedom fighter. Muslims are suicidal, as can be seen in the way they use children, and women and even themselves to bomb innocents. Secular Jews are also buying this lie- and it's going to be the cause of their extermination. They seem not to care if they're murdered- as long as the cause is furthered. Kill us, kill them, let's all just kill. It should be obvious what is really behind this killing locomotive. This force hates human life, and is a liar.

We've already discussed at length the acceptance of communist/socialist ideology by gays. But it's noteworthy that both Hitler and Castro insisted that homosexuals be put to death. The gay community also jumps to the defense of the Muslims that want them exterminated. Do they want to die too? Why? Their lust for self-satisfaction and revolution blinds them from knowing God and the truth. The moral of the story: any causes that ignore/marginalize God in this lifetime are suicidal.

Lucifer hates humans and is jealous of what we have been promised. He wants to take as many with him as possible before it's all over with. He is the father of lies and loves to cause hatred in as many of us as he can. It is obvious he has succeeded in a good portion of the population in the past and present. We (who are loving and truthful) are his enemy. These people are deluded into thinking they are part of a revolution to free others- but actually are serving their god, Lucifer (whether they know it or not). It is up to us to show them what freedom really looks like. We need to show them what love and truthfulness looks like. So we have to be what we promote first. Then they will see what a loving, peaceful world they could have. Then, maybe we can save some of them- feminist, gay, Jew, sociopath, Muslim, communist, et cetera- from their suicidal tendencies.

Chapter 11

Communists or Communalists?

Do you think everybody that buys into communist ideology actually believes in communism? I don't think so. I don't think many of them even know what communism is. The way it is presented to them it must seem like, something like...communalism. As in a community, all loving each other and sharing everything. Just listen to the words of John Lennon's 'Imagine' and, well, imagine...

Imagine no possessions
I wonder if you can
No need for greed or hunger
A brotherhood of man
Imagine all the people
Sharing all the world

Look, we know that the way it always turns out is quite different than the way communism is presented. But why don't today's Americans know that the old USSR, Cuba, North Korea, Venezuela and China are just typical communist countries? If they did, they'd realize that they're currently being indoctrinated with those countries' philosophies. Also, in these countries the people are trying to escape, usually hating their leaders/captors. Why don't they know that the 'green' movement, the 'free love' movement, women's rights, animal rights, and global warming is just communist sociopaths trying to make their philosophy more palatable? They're liars and sociopaths who have no intention of providing the world they expound if they come to power. And people are oblivious.

The reason Americans don't know is obvious and I've said it all before: they're busy. They don't think about these things. They have an X-box. Fantasy football. They watch E! entertainment television.

Yet even the people who are not so media enveloped seem to be unaware of the ramifications of their own beliefs. When I was a trainer at Gold's Gym in Hollywood we had a saying: "All you have to do is attach the word homeopathic to anything- even if its golf balls- and you will have all of Beverly Hills down here writing you checks." I'm quite sure all of the people I trained voted for Obama because he was a black man and would be mortified to find out how many communists he has in his cabinet. Some wouldn't- they would applaud it.

A lot of the people I trained- when not working on their movies or TV shows- were usually catering to themselves or their pets. Almost none of them ate meat. Animals were not for eating and were deified. This attitude is certainly not limited to Hollywood. Even Tucker Carlson, a conservative and Fox News contributor, said after the Philadelphia Eagles gave Michael Vick a second chance after doing time for fighting dogs that he thought Michael should be executed. What happens when people walk their dogs and other dogs come by? Snarling and barking? What does this mean? Dogs fight. Its true, dog fighting is cruel- but executed? Tucker, Christ did not give himself for the dogs. You are deifying the creation rather than the creator.

I call these people 'lay communists' because they don't even know what drives their opinions. And I'm quite sure they're not thinking,"oh, those stupid people out there they don't even know what's good for them. I need to be dictating their every move." That's what the sociopaths are doing. They have just bought the lies told them, that it's all about "fairness to the downtrodden" and "protecting the animals" and "mother earth." But they are very adamant about their philosophies nonetheless. They don't even know they are expounding communist ideology and some, if they figured it out, would probably say "so what?"

I got a call recently from an old friend in Seattle and he said he had been trying to reconnect with Jesus. We talked for a while about that and then he asked who I was listening to these days and I said Glenn Beck. Silence......I said, "just listen to him." He replied, "Oh, I did once and couldn't take it." Bullshit! You see, all you have to do is listen to the sociopaths a little while and already you're lying!

My friend is the same age as myself and I know where his philosophies come from. Crosby, Stills and Nash. And don't forget Neil Young. Carlos Santana wears Che' t-shirts, totally unaware that Guevara was a monster who loved killing. They think he was a freedom fighter. I used to listen to "Four Dead in Ohio," and was outraged. I would hear, "Please come to Chicago or else join the other side" and was rallied. I was a rock musician. I understand.

This mindset is very hard to beat because it is all about loving and peace and respecting the Earth and its creatures. I mean, who isn't for these things and if you're not- well, you must be one of those haters. If you could sit with any of these people and explain where their philosophies come from and what they were designed to do, they would certainly say..."but I'm not for people control!" They would be right, they're not. The problem is, the ones who gave them their wisdom are subtlely brainwashing them. I say "how does it feel to be *that* easy to influence?"

I'm also quite sure that any lay communist (who doesn't even know they're communist) would say they want freedom, not servitude. But what are they buying into? A philosophy that denies them even the right to make their own decisions! What they don't realize is that communists are, first, LIARS! I mean 'The Peoples Republic of China.' Is it the 'peoples' republic? Of course not. Then why is it called that? Because they are LIARS! The 'people' really have a lot to say- don't they? The government over there tells them how many (and what gender) children they can have. People that want dominion over you will not tell you the truth! You would never accept that. So they are not truthful and tell you things they will do for you with absolutely no intention of making good on their promises. LIARS!

If it all is about loving the Earth and equality of people, then why all the lying? *You don't have to lie about those things.* Take (for instance) the names for their organizations. SDS is the Students for a Democratic Society. Tom Hayden, its co-founder, used to take students on field trips to Cuba to see what a sweet thing Castro had done. Democracy, in theory, means the people rule themselves. Does Cuba look like that? Then why do they get on inner tubes trying to escape? I live in a Russian neighborhood in West Hollywood and the fear on these peoples' faces when anyone walks by is amazing! The suspicion in their eyes tells me there's nothing good that happened with the KGB having 'rats' on every street corner. Tell me: is living under communist rule progressive or is it regressive back to the days of kings? Is communism democratic? Do the people really make their own decisions?

George Soros, the Hungarian Jew who made billions on his hedge funds and collapsed many countries' economies for the 'fun of it,' funds many of these organizations. He has made his money from betting he can force a large scale movement in the markets, and then plays against those moves selling the original investors short, and cashing in on their losses. His 'Open Society' promotes communism and his 'Media Matters for America' goes after conservative media figures and attacks them in any way they can find. Also, his organizational website, moveon.org, has 5 million members- ordinary Americans- who believe they can unite and find a political voice in a "system dominated by big money and big media. Hmmm...who is funding MoveOn? Doesn't "big money" and "big media"= George Soros? This man funded the supposed energy saving and job creating Apollo Alliance (which also was responsible for drafting the first stimulus package). They also drafted the 'Cap and Trade' bill, where America gave millions to poor countries via the U.N. to 'punish' us for our carbon emission standards being so lackluster (then again, who is creating the standards?) Lastly, there's his money laundering charity, the Tides Foundation, which is the charity 'agent' that funds all these corrupt organizations. And here's the kicker: he says the main obstacle to a stable and just world order is America. Really? Not Iran?

Soros' Center for American Progress (CAP) is a progressive think tank designed to find out just how to successfully bring America down in a graceful managed decline. It was started in 2003 by Hillary Clinton and 'Generous' George. Clinton and Obama pretended to be adversaries, but the minute Obama was elected, his administration was filled with CAP alumni. One is John Holdren, who says we should force abortions and put sterilants in our drinking water. Another is Carol Browner, head of the EPA (Environmental Protection Agency). She wants us to avoid drilling for our own oil- leaving us dependant on Muslim countries. A third is 'Safe Schools' czar, Kevin Jennings, a longtime homosexual rights advocate who had much praise for Harry Hay of the North American Man Boy Love Association. He even advocated teaching 14 year olds

about 'fisting,' meaning using a fist in the rectum as sex organ, and asking them whether it's rude to 'spit or swallow.'

Also, there is the aforementioned Cass Sunstein, Obama's regulatory czar, who says "there's too much Homer Simpson in the average citizen which prevents them from making right choices on things such as food,' and this makes them 'easily manipulated' by the progressive elitists. Cass' agenda includes regulating education (indoctrination), banks, religion and charity. Cass wants to ban hunting for sport and believes animals should have lawyers and be able to sue people in court (he said this in 2004) and is now married to fellow Harvard-trained lawyer Samantha Power (both are educators and advisors to President Obama). Samantha Power is the driving force behind the US intervention in Libya and seems to be someone who sees war as an answer to anything and her radical views are heard by our president. She has authored the 'Responsibility to Protect' act, which is legislature that gives license to bombing in Libya and Jordan and paints Israel as the ones inflicting all the damage to civilian infrastructure when they are really only defending themselves. There were 35,000 killed in Mexico in the last 4 years, many being dumped into mass graves by drug cartels. But we have a 'responsibility to protect' in Libya? How about *Americans*, or are *we* worthless? Looks like George Soros is more than just a financial terrorist.

Look, a government big enough to give you anything you want is also big enough to take everything you have. Sherle Schwenninger is the director of economic growth and American strategy program at the New America Foundation and says there are 8.5 million people in the US receiving unemployment insurance and over 40 million on food stamps. Middle-income jobs are disappearing from the economy; the share of middle-income jobs in the United States has fallen from 52% in 1980 to 42% in 2010. Middle-income jobs have been replaced by low-income jobs which now make up 41% of total employment. 17 million Americans with college degrees are doing jobs that require less than the skill level associated with a bachelor's degree. Over the past year nominal wages grew only 1.7% while all consumer prices, including food and energy, increased by 2.7%. Wages and salaries have fallen from 60% of personal income in 1980 to 51% in 2010. The bottom line is, the middle class is shrinking, which threatens the social composition and stability of the world's biggest economy. I worry that we are becoming a barbell society – a lot of money and wealth and power at the top, increasing hollowness at the center, which provides the stability and heart and soul of the society...and then too many people in fear of falling down.

Obama's followers keep saying our debt problem is the fault of George Bush. Then why has Obama tripled our debt since he came into office? Its true, Bush started spending way too much near the end of his second term and I personally think that was all part of the plan. To allow Obama to pass the buck. The Bilderbergs have had this plan all along and have been grooming Obama for his exalted position for some time. China now is the most capitalist country on earth! They have been through communism and seen that it doesn't work. They're repressive- but capitalist. Trust me, very soon they are going to tell America they will not buy anymore of our debt and will tell us we are not fiscally responsible enough to work with anymore. We will be on our own and will have a Marxist president who will bring *everyone* to poverty.

In the book of revelation it speaks of the battle of Armageddon where the kings of the east war with the beast from the west and I believe this will come about because the leader of the New World Order will be a diehard communist/Islamic dictator and will be worshiped and the eastern kings will not want on board as they have gone through communism and found it wanting.

Well- well, so you elected a president on behalf of his skin color and didn't look into his background. Boo hoo! This, friends, is what you get when you elect someone for this reason. You get a Marxist president. This is what he wants. Enjoy yourselves!

Van Jones, Obama's green czar and, has called for a protest at every state house in the union and is sponsored by progressive organizations. Many have called this the "American Dream" movement. He is saying to them, "Have your own tea party," effectively co-opting the real Tea Party movement, which is all about fiscal responsibility and supporting the family and private enterprise. They say this is to defend the American dream against Republicans' 'slash and burn' agenda. He says "Let Saturday February 26th 2011 mark the beginning of the national movement to renew the American dream and return us to the MORAL center, where everybody counts and everybody matters." This really is just a movement to revitalize unions. Van Jones was the man ousted in

2009 from the White House after it being revealed he was an unabashed communist. What has this to do with the real American dream? LIARS!

The real American dream has always meant that anyone can work hard or be creative enough to bring themselves to prosperity.

Now let me tell you what the *real* Tea Party is. These Americans do not want federal programs that are wastefully expensive and just redistribute wealth from the working people to people not working. They want equal opportunity for ALL Americans; whether Americans take advantage of those opportunities or not is another story. Tea Partiers don't want to get in line for government handouts; they want handouts to stop. For bankers, auto makers and irresponsible people who have defaulted on their mortgages. They want the government to get the hell out of the way of the free enterprise system that brought America into prosperity. They want to battle (just like the originals), "taxation without representation."

The way the left paints the picture, the Tea Party people are racist haters and violent. But who is really racist and violent? SEIU thugs, or the Service Employees International Union. They snuck in a side handicapped entrance at a town hall in south St. Louis on August 7, 2009, attacking Tea Partier Kenneth Gladney as he handed out yellow flags saying, "Don't tread on me" on them. Kenneth is also a black man. No respecter of races, these thugs are just mindless robots obeying their union bosses! There have never been any violent incidents at a Tea Party gathering that wasn't union thugs creeping in and doing it, yet they say the Tea Partiers are violent. LIARS!

The National Endowment for the Arts in 2009 was exposed by Glenn Beck for giving grants to artists to put out communist propaganda. Hitler did something almost identical by placing state sponsored fliers supporting his ideals throughout Germany.

President Obama campaigned on a platform of not doing business with lobbyists but we knew it was a lie, given the number of them he let into the White House. He is having his people take secret meetings with lobbyists routinely, but they are doing it outside the White House, across the street. Why? It's because the Secret Service does not keep logs of where they meet, so there is no way to track who is going into and out of the meetings. And to think: this was promised to be the most transparent administration ever! LIARS!

Look, in 2009 the White House issued an edict asking people to email them with any "fishy" information, clearly meaning any information that was anti-Obama Administration. Does this bother you? This will be communist Russia; in other words, the USSR with KGB roaming the streets, if anything like this is allowed to continue. Venezuelan dictator Hugo Chavez was adulated by Mark Lloyd, President Obama's diversity czar, as having done a good work by taking complete control of the media, including the internet. Only state-sponsored propaganda is allowed. Is this what you want?

Egypt has been in what is referred to as 'emergency mode' for the last thirty years. This hit a tipping point in Feb. 2011 when citizens rioted against dictator Hosni Mubarak in Tahrir square in Cairo. This 'emergency mode' is what we here in America would consider 'martial law.' Now do you really think this cannot happen here? Do you think any leader that buys into the "dependent society" kind of mindset, after securing the internet, all television and radio channels, and having all transportation locked down, would give this up? Are you kidding? He could be a king! You would be isolated. Helpless.

Why do the democratic lawmakers want rioting in the streets? They want to destabilize the country. Just like Egypt is now and many more countries around the Middle East are also. They want this to be global. Europe has been undergoing civil unrest now for a few years over the same thing (entitlement reductions) and now they want to bring it to America. At this writing there are revolts going on in Algeria, Bahrain, Libya, Yemen, Jordan, Lebanon, Syria and Iran. Italy is also undergoing protests in the streets. So is Greece. In England there were 500,000 in the streets in early April 2011 and it was all motivated by trade unions. It also happened during the same period in Wisconsin and Ohio. Also motivated by unions.

The main impetus for the civil unrest will all start with unions. Lawmakers who are trying to be fiscally responsible will be the bad people. The progressives want the states to go bankrupt so the feds can bail them out and then they will then be beholden to the federal government. States' sovereignty is written in our constitution but the communist sociopaths want the federal government to be the ones dictating what happens in the states. They want control. Where do you think this all will lead? Revolution is what both the communists and the Islamics want. Revolution all over the world will only lead to one thing. First it will be chaos and rioting and then there will be someone that comes in and tells everyone that he has the solution. This will be a world leader that will be able to have control over every human. The Christian scriptures tell us he is the "man of lawlessness" who exalts himself above God, takes his seat in the temple of God in Jerusalem, and has the whole world under his sway.

President Obama already has been trying to piece together a civilian national security force. Do you know what this is? Think about it for...oh...two seconds should do. This will be used for crushing freedom of speech and any dissent whatsoever. Sound like the KGB? It is... Even Henry Kissinger, the Secretary of State under President Nixon (and longtime Bilderberg member) said of President Obama, he is the one person perfectly positioned to bring in the 'New World Order.' Wow, and we wonder why he won't listen to the American people?

Speaking of the 'New World Order,' which is something that no one seems to be able to define, did you know that President Obama is allowing for the indefinite detention of prisoners at Guantanamo Bay even after their acquittal? Why would he do this? Does he, at some point, want to be able to do this to you? Power corrupts.

Is this where you want to live? Well...then get involved. Do something. There's the 9/12 project. There's Freedomworks. Many others...just look them up. Glenn Beck is one of the very few addressing our problems accurately right now. Just look at how hated he is. Then look at WHO it is that hates him. This should tell you everything. I'm telling you now that EVERYTHING Glenn has said would happen has. Everything he has said regarding anyone has been supported with their own words. Glenn Beck is the ONLY ONE with the balls to say what he sees is happening and if you do not keep up with him *you deserve whatever happens to you!*

The environmentalists that closed down farmers in the San Joaquin Valley, in California (and more recently shut down businesses in North Carolina), are not interested in the preservation of wildlife at all. They know that if they can shut down some large industries for the protection of particular species of fish, bird or rodent, they will have dealt a huge blow to capitalism. They hide behind the environmentalist masquerade just to justify their actions.

From the beginning, the global warming issue has been all about bringing down industrialized nations; namely, the United States. Burning fossil fuels or man-made carbon dioxide has never been the cause of any hole in the ozone layer nor been responsible for global warming. The global warming hoax was proven to be just that, with the release of many emails from the scientists in England who were responsible for the studies that supposedly 'proved' man-made global warming. They took center stage, marginalizing the opposing scientists from publishing their works, and were paid well. This, from the very beginning, has been about taxing Americans because of carbon emissions, damaging our economy and leveling the playing field between countries by reducing an exceptional America to just another 'nation state.' Al Gore (previously worth about $2 million) is now worth approximately $200 million and has made many of his fellow 'corruptocrats' millionaires as well. If they can establish global environmental laws, which they *are* trying to do, the U.S. constitution will suddenly cease to be the laws of our land. This will be because we will suddenly be answering to a new global authority- and not our constitution. This is all about money and power. All you stupid little people out there will just keep playing video games, talking about the Lakers, be good little puppets and regurgitate the horseshit fed you.

By the way it is right now January fourth 2011 and we just had four inches of snow in Las Vegas!

What these people want is a government takeover of what once were private industries. What once were mom and pop businesses will become so state-regulated they will eventually disappear. This, in a nutshell, is Fascism. State-controlled agriculture and health services lead to state-controlled speech and behavior with a paid individual on every street to inform the government of any speech that does not follow what is deemed "accepted speech." What a pleasant world that will be!

All the left wing pundits praised the pandering rhetoric of President Obama's Jan. 25, 2011 State of the Union speech. He said we must keep putting more money into our infrastructure (investing) and funnel more money into schools. For one thing the problem with our schools is not something that can be solved with more money, the problem is lazy teachers that spew communist philosophies. Our infrastructure always could use something but not when we are underwater financially.

He also wants to build high speed transit for cities. I'll tell you what this is for. This is for all the 'great unwashed' to use so they will stop driving cars (that is, if they can afford them). Do you notice that all this just means more spending? The code word now is 'investing.' We're investing in our future. This means spending. Our president wants to bankrupt us by 'spending' our future, leaving us beholden to China, another communist country. We have borrowed from China to the point of owing them our future. China is now beginning to sell off a lot of our debt to other countries. Sixties radicals Cloward and Pivin taught this: "Spend, spend, until you collapse the system."

At present oil drilling is forbidden in many parts of the US as groups like Greenpeace and the (EPA) Environmental Protection Agency have successfully made it impossible to drill in some areas of Alaska and also off the coast of Florida. Environmentalists have closed 83 percent of our land for oil drilling. President Obama has extended a freeze on oil drilling after the gulf oil spill. But on March, 20[th,] 2011, Obama OK'd Brazilian oil giant Petrobras to drill into our environmentally-forbidden Gulf of Mexico. This came after the US loaned them $2 billion taxpayer dollars last year on September 11[th.] What this is really about is keeping us dependent on big oil despots in the Middle East (and now Brazil) and building up the other countries. What does this do for them?...redistribute our wealth to Brazil because they are a poorer country than us- and that's the point. Never mind that they (besides being one of the most resource-rich countries in the world) are poor because their government is corrupt! Our government likes corruption.

One of the Forbes brothers was on a news program on oil and the host asked him, "How much oil does the US have in the ground?" Forbes replied, "More than all the Middle East together." The Bakken formation in North Dakota is the largest domestic oil discovery since Alaska's Prudhoe Bay, and has the potential to eliminate all American dependence on foreign oil. A recent technological breakthrough has opened up the Bakken's massive reserves and we now have access of up to 500 billion barrels. Because this is "light, sweet" oil, those billions of barrels will cost

Americans just $16 per barrel. That's enough to fully fuel the American economy for 2041 years straight.

Brazil and Mexico are now using our old drilling sites and equipment for their own drilling. I'm telling you, our government wants us to be equal with them. Do you want to be equal with countries like Brazil or Mexico? Is life there better than here? This is nothing more than redistributing the wealth. We are not short on energy supplies. We have enough places to drill for oil. If we open up the Arctic National Wildlife Refuge (ANWR), use Canadian oil, and also work with Brazil, we have everything we need- even if we never tapped into Bakken. Sociopaths want to even the playing field amongst nations, making us all the same so their one world government will manage every person on the planet.

Have you ever looked at the UN? I mean- not only the member states- but also their representatives? Some member states are Venezuela, Libya, Iran, Afghanistan, Cambodia, Cuba, Egypt, Jordan, North Korea, Pakistan, Russia and United Arab Emirates. Look at the leaders of these countries. Men like Muammar al Gaddafi of Libya, Hugo Chavez of Venezuela, Kim Jong Ill of North Korea or Iranian President Mahmoud Ahmadinejad. Do you realize that these people are the elite that will rule the world? These are the people that think you are stupid enough to warrant their rule over you! Listen to them! Do they even sound intelligent? No, they're just brutal dictators.

Now let's look at organized labor. This is responsible for bankrupting many cities, states and even our country. It, really, is just immoral. Our government cannot tax us enough to pay for the exorbitant pensions given to their own employees. If you make a pact with someone to work for a certain period of time for a certain amount of money, this is a covenant with this person or company. You made a deal. So how can you expect more than that? That's what unions attempt to do. Unions stand up for you (even after you made a covenant), when you should be standing up for yourself.

They are *always* corrupt and do not need to exist. Abusive employers should, under free market principles, lose employees, as they would eventually move on to work elsewhere. Companies would be forced to be competitive. But with unions, this never happens.

Unions' functions are to extract greater compensation for political support. Unions sound like a good idea, but have always been nothing but a tool for corruption. Unions always end up funding the most insidious 'corruptocrat' politicians, making their organizers rich.

President Obama was a community organizer before coming to the White House, which, in function, is just about the same thing as a union boss. The unions he worked for (SEIU and ACORN) leaned on the banks, calling them "racist" to extract loans. The banks obliged, making loans to low income buyers (who could not possibly qualify for or pay back the loans), thus collapsing our housing market. ACORN also committed many cases of voter fraud around the country during Obama's bid for the White House. Both these unions went into the cities and rallied the poor in favor of Obama. It is my opinion that we would have another politician in the White House if not for Obama's ability to mobilize these unions on his behalf. Unfortunately this 'other' politician would have been John McCain. Just great! Fast death or slow death.

Wisconsin is now being called "the new Egypt" by Congressional members, due to recent union protests in the streets over Governor Scott Walker's (Tea Party) decision to strip them of most of their collective bargaining rights. This is exactly what the communists want- rioting in the streets. They want people dependent on their entitlements. Truth is, they shouldn't have entitlements in the first place.

But that is what the sociopaths want. They want the whole country to be financially desperate so they can come in and provide the solution: which is a communist state. Our socialist President has sided with the rioters, because he loves the way he can use them for his political support.

Union leaders (who are always Democrat) are saying that Republicans are trying to keep them from being able to bargain their way to adequate compensation with benefits and pensions. But in 2011 in 41 states, public union workers' pensions rose tenfold, slashing school, road building and maintenance funds. I guess their bargaining works. But when these are bankrupting the states, what's a mother to do? Fourteen Democratic lawmakers even left town on the eve of the protests to avoid having to vote on the bill. These senators should be put out of office for this. In any other job they would be fired.

The teachers' unions in Wisconsin have put their union privileges ahead of educating children by staging a 'sick in,' calling in sick *en masse* to protest. They have been 'fixing' the system

through spending millions to elect politicians, who in turn reward the unions at taxpayer expense. They then increase the role and size of government. Unions are the Democrats' moneymakers. The left has really gone overboard trying to protect their stranglehold on taxpayers. They have made the issue about their 'right to be unionized' and their right to collective bargaining. They are trying to make it a civil rights battle. Despots! And teachers, firefighters and policemen are the political pawns in the communist labor organizations' plans to take American wealth.

There is nothing in the US constitution requiring the government to negotiate with collectives of workers. Collective bargaining is something that's solely designed for employer-employee relations in the private sector (private businesses). Public sector (government employees) bargaining distorts democratic government by using political clout to elect public officials. They later negotiate with the very same officials. Public sector employees should not be able to collectively bargain because they are being paid by the taxpayers! Public sector unionization WILL create a situation where eventually all jobs will be government jobs. The private companies will be "bailed out," or taken over, ie. General Motors.

And people are oblivious. You know how I know this? Because a Rasmussen poll in Wisconsin found that 48 percent of the citizens were against Gov. Walker and 34 percent were for him. Unions are bussing in demonstrators and comparing Walker to Hitler. This precisely describes their ignorance, as Hitler loved unions.

Gov. Walker gave tax breaks to businesses that wanted to relocate to Wisconsin. This would bring jobs in and help the economy. The locals' problem with this: the businesses aren't unionized! Van Jones says Walker is helping his 'big business' cronies and stealing from workers. You see, this is what the communist union people want you to think. What I want you to see is how this would *make sense* to someone that didn't know all the facts. They want you to think they are going to give you things like job security, which they will- for a season. They want you to think they will give you higher pay and multitudes of benefits; this also, for a season. And then if they can win, which means get all employment unionized, they will not be able to live up to their promises, and eventually take your job, leaving you with nothing.

This is exactly what happened in Russia after 1917 and China decades later. They don't care. They got what they wanted (which is power), and now you are worthless. When they manage to get you dependent on their pay and benefits you are just that- dependent. All they want is power but they promise you everything. Sociopaths are clever liars. YOU need to become educated enough to know what is going on so you can stand your ground with these dishonest people.

Unions are communist tools. Just listen to the slogan given by Stalin's forces before coming to power: "Workers of the world unite." Is that what happened? SEIU's Andy Stern (of SEIU) says that 'workers of the world unite' will not be just a slogan anymore, it will be a reality. This is the man who also echoed Mao Tse Tung's saying that 'power comes from the barrel of a gun.' Also that if the 'power of persuasion' doesn't work the 'persuasion of power' will. Do you think people like this care about you?

As a matter of fact, SEIU has been bussing in protestors to Wisconsin now. 88 percent of Americans do not belong to a union or work for the government. We Americans are held hostage by a loud minority of thugs who feel it is their right to force the vast majority of Americans to give in to their demands. What this causes is a battle between the public sector and the private businesses. One cause of long term unemployment is unionization because high union wages exceed the private sector rate. Union members have absolutely no say in what their mandatory dues are spent for. Their dues are invariably spent funding Democratic organizations and candidates. Richard Trumka, the president of the AFL-CIO, is a weekly visitor to the White House. The AFL-CIO solidarity center is trying to create a global labor movement. Great!

Don't get me wrong- not all public sector union members are bad or thugs or anything like that but are just working people trying to make as good a living as they can. It's their union bosses that are the ones who want their obedience and stir up the hatred. Most of the workers don't even realize what is going on. They really think evil Republicans are trying to take from them. They don't realize that their exorbitant pensions and their wages (which far exceed that of private sector workers) are bankrupting their states and are going to make states' rights a thing of the past because they will be

owned by the federal government. They are just being used as pawns to make some people very rich and powerful. 'Useful idiots.'

Here is the extent of their union bosses creating 'thugs' to get their way. There was $6 million in damage to the Wisconsin capital by protesters. They climbed through the Statehouse windows, breached the assembly chamber and got in a physical struggle with people trying to work. Police refused to move the protestors because they, too, are union members! Nice. Controversial documentarian Michael Moore showed up with handcuffs, threatening to take their wealth away. Fatboy...to the rescue! Andy Stern (mentioned earlier) said "We took names, we watched how they voted, we know where they live." What is happening to our country?

If you are a fiscally responsible Republican (or Democrat for that matter) and your life is clean so they don't have any dirt they can bring up to smear you with, you know what happens? Death threats! 15 Senators who voted against public sector unions received an e-mail that stated they and their families would be targeted for assassination. The e-mail started with, "Please put your things in order because you will be killed due to your actions in the last 8 weeks." It goes on to say, "you will be killed and your families will also be killed" and "I as well as many others know where you and your family live, we have planned to assault you by arriving at your house and putting a nice little bullet in your head" and "we have also built several bombs that we have placed in various locations around the areas in which we know you frequent." Now you tell me....is this the actions of honest people just wanting their due? People wanting a decent wage and retirement? No...these are criminals and sociopaths wanting to have everything! They don't care who they take it from to get it!

I would like you to note an interesting bit of very important symbolism: the fist in the air, which is the symbol that represents both the AFL-CIO and the International Socialists' Organization (ISO). The ISO is involved in Van Jones' "Renew the American Dream" rally. 'Renew the American dream,' now isn't that noble? Do you know how many people are fooled by sociopaths' phony names for things? LIARS! In case you were wondering, the 'fist' is attributed to "Rotfrontkampferbund," a paramilitary organization of the German Communist party pre-World War II. Since then, it's been associated with Marxism, socialism, anarchists, black nationalists, and, (yes) trade unions. It indicates 'solidarity' and *defiance*.

Organized labor makes up 12 percent of the middle class in America. Right now, government employees make more than private sector employees do with their bargaining rights. But America is now in a MANAGED decline and our currency will fall to unforeseen lows. The dollar will be replaced by a global currency. In time, ALL workers will make very little and the United States will become just like China, which is the new model.

Capitalism means we are free to innovate and challenge ourselves to succeed. As soon as the government begins to start regulating things, capitalistic innovation and personal drive begins to disappear. People then have no freedom to attempt to create economic strength for themselves. They become helpless. Now they can't even help the less fortunate. In a truly capitalist society some of the wealthy always help those in need! We would be truly capitalist if nothing were instituted. It is the natural state of things. Think about it. What's more natural than free trade and an open marketplace? Where did your iphone come from? Your car, your dishwasher? Private citizens' entrepreneurialism. This is what will go with the communist takeover. There will be no more innovation.

There was a time when America was self-sufficient. We can be this again. How? Simple, get the communist sociopaths (who have attempted to implement their ideas) out of our country and start over again. Throw them into prison!

Across America, the same thing is happening. Lumber mills are going into bankruptcy and textile plants are moving to the Caribbean, Mexico and the Far East. Auto plants are closing and reopening overseas. Thirty years have gone by since our free trade era began, and the United States is no longer the manufacturing giant it once was. So, what were free trade agreements supposed to do? All it has done has made America into simply a consumer nation. It is obvious that the forces behind the free trade agreements were the same forces that want us to be just another nation state and rid the world of an exceptional America.

You know how this is done? Trade unions. Manufacturing jobs have been shipped overseas because of these unions' demands. This is now being done with much more than just manufacturing- but service positions as well. Every time I need to call about my Norton firewall I'm talking to someone in India!

Unions and high taxation have driven our lifeblood from us. Ronald Reagan brought prosperity back to the United States by *lowering* taxes. Businesses could afford to hire and invest. Taxing the rich just hurts everybody. *They're the ones that hire people!* President Obama, after extending the Bush-era tax cuts, is now reneging on his decision, (to appease his left wing base as he is campaigning for re-election in 2012) and deciding to impose heavier taxation on the wealthy. LIARS!

This will hurt workers because it will hurt businesses. Jobs will be scarce because hiring will freeze. Taxing the wealthy sounds noble and all, but everybody loses. Do you know that the upper 2 percent of Americans already pay 97 percent of our taxes? America was the land of opportunity where everyone could try to become wealthy. *Now success is persecuted.* What have we done? Who the f**k have we elected?

As I say elsewhere, the communists want all jobs to be government jobs. The Wall Street Journal's Steve Moore recently reported that we now have more government workers than manufacturing, construction, farming, fishing, forestry, and mining combined! We now have more people on the government dole than anytime in history! Well, hallelujah! We really ARE becoming red China!

The communist sociopaths have a phrase referencing to the people they use to initiate their collapse: 'useful idiots.' These people are quickly discarded after the sociopaths come to power. They claim to be for you...but *are* they? What 'useful idiots' are the American poor? You really can get welfare recipients to do anything for you. They, as a rule, don't read, but lounge in front of their indoctrination boxes (television sets) and listen to anybody that claims to have (or looks like they have) something in common with them. It's the same with low wage workers like home health care providers. Do you think any of these people voted for President Obama because they looked over his past and thought he was the best man for the job? No, he was black and very charismatic. And he fed everybody his anti-colonialist, 'redistribute the wealth' rhetoric which was nothing but the rantings of his alcoholic, Marxist father.

The first stimulus bill under President Bush was supposed to boost the economy and create jobs. Results were minimal. President Obama's stimulus was all about creating jobs. Unemployment rose from eight percent to ten and, as of April 2011, has stayed there since. Do you know that our Republican congress has decided to mandate reading aloud our Constitution because congressional lawmakers don't even know it? Think about that- will you?

Obama's health care plan is/was nothing but a power grab. First, just look at what was inside the bill. A government takeover of student loans. Will someone please tell me: just what do student loans have to do with healthcare? That should tell you there's something's fishy. Now will someone tell me why are Congressional people given a full pension after one term? Why their entire families are are exempt from having to pay back student loans? This means us taxpayers foot the bill. Why are congressmen exempt from the limited provisions of Obamacare? After passing the bill many healthcare companies have closed their doors- at least for healthcare insurance. Premiums have gone up and employers have dropped coverage by cutting hours.

Think about this. This plan mandates that you, a private citizen, buy something (health insurance) with your money *you* worked for. If the state/government can do this, then what's next? Gym memberships? Eco-cars? Condoms?

Obama promised that people would be able to keep their current health plan- ain't gonna happen. The taxes imposed on small businesses would be crippling, causing further job loss. With this wonderful plan, not your doctor- but a Washington bureaucrat will be deciding your treatment. Also, the bill would cost a trillion dollars over the first 10 years, putting your children further in debt to China. This bill is European-styled socialism and won't turn out to be ANYTHING like what they promise. England has socialized medicine. In England people are drinking water out of potted plants just waiting for care in hospitals! No government programs of any kind ever work efficiently. They are always bound in so much red tape and bureaucracy that they are inefficient and slow moving. The regulations that will naturally come from government-run health care will stifle innovation in medicine, as the bureaucrats in Washington will decide that groundbreaking advancements are just not economically feasible. Cool!

The aforementioned Cloward and Piven strategy for causing the collapse of the American economy (studied at length by Obama while at Columbia University) says to just spend until resources are gone. Your freedom is compromised as everyone is mandated to purchase government approved healthcare, and wealth is redistributed. Take from people that work and give to those who don't.

Then look at the size of the bill. Two thousand pages- totally indecipherable to anybody- even with a law degree. Nancy Pelosi actually said right in front of a huge crowd of people, "Well, we have to pass the bill so we can see what is in it." Unbelievable! She really thought she was talking to kindergartners. Do you see? These people *really do* think you are stupid!

If the Obama health care bill is so good then why are so many getting exempted from it? There have been 2.6 million waivers across the country, many of which are SEIU members who lobbied for the bill. Also 20 percent of businesses that have applied for, and gotten, exemptions from having to participate are in Nancy Pelosi's district and include Spa's, gourmet restaurants and hotels. Rep. Michelle Bachman just found $105 billion in appropriations hidden in the "Obamacare" bill that were not disclosed to any of the house members voting on it. 'Spend, spend' until you collapse the system.

Do you know what would totally solve all the health care problems? Simply allow health care insurance companies to compete across state lines. This, by itself would drop the cost of healthcare because the free market would take over and the companies would be forced to price themselves competitively. Cost goes down but we maintain quality patient care, which has been the best in the world. And... you might even be able to drink water from a glass or cup when waiting for your doctor!

China right now is becoming the model that world governments are using in terms of economic policy and streamlining. They don't need to over-regulate; they already have complete control over their industries. And it's seeped over into America: in Chicago, lawmakers are even starting to mandate that some students learn Mandarin Chinese!

President Obama, while still campaigning in 2008, said our constitution was 'fundamentally flawed' and is a document of 'negative liberties.' Well, if our constitution is flawed, then why did we, in our first 150 years of existence, become the richest, most powerful nation in the world? And the most giving. 'Negative liberties?' Liberties by nature must be of the negative as this means a absence of external control of the citizens by the government.

'Positive liberty' can only mean the states' power to coerce, which is not liberty at all. This is nothing but Orwellian newspeak.

Since Obama has been in office, we now have 20 percent of the American population living on government money. That's right; I said 20 percent on entitlements! Only 51 percent live on their salaries. Obama continually talks about getting Americans back to work. LIARS!

President Obama promised to cut the federal deficit in half by 2012. As of April 2011, this would be impossible. He promised to ban earmarks (legislative provision allowing funds to be spent on specific projects), but the first spending bill he signed had over 9000 of them. LIARS!

Mr. Obama promised he wouldn't force Americans to buy health insurance. He then told Congress, "Under my plan individuals will be required to carry insurance. He promised he would cut government spending. Two trillion dollars later, it's obvious he (along with Cloward and Piven) knows exactly what he's doing. LIARS!

Obama promised not to raise taxes on families making less than $250,000 a year. He began taxing their health plans and is trying to introduce the 'cap & trade' legislation for carbon emissions (which has been proven to be a hoax). He promised to put all bills that end up on his desk online and be the most transparent administration ever. This has not happened, as this administration has made more backroom deals and held more secret meetings than any ever have to date. LIARS!

President Obama promised to end the wars we were in. 2014 is the most likely year for us to pull out of Afghanistan and we're dropping bombs on more countries today than at any point in the Bush administration. LIARS!

And guess what else: do you know that President Obama is trying to close many of our military bases? Why is this? To cut wasteful spending? On the contrary: to make us vulnerable! Close the military bases and keep the prisons open! Do you know why the sociopaths are so fearlessly proceeding despite the opposition from the right? They have the youth. Young people don't know any better- I didn't! This is why I'm writing this book.

After extending the Bush-era tax breaks to Americans who make $250,000 or *more*, because of pressure from Republican congressional leaders, President Obama is now sneaking them back in under new legislature. Now why does he want to tax the wealthy so much? Answer: the people making this amount are the ones who employ Americans. He doesn't want Americans working, because people *not* working usually end up ironically feeling entitled (even without unions!), thus becoming dependents.

One must remember our media figures that disseminate this communist propaganda *do not like you*. They think you are stupid, backwards and primitive. Sheryl Crow, our beloved singer/songwriter, when questioned about forest destruction and subsequent paper production, said she thought people should limit themselves to one square of toilet paper. I don't know about you, but that wouldn't even begin the project for me and I seriously doubt Sheryl uses that either.

So when our celebrities exhibit such disdain for us citizens, why are we following them and reading about everything they do? This is worshipping the very people that hate you. Now THIS really is the definition of insanity. What Americans really need to do is to stop watching Hollywood! Stop living vicariously through musicians and actors, and start living your own lives!

And don't think that she's alone! For example, Microsoft billionaire Bill Gates *denounced capitalism* on a late 2010 CNN interview. Bill Gates=capitalism!

I personally think people just do not want to think other people can really be this evil. I understand- I don't either. They seem like nice intelligent people with a good sense of humor and have families like us. They talk a good story. Can they really be this evil? The answer is no- but the end result is yes. They just have been brought up with this 'tear the system apart' worldview. This is the foundation of the 'lay communist.' They have thought like this since they were young, thinking they are doing what is right, when it's, in fact, downright sinister!

I know! I did! The only thing that changed me was finding Christ. My heart changed. Then my mind followed.

Obama was right; we really do need fundamental transformation. But the true transformation needs to happen in our hearts and minds. That's what happened to me and I'm the better for it.

I would like to say something about our supposed inalienable rights so many Fox News people like Judge Anthony Napolitano and Glenn Beck, whom I do admire, talk about. I don't see this anywhere in scripture and know that when the New Testament was written, Israel was under Roman rule and people didn't have any rights at all. Our inalienable rights were given to us by our Constitution and are valid. As should be obvious by reading any Bible, God allows you to go into slavery if you do not know how to maintain some kind of check on your passions. What I'm saying is that we DO NOT HAVE INALIENABLE RIGHTS!

We have the right to go into slavery, if we are stupid enough to want it.

In case you don't know already, sociopaths need those they can fool into thinking they will redistribute wealth to them. These people (ie. servants) are the ones that elect them. When all is done they will reduce ALL their subjects to abject poverty (slaves). Study for yourself the communist programs of Stalin, Mao or Castro. They too promised education, healthcare and a transfer of wealth. When they were finished taking over, is any of this what happened? Nope- they just helped create more 'useful idiots,' shackled with chains that they could 'off' or use in whatever way they want.

Lay communists really are just plain stupid. Think about it, do you think any of them want to live in a country like Cuba? The USSR? North Korea? Then why do they rehash all the bullshit fed them by the communist-minded Hollywood stars and left- leaning politicians? They don't want to live like that! There are only two reasons to talk like that. You are brain dead and shouldn't be talking but talk because you have nothing better to do, or you have some reason to believe you will sit in a palace when the revolution is over. Either way you ARE evil- when push comes to shove, what excuse do you have for being unaware? It's all there for you to see.

Two young journalists, James O'Keefe and Hannah Giles, attempted to expose the lay communism of ACORN in September 2009. They went into ACORN offices, posing as a pimp and a prostitute, and received aid and advice from ACORN counselors in underage sex trafficking. The same thing happened again in February 2011 at Planned Parenthood, which receives 360 million dollars a year from your tax money to abort fetuses. Journalists at Live Action posed as a pimp and a hooker at a Planned Parenthood in the Bronx in NYC and a staff worker and a medical practitioner willingly helped the couple in assisting their invented stable of underage prostitutes as young as thirteen. Well, why do they want abortions so bad? Because it's population control, baby. Less people=easier to control.

Larry Grathwohl was an undercover agent for the FBI and infiltrated the Weather Underground in the 1970's at a time when they were trying to take power. These people decided that they needed to kill off 25 million Americans who are diehard capitalists that can't be reeducated (it failed- *then*). Bill Ayres has had a close relationship to President Obama and was (along with Bernadine Dohrn) running the Weather Underground at the time. In the mid 1990's, Obama was hired to be the chairman of Ayres 'brainchild': the Chicago Annenberg Challenge. This idea poured more than 100 million dollars into the hands of community organizers and radical education activists. What I'm trying to illustrate to you is the fact that these people DO want to kill you whether or not you are instrumental in helping them bring communism about in America. They *don't like you* and want to be kings.

Remember what Jesus said of the end times, "that which is whispered in secret will be shouted from the rooftops." Those young men and women and the people that leaked the scientists' e-mails regarding global warming were doing God's work by exposing these things. The function of this is so that the information is out there for you to see. This way you have no excuse for not seeing what is happening. This isn't to condemn you; it's so you can see it and potentially act on it. If you choose not to, whose fault is it? If you find yourself someplace you do not want to be in the near future, just don't say "I didn't know." The opportunity was there.

These people want you to have almost nothing for yourself, be it private property, a good supply of food or anything else, because they want it all for themselves. They think they are more intelligent than you and deserve these things. Worse yet- they think IT WOULD JUST BE WASTED ON YOU!!!

Do you think I'm making this up? Interior secretary Ken Salazar has just directed the Bureau of Land Management to survey its huge amount of acreage to determine which should be designated as 'wild lands,' so the administration can make millions of acres of public land that's off-limits to development through regulatory fiat. Why?

They want regular people like you and I to move to the cities and live in little eco-apartments where we will work and live. Amazingly, this is really all laid out in writer/journalist George Orwell's fictional book, "1984." They want these beautiful pieces of land to be their private places to live and be served. They are laying the groundwork now under false pretences.

These progressives will be the real pawns in the totalitarian society that follows their revolution. They are duped into thinking it will be communal (communalists) instead of a kingship. They don't know that only the elite will be served. They will bring it about with THEIR hands and then give it all to a group that will eliminate them for their service and then sit in power over everyone. What a joy to be part of that!

They are taught that capitalism is oppressive. Yet the United States has been the most giving nation in history. We have propped up more faltering countries than anyone. And the reason for this is our love for God and our free enterprise system. 90 percent of the aid to Pakistan and Haiti after their terrible earthquakes came from America.

Besides rebelling against the establishment, another reason 'lay communists' desire to rid the world of capitalism is the idea of eliminating competition. Competition means the strongest, smartest or most talented will get ahead faster. Usually in these cases, those who get ahead will help the less fortunate.

But these people don't see it that way. They would like to see an even playing field. No losers: everyone gets a prize. Everybody 'loves' everybody (although the 'love' is fake). Do you think we were all created to be the same? It should be obvious we were not. Some are taller, smarter, quicker, blond, black, slender, fat, developmentally disabled. Sorry, there *are* exceptional people.

Some people are musically inclined, some are not. Some are athletic, some not. Some are really good at math, I am not. It's the same reason that not all flowers or fish are alike. Dolphins can actually communicate with humans, while other animals cannot. This kind of thinking is directly against nature: the *very* thing these people are trying to worship!

Now right here I'm talking about the 'educated' communist sociopaths: the ones who actually have a philosophy. Not the ones that are simply buying the rhetoric and have no idea what they are talking about. My friend in Seattle clearly heard someone say that Glenn Beck is a monster (I've heard this before) and because it was someone whose opinion he trusted he decided, 'Yeah what a monster.' He is, while being a friend of mine, is sadly a 'lay communist,' just buying the rhetoric. Funny thing is that my friend has a beautiful wife and a handsome young son and a home. He has everything that a good capitalist society will bestow upon a good citizen, and yet he still buys into the 'down with capitalism' rallying cry. It breaks my heart.

What these people don't realize is that struggle is necessary. Failure is necessary. Think about who you would be if you never had to struggle. Look at the personalities of people who are never had adversity in this harsh world. Are they nice people or spoiled little demanding brats? Don't a lot of the communists act like the latter? Find most of the publicly acclaimed ones and look at their upbringing. They don't care if most of the world is impoverished. All they know is providence. All those 'little people' out there just need to be tamed.

Failure is necessary so you don't think the world revolves around you. You have to pull yourself up by the bootstraps and try again. Your character is being molded- whether you like it or not. I have fallen so many times that down is the only place I know anymore. I don't like it, but as the years go by *I see something in myself that I only used to see in the men I admired most....*

The fact this happened is through the grace of God.

The communists say they want everybody to be equal. This is a lie. They really want everyone to be alike. Anything that makes us all alike is destroying what God created. Bear it in mind that, "A nation of sheep breeds a government of wolves." They want you to all be alike so you are easier to control.

Michelle Obama is trying to make school lunches healthier for kids. Great idea, right? The real idea is, you don't teach your kids; we will. They are already indoctrinating you and your kids with Communislamic propaganda and have been for decades. All this 'helping' is doing is transferring power to the government. We are all supposed to quit smoking and eat healthier. Wear seatbelts and helmets. All of us. No choices. Kinda sounds like people-control in action, doesn't it? Why would anybody want to rid the world of unhealthy people? They're people too. No unhealthy people means no really healthy people. We are all alike. Is that what you want? I never wanted to live in Thousand Oaks, California because all the girls are blond and white and say "oh my gosh!" I like diversity. It's what makes this world beautiful.

The FCC recently passed a net-neutrality bill that is totally unnecessary but is just one step closer to regulating free speech on the internet. They want to isolate you. Do you know why we have an internet in the first place? They brought it about so that eventually all communications would be electronic or digital. This is so they can control it. Eventually be able to shut you down if you cross them. Make you feel alone and defenseless. That's just for now because that's all they can do now. In time you will be sent to reeducation camps or simply be killed for any dissenting speech.

And what about the digitalization of all TV sets? Is this all solely for your Hi-def viewing pleasure? Or is it the future restriction of *all* freedoms?

Speaking of freedom, the ACLU (American Civil Liberties Union) has just recently filed a lawsuit over a Point Pleasant Beach, NJ city council member's NJ decision to pray when the council is in session. For years, the council members have been opening their council meetings with prayer. They were just doing what our founding fathers did. Point Pleasant Beach cannot afford to oppose the lawsuit. Christ is the enemy.

Something you need to know here is that the people that have been trying to own you in so many ways have been setting this up for a long time. They have been placing the right candidates in the front lines for election and watching while you think you are choosing between candidates. They alternate, this one good, this one bad, this one Republican, this one Democrat. There would have been absolutely no difference between Barack Obama and John McCain. Don't get me wrong, they are different personalities, this one is willing to simply play his role, this one wants to do it all in his term. President Bush spent quite a lot on unnecessary things. Each one has been bringing us just a little bit closer to their intended goal of complete subjugation.

They really have set up a win-win situation for themselves here. The Tea Party candidates have just won most seats in Congress and want to start making cuts to union entitlements. So let's say this happens. What do you think will follow? Wisconsin times 50. There was utter revolt and chaos in most large European cities last year, which was all about entitlement reductions that were necessary just so the governments would remain solvent. So, if we cut these entitlements, we will have rioting as people will not want to give up welfare or Social Security checks and go find work. If we don't, we will officially lose our place in the world's economic balance. Bankruptcy will decline us into a third world country- and the sociopaths will have won.

So, if there's rioting here in the US, do you think we will have our entitlements restored so we can lounge around on government money and live for ourselves? Really? This kind of rioting is described in a book called "The Coming Insurrection" by a group of communists from Europe. Will this insurrection result in freedom? The opposite: martial law. Martial law that will not be removed. You must know that every revolution ends with a strong man. There WILL be a man at the end of whatever happens and *he does not like you.*

Remember what Margaret Thatcher said: "Socialism cannot work because you eventually run out of other people's money."

Remember something. Communism is Socialism is Marxism is racism. At some point it will all boil down to a race. In America today, it takes the form of feminism, homo-eroticism, unionism, racism, and soon enough....Holy war...to be explained further later- in the form of CommunIslam.

No matter what form it comes in, they want us to worship man. As in mankind. In time you will worship A MAN. He will have a name, will hold the whole world under his sway, will sit in the temple of God in Jerusalem and claim that he is God.

I know nobody wants to believe that our government officials (or anyone for that matter) are so evil, but this, my friends, is just burying your head in the sand. Silly example to some, but seriously...look at the way people drive...for God's sakes! Look at the numerous cases of corrupt businessmen who steal from the elderly! Do you mean you can't believe these people think you are stupid and want to make you dependent on them? Open your eyes!

Listen to the people that are trying to get you to follow what they think are good ideas and see how they lash out at any dissenting opinions. Is that how someone acts that knows they are right? Look at their smugness. Listen to their hatred. Look at how viciously they attack any opinion other than their own. Liars and sociopaths- all of them! They're pandering to you, but what, really, do they think about you? Do they love you? Do they even *like* you? YOU NEED to think about these things!

Northwestern University Associate Professor Bernadine Dohrn is teaching students now to 'embrace their rage.' Bernadine is a communist sociopath. These people want you to be angry- it is useful to them! Please do not listen to anyone that tells you to 'embrace your rage.' I am telling you to embrace your love.

Yeah, imagine no possessions, its easy if you can. No winners or losers. No people with a strong desire to succeed and only apathetic people. Apathetic people usually fear something, like competition. People who are driven usually fear something too. Like mediocrity. The sociopaths would like all the driven people to be in

their 'kings' court' and all the others to be the 'great unwashed' serving them. The only prerequisite is the absence of God. The absence of God means you don't have to value His people. If you want to rule over them, you obviously don't value them. They are for your use. You are a sociopath. This isn't the result of you winning a competition; it's the result of you devaluing every human you come into contact with.

Know this.... communists are losers. They have nothing to do but destroy. Anything. If the world were perfect, they would have to bring in some kind of hatred or create a problem so they would have something to rail against. These are my generation. The sixties really were all about "love and peace." Yeah, right. LIARS!

The Bible says "Fear not," or a form of this phrase- 365 times- incredibly, one for every day of the year. It also says, "The fear of the Lord is the beginning of understanding." This clearly means we are not to fear men (or man). If one lives by this principle, you can never devalue or fear any human you come into contact with.

Americans have been trained over the last forty years to be a people that serve only themselves. Yet a nation of sheep that serves themselves will go into servitude to someone else. This will teach them obedience and also will teach them to serve others, even though it is unfortunately based out of fear. If you will not love enough to serve others, you will be forced to live in a way that imitates the serving kind of love (which is the only kind of love) - even if this is your own servitude. If this is the only way to open your eyes, so be it. They are of much value to God- but an undisciplined, self-serving people are worthless to anybody but themselves. A people that serve others without expecting anything in return are of so much greater value, because it's based out of true love.

Look, I love you. I am writing this book because I love you. I just happen to know that sometime in the near future you are going to HATE your life if you don't wake up. So, wake up and realize this before it's too late.

Compassion doesn't strike at the surface of things. It goes to the root of the problem. That's why it always succeeds. Call it tough love or whatever you want- if enough Americans want God out of the way, He will let go. Then watch where you find yourself. You will be part of the CommunIslamic plan for you to serve man.

Stop listening to hateful people and see that God is love.

Chapter 12

Why Peaceful, Moderate Muslims are Irrelevant

In this country and many others, right now we are faced with a threat. This threat challenges us: not only to know what we really believe in, but to face this threat and know we are right. We know this threat threatens our very existence as a nation. The people behind this menace want to dictate our beliefs and our activities. As mentioned many times already, the first thing they want to do is remove our choices. But we know that our choices are all we have. Our God wants us to make these choices. And He gives us freedom to love or reject Him.

A secret meeting was just scheduled in Germany to put together a party that would address the growing Islamic threat to European security. Both France and Switzerland recently issued edicts against building new mosques and face coverings. Islamic extremists have tried or detonated bombs in many European countries, and have killed innumerable people in America as well. They killed kindergarten-age children in Beslan. They assassinated more than 50 worshippers at 'Our Lady of the Holy Salvation' church in Baghdad. They slaughtered 3000 in the Twin Towers on 9/11, savagely murdering any who will not sing the praises of Allah. Forty Christian churches last year were bombed in Iraq. These people are called extremists by both their moderates- and even our own government.

Take one look at certain scriptures in the Quran and you can see that all these hateful actions are quite valid, given their Quranic mandate. They hate our freedom and openly express this. But our freedom is necessary for our choices. We cling to our God-given freedom because we want to be a people that make choices, like the choice to love and worship Him or not. Our Holy book says "Be fruitful and multiply." Theirs tells them to kill and make war in the name of Allah.

"Multiculturalism has totally failed," says German Chancellor Angela Merkel. "It's a failure," says French President Nicholas Sarkozy. "State multiculturalism has had disastrous results," says British Prime Minister David Cameron. Ex-Spanish Prime Minister Jose Maria Aznar declared multiculturalism a failure as well, saying it divides and debilitates Western societies. Thilo Sarrazin published a book titled, "Germany Abolishes Itself," arguing that Germany's 'guest workers'- Turks, Kurds and Arabs- are dumbing down the nation. Germany's birth rate fell below the replacement levels, and these foreigners with less intelligence and higher welfare and crime rates are rapidly replacing the German population. He says Islam is the culture and Muslim immigrants have proven to be "socially, culturally and intellectually inferior to most everyone else." Germans want to *return* to a nation of, by, and for their own kind, with their own history, holidays, heroes, language, music and art. The Muslims are pouring in and creating sub-nations within the country. They're unwilling to embrace a new identity, as Englishmen, French or German. The former Prime Minister of Australia has issued the same verdict as Sarrazin.

Do you know what multiculturalism leads to? Political correctness- like the Fort Hood massacre, where Maj. Nidal Hassan killed thirteen people while yelling "God is great" (*Allah Akbar*) in Arabic. People knew Hassan was becoming radicalized but said nothing, for fear of being politically incorrect. "*Allah Akbar*" is also what a young man yelled in Frankfurt, Germany recently when he shot two US soldiers. The White House still refuses to call this an act of terror. Tell me: just how long are we going to take this shit?

Innocent people are losing their lives and we are playing 'word games' and being nice to murderers!

Muslims do not believe all religions are equal. They believe there is one god, Allah, and submission to his law is the path to paradise. They do not believe in freedom of speech and the press, if it means saying anything against the Prophet. They do not believe in western dress codes or mixing men and women in schools and sports. They believe that women who dress in western style clothes are whores and are 'fair game' for sexual assault. They do not believe all lifestyles are equal, and many believe adulterers should be stoned. They want to live THEIR faith and culture in OUR countries to live alongside us, but dwell apart. What they really want is for *our* culture to submit to Islamic law. Living alongside us is just the path to this.

We have been at war in two Muslim countries for a decade now (and as of March 2011 we are in a third). All three are useless stupid wastes of taxpayer money and will not accomplish anything. We are trying to teach Muslims in Afghanistan and Iraq how to form democratic governments. What a crock! This is impossible. These people do not even know HOW to live in a free society. Why? Because of their 'holy' book! Their scriptures demand an autocratic, 'top down' world in which every move one makes is subject to the scrutiny of their Imams. It's the only way of life they know. They are not ready for freedom. The Karzai thugocracy in Afghanistan will never be anything but that. In either country, we can set up a government that looks like a democracy, but upon our departure it will return to its original form in weeks. This is because Shariah law is not democratic.

Look, in Iran in 1979 the Shah was overthrown, because the people wanted out from under his rule and protested for democracy. The power vacuum was filled by the Ayatollah Khomeini in just one month, who set up a far worse situation than had previously been endured by the Iranian people. Now they have

Mahmoud Ahmadinejad as President and have been protesting again- only to be put down and (sometimes) killed. Ahmadinejad wants nuclear weapons, so he can destroy Israel and the west, which they consider 'the great Satan.'

The current situation in Egypt is a mirror image of Iran. The people say they want democracy but the Muslim Brotherhood is perfectly positioned to walk right in and take control. They have very strong ties to Al Qaeda, want to eliminate all Jews, and bring down the west. Isn't it interesting that just when Tunisia had riots, suddenly Egypt, Yemen, Jordan and the Ivory Coast follow? What do you think will come of this? What do you think is being prepared? Trust me: when any society goes through changes, the people will ALWAYS go towards the familiar. In Egypt, Islam is familiar and the Muslim brotherhood WILL be there to help.

A fitting example of this is the March 9, 2011 fighting in Egypt between Muslims and Christians. The Associated Press says this violence is what to expect from a once police state that has been given freedom. I say- when it is Muslim. Less than half its security forces are back to work, and the military does not have many troops on the ground. The fighting began when a Muslim mob attacked thousands of Christians, protesting the burning of a church in Soul village, south of Cairo. The Muslims torched the church because of a love affair between a Muslim woman and a Christian man. The woman's father and a cousin of the man were killed. Do you see what I mean? These animals do not want democracy, they want war! Give them freedom and...?

They are now protesting in the streets again on the Syrian border over today being the day Israel was founded, which is the 'great catastrophe.' They have been lighting fires in Israel (Palastine) too. I say 'get a job.'

For example, the radical Shiite cleric Muqtada al-Sadr, whose fearsome militia once battled American troops and has been in Iran for four years, has returned to Iraq. He is back telling Iraqis to resist the American influence. This comes just as President Obama has decided we have successfully set up their democratic government and will be pulling our troops out. You see!

The communists are such 'butt buddies' with the Islamics that they want us out of Iraq. Here's where I agree with them, but for different reasons. The communists, like the Islamics, want to overthrow capitalism. I think Americans need to keep our forces at home and pay more attention to domestic issues. We have welcomed in both these groups to the point of our own instability.

Louis Farrakhan, the Nation of Islam's leader in the US, gave a speech in early 2011. He told thousands of Muslims to "love war over peace and love wrong over right, to love injustice over justice and that this is the day of your doom and the end of your world" (speaking to Americans). "What you're looking at in Tunisia and Egypt and Yemen and Jordan, Libya and Bahrain and soon in all the nations of the world and is going to take place in America, it will be coming to your door. God is stimulating the rise of the masses and it's coming to your shores. This is a sign that the Mahdi that the Muslim world has been looking for is present in the world. The Christ that you hoped for is here." Right...

We are not going to change Muslims as long as they are Muslims! Their Quran will not tolerate this anymore than Muslim men will. Communists will not change unless they have an awakening and see that God is not their enemy.

This is where the peaceful Muslims are unaware. Peaceful, moderate Muslims are loved and appreciated- but are deluded. We keep trying to find a way to make peace with a worldview that only wants to dominate the rest of the world. These moderate Muslims think they can convince people that the way *they* believe is true Islam. Their holy book says different. These moderates are misguided because they feel no animosity towards others and feel that somehow the rest might eventually see things their way. They won't. They hate choices and they want to dominate the rest of the world for their own satisfaction. And the peaceful, moderate Muslims will continue to try to sell their 'religion of peace' to your sons and daughters and friends with some accepting this out of their own ignorance! They're the Muslim equivalent of 'lay communists.'

Daniel Pearl, while researching Islamic militancy in Pakistan after 9/11 was abducted, beheaded, and presented on videotape presented to US officials in Pakistan. We've even had American converts go awry...in 2001, San Francisco bay arean John Walker Lindh made international headlines for joining the Taliban. He even garnered the name, "American Taliban." When looking into his background, you see that his father became estranged from his Marin home, taking frequent visits across the Golden Gate to San Francisco to visit his gay lover. Following his intense love for rap music and posing on internet chat rooms as a black rapper, Lindh converted to Islam after admiring the Spike Lee film, "Malcolm X." He began attending mosques in Marin county and 1997, traveled to Yemen in 1998 to learn Arabic so he could learn to read the Quran in its original language, and the rest is history. He is now serving a 20-year prison sentence under the name Abu-Sulayman al-Irlandi. Is Islam the best 'escape' for angry young American males? Clearly not in this case.

Unfortunately it doesn't work well when it's the other way around. On November 22, 2005, an Iranian convert to Christianity was kidnapped from his home and stabbed to death. Ghorban Tori was pastoring a house church of convert Christians. Shortly after, local secret police searched his home (and all other known believers' homes) for Bibles and other banned Christian books in the Farsi language.

During the recent uprising in Egypt, a CBS news correspondent named Lara Logan suffered a brutal and sustained sexual assault and beating on Feb. 11, 2011. She was in Tahrir Square, preparing for "60 Minutes." There were over two hundred men in the mob. "They blindfolded me, beat me with flagpoles and tried to rip off pieces of my scalp" she told a magazine and stated on her show. "They kept us in stress positions and wouldn't let me put my head down; they put their hands inside me front and back and tried to rip me apart." Lara has two small children at home. Now these may have been pro-Mubarak (their dictator) supporters here politically, but they really were just Muslim men just being, well, Muslim men.

They are barbaric dullards only a small step from cavemen or total retards (and we try to *reason* with them?).

A poll was taken in Egypt just after the uprising that showed 84 percent of Muslim men still think that apostates from Islam should be put to death. Peaceful, moderate Muslim people, living in harmony with the rest of us...right? And these people *say* they want democracy?! This is laughable!

Note: when the American revolution took place and the Declaration of Independence was written, Americans may have celebrated, but do you think groups of men took innocent women, raped and beat them? Then why, when Muslim men (sorry, just men) secure a similar victory, do they do things like that? Because these people are savages and cannot possibly handle freedom.

The vengeful, angry, hate-filled Muslims who want to see the end of freedom and the beginning of world dominance by Shariah law have hit some roadblocks recently. Our security has been beefed up and has prevented them from smuggling bombs into our country or taking control of airplanes.

So they have decided upon a strategy. It is called "Death by a thousand cuts." What this means is first sharing their faith in the US. The next is setting up websites and convincing American men to convert to Islam and showing them on the sites how to construct bombs out of common household items. The other is teaching them to organize within our cities. Another is using our prison system to win converts. There are so many out of touch, feeble-minded, wayward American males out there (Exhibit A: John Walker Lindh) it is no doubt they will be successful. And, like so many other things, it only takes *one!* But there are many.

A powerful virus was inserted into the computer systems of Iran's nuclear facility that set back their nuclear ambitions; prolonging the time they have before having the ability to bomb Israel. It was attributed to Israeli intelligence. Supposedly the name of the virus, when translated into Hebrew, is: the 'One who restrains.' This is one of our scriptures in the New Testament. The true One who restrains prolongs the time of the end for those who do not know the Savior to come to know Him.

This plan is old- as old as mankind. Mankind has wanted God out of his life since the beginning. This man-centered mentality has wanted to have a world that is fashioned after his own desires, and he will not stop until he sees this. He will eventually see this- and scripture tells us it will be taken from him. Those of us who have seen our own sin and have repented of it will be taken away prior to the wrath of God.

Moderate Muslims will never act against their counterparts with any success. They cannot. These extremists are NOT extremists. They are acting according to the mandates of their holy book. Any who think differently are either delusional or have an agenda that is similar enough to warrant turning a blind eye.

This kind of rage is evidenced in the way they killed four US soldiers in Iran a couple years ago. They had to drag them down the street, light them on fire and then hang them from a bridge. Just look at the hatred here! The citizens (yes, I said *citizens*) cheered at the bodies being drug down the street. Do not tell me common Muslims want only peace and harmony. If this were true, why were common citizens cheering?

Common citizens cheered as the Lockerbie bomber, who murdered 270 innocent people, finally was released from prison in Scotland in July 2010 and returned to Libya.

Palestinian assailants cut through the fence surrounding the settlement of Itamar and killed the Fogel family in Israel in March 2011. Udi, Ruth and three of their four children (Yoav-11, Elad-4 and Hadas-3 months) were savagely carved up with knives. An older daughter who was absent returned home to find this grisly scene. The next day Palestinian citizens passed out candy on the streets in celebration of their victory. Carving up a three month old baby? Victory? Then, celebrations?

Based on the *citizens'* reactions are you still going to tell me that these savages are extremists? No, this is just ISLAM!

Surah 4, verse 56: Those who have disbelieved our signs, we shall roast them in fire, whenever their skins are cooked to a turn we shall substitute new skins for them, then they shall feel the punishment.

Surah 47, verse 4: Therefore when you meet the unbelievers smite their necks and when you have caused a bloodbath amongst them bind a bond firmly on them.

Surah 4, verse 89: Try but wish that ye who reject faith as they do and thus be on the same footing as they, so take not friends from their ranks until they flee in the way of Allah, but if they turn renegades, seize them and kill them wherever you find them.

This is a religion of peace?

Now I have shown you three of the verses from the Holy Quran- the book that the peaceful, moderate Muslims read. I'm sure that, just like some Christian groups do with our scriptures, these Muslims piecemeal the scriptures together to see what they want to see. These 'lay Muslims' do not want to harm anyone but just want to live peacefully and support their families. Some people just want peace. Others just want war. So as long as their holy book says these things, how can we ever think we can make peace with people that follow Islam? There may be moderates- but there will also be those that want bloodshed. And as long as these things are in their scriptures they have reason to believe it is right to kill in the name of Allah. The peaceful Muslims will have no footing for their belief. Sorry, they will not police the others. IF THEY DID THEY WOULD HAVE TO FEAR FOR THEMSELVES!!!

When all is said and done, "All nations will turn their face against Israel." This is biblical. That means ALL nations. Yes-this must include the United States. It is obvious that someone in biblical times (God) knew that the US would eventually turn against Israel when we have been friends with them since they began the resurrection of their nation in 1948. Isn't this proof enough for you to see....?

Can you see now how our political correctness is going to kill us? Many among our ranks are now in a battle to control us and eventually enslave us. These are the communists, and nothing will stop them from trying to make their goal a reality.

We are fighting a battle that our scriptures tell us that we will not win- not on this earth. But we must fight this battle because we need to save the ones who are not infected with this hatred and are simply misguided. We must not fear for our safety; we will be taken care of. Anything else would be denying what our Lord has told us. We know from Scripture that there will be a 'man of lawlessness' who will say he is God, and sit on the throne in the Jerusalem temple. But soon after, this Antichrist's 'kingdom' will be taken away and we will win. We are told we will 'rule and reign' with Christ Jesus for one thousand years, after which 'the beast' must be released for a short time.

It might be interesting to ponder just who it is that we will rule and reign over? (Sorry the scriptures do not say).

Islam teaches believers that if they follow their path and make holy war they will receive 72 virgins for their personal pleasure/use. Our Scriptures tell us, simply, "man has not seen nor heard what the Lord has prepared for you." Which *sounds* more like God as you imagine Him? Think....

You must know something about the life of Mohammed to know the origins of their faith. The basic tenants of their faith tell them that any criticism of Mohammad shall be met with the death of the individual who blasphemes him. It also says that anybody who leaves the faith should be executed. This by itself proves that the author of Islam feared scrutiny (and simply *feared*, in general). Most Muslims do not want to execute people; but they are mandated to. It should be obvious that this is not a religion. It is simply 'people control' and is meant for the few to control the many, to use as an instrument for their anger.

Mohammed survived by raiding caravans in the early days of his 'ministry.' What is a caravan? It's a group of people that are traveling to another place (usually in search of food or work) consisting of families and friends. To raid a caravan in the sixth century meant to take a group's water, food and valuables, and it also meant to rape their women and take for themselves young servants. The rest were left to die in the desert.

Mohammed also spoke what ended up as scriptures, passages that ended up reversing things he said earlier, saying that Allah had something 'new' to say that negated the earlier passages. Does this sound like God? Does God change his mind? How 'holy' can your book be when your Prophet contradicts himself? Mohammed also had men beheaded that left the faith or got in his way. Mohammed's second wife was a seven year old girl. This is the man who gave birth to their religion! A thief, liar, murderer and a pedophile! Is it no wonder that anyone who says something bad about Mohammed needs to be assassinated!

Mohammed IS the model for Muslim men.

Mohammed was also an illiterate. He did not know how to read or write and this is the same for a large portion of the Muslim population in the Middle East.

So what are we to do with a religion that mandates the execution of both the Jewish people and the other 'people of the book,' which are the Christians?

Well, the first thing is to be truthful in all things, so those around you (including the Muslims) can see that you are honest. Most of the Muslims who want to dominate the world and impose Shariah law, by necessity, need to be dishonest to support their desires. They need to play with words and distort the truth to paint a picture of good Muslim people living in harmony with the rest of the world. We know already that this is not the truth.

The second way is to love them. Yes- I said love the ones who are trying to kill you! Jesus told us to love those that persecute you. This is very difficult- I know. But this is the only way we can be seen as the ones that are bringing the good news of Christ's redemption to an evil world. If we are trying to kill them, we will become like them. This is not Christ-like. Jesus was beaten and hung on a cross by people that he had come to save from peril. He did not curse them nor desire war with them; in fact, He loved them. This was the only sinless man in history- and at the same time He was God in the flesh.

The time has come, my friends, when the dark is getting darker and the light is becoming lighter. We need to be that light. We need to walk in truth and in love; for these are our brothers and sisters. Evil, liars, and murderers who plan to kill us, these are the ones we are mandated to save. Someone who sees us living this way will see the truth and repent- even if it is in secret. This includes the 'lay Muslims' and the ones who are trying to kill us. This is difficult- but wasn't what Jesus did for us difficult too? You have been bought for a price. That price was Jesus' earthly life. That price could give you eternal life with your acceptance.

Jesus told us to count it as blessings when we are persecuted.

Matthew 5: 10-12- "Blessed are they which are persecuted for righteousness' sake, for theirs is the kingdom of heaven. (11) Blessed are ye when men shall revile you and persecute you and say all manner of evil against you falsely for my sake. (12) Rejoice and be exceedingly glad, for great is your reward in heaven, for so persecuted they the prophets which were before you."

Something frustrates me with the people who are currently leading our movement toward a healthy nation right now. Our leaders are well-intentioned, but a bit misguided. I love men like Karl Rove, Charles Krauthammer, Sean Hannity and Dick Morris, but they seem to think we are going to fix things with our own hands. Sean Hannity is doing a great job fighting the good fight. But they think winning the House of Representatives and/or the Senate, or even replacing our man in the White House will repair our country. This is wrong. Our nation is very sick right now, as evidenced by the tight races for seats in government. Most Americans don't even know what is going on, as you can see, by the way people are still just following whatever desire they have even while their own country is being disassembled!. This is not going to work by simply having a respectable government and a good economy. THIS IS JUST TREATING THE SYMPTOMS! Americans need to have a real heart-changing event happen that transforms their awareness and causes them to want righteousness in their lives. What I'm saying is we are not going to fix this with our hands, BUT ON OUR KNEES!

I want you to notice that it is always during periods of extreme adversity that people reach out to their God. The two periods in which the greatest Christian literature appeared was in the time of the American Revolution and the Great Depression. At both these times there was a great awakening.

Hardship is coming our way---and it is necessary. This tribulation is the only way people change. Change is hard, change we must. We need to stop thinking we are going to do this ourselves. If we continue to think deceitfully, our trial may come by fire- literally. We need to be in constant prayer. We need this for ourselves and for our lost brothers and sisters. Jesus said, "If you deny me, I will deny you before my father in heaven." Let's not think we can do this alone. We are not alone. We are going to inherit a Kingdom we cannot even imagine.

Chapter 13

Cowards Kill Women

Why would anyone want to kill women? Tell me please, because I just don't understand. I think women are such beautiful creatures, even when they are not pretty. Just the fact that they're female. Girls. That's why I just can't wrap my head around why a man would want to kill a woman. Okay- I've met real witches before. I try to ignore them because they skew my view of the fairer sex. Some of them are real monsters. Conniving, hateful, vindictive and evil. But for some weird reason these are not the women that keep turning up dead.

On January 8, 2011, Rep. Gabrielle Giffords was shot in the head by a crazed lone 22 year old. He then shot a nine year old girl and several other people.

My wife and I recently spent a week in Las Vegas, and when we were there a dancer turned up missing. A lovely black haired beauty with a law degree is now dead. The ex-CEO of Anheuser Busch recently had a beautiful model discovered dead at his residence. It just keeps happening. Over and over again women are turning up murdered all over this country and all over the world. If you will notice it is overwhelmingly women and not men that are turning up murdered. I'm not saying that men are not killed too; it's just that women seem to be the targets in so many cases.

Something I really wonder about is what men who do these things feel like after they do this. Do they feel like a real stud? Or are they regretful? Is it "Yeah I killed the bitch" or is it 'What have I done!?" The life of a beautiful girl abruptly ending because of one man's rage is unthinkable to me. Do you know what kind of hatred this instills in me? I hate feeling this way about anybody! *I hate dead women even more!* I just want to break bones. I know how to do this; the grace of God has kept me from sending myself to

122

prison for violently destroying these monsters. I love women and want to annihilate the men who don't see how beautiful they are. I need to know why these men don't fear retaliation from other men. If men were real men, these cowards would fear walking the street.

Another group of men who seem to relish the thought of killing women are the Muslims who abide by Shariah law and see fit to kill women for what they think is dishonoring their family. All they want to do is go outside and see what the outside world looks like. Or they want to choose their own boyfriend. Or shed their stupid face covering. And this is a cause for death?! Detestable!

An eighteen year old girl was found by American soldiers on a hill in Afghanistan, totally disfigured, with her nose and ears sliced off and left there to die. She had ventured outside her home and had dishonored the family by doing so. Her father and brothers did this to her. She ended up on the cover of Time magazine. I bought a copy, just to read the story, and was sickened.

Faleh Hassan Almaleki, a native Iraqi, ran over his daughter in Arizona in his jeep allegedly because she was becoming too westernized. This is an honor killing. What Faleh doesn't recognize is that there's not any shame involved in his daughter becoming too westernized in America! This isn't Iraq. I say, you dumbshit, you're the one that moved her to America! Then you kill her for becoming too westernized!!??

An actress on the Harry Potter movie named Afshan Azad's father disapproved of her decision to date a Hindu boy. Her brother beat her and her father threatened to kill her. Afterwards, the actress refused to testify, as she would surely be marked for murder by Islamic Shariah law.

Jesse Marie Bender ran away from her home when her mother's boyfriend, Mohammad Khan, decided to take her on a trip to Pakistan. She was afraid she would be forced into an arranged marriage. She was thirteen. She was later found in a motel in Apple

Valley, CA. She lived in nearby Hesperia with her mother and boyfriend. Her mother, Melissa Bender, said she thought her daughter was abducted by someone she met on Facebook. Jesse and her three siblings have been taken into child protective custody pending an investigation because it seemed like her mother had lied.

A Muslim cabdriver in Texas shot his two teenage daughters in his cab, Amina and Sarah Said, to death in January 2008. The murders were prompted by the girls having 'unsanctioned boyfriends.' Later that year a Pakistani man beat his 25 year-old daughter to death in Atlanta, reportedly because she opposed her arranged marriage.

In Ontario, Canada, a 16 year-old girl was stabbed to death in 2007 by her father while her mother held her down. The teen had reportedly fought over wearing a hijib, the Muslim head covering. In another Canadian case, three teenage girls were drowned in their father's car in 2009. Also found dead was the father's first wife, who (relatives say) he never divorced. The father, his current wife and the girls' 18 year-old brother were all charged with first degree murder. Relatives told the media the killings were the result of one of the daughter's dating decisions.

In 2004, a 14 year-old girl who had been raped in Newfoundland was strangled to death by her father and brother to 'restore the family honor.' A 20 year-old Afghan daughter was shot dead in 2006, allegedly because she had moved in with her fiancé before their wedding. The killer was her brother.

Seattle cartoonist Molly Norris went into hiding at the FBI's recommendation last spring after her 'Everybody Draw Mohammed' day hit Facebook. A Seattle newspaper said Norris was 'essentially wiping away her identity' in reaction to a fatwa urging her killing. The contract was issued by Anwar al-Awlaki, the Muslim cleric who had hovered around a schoolyard and solicited prostitutes. He was connected to the Fort Hood shootings, the failed Times Square

bombing and the attempted Christmas Day, 2009 airline bombing over Detroit.

An Ohio teenager, Rifqa Bary (who secretly converted to Christianity), fled to Florida because her father threatened her with an 'honor killing' for abandoning the Muslim faith. She was returned to her parents by our courts. Deplorable!

So why is Shariah law so malevolent towards women? The following paragraphs are some key tenets of Shariah:

Female genital mutilation is what amounts to the clipping off of the clitoris of a young girl to relieve her man of the need to please his servant (his child bride). I'm quite sure that a young girl with her clitoris removed is worth more money than one with it intact as that is what girls are for: sale.

Muslim men are given permission by the Quran to beat their wives and commit marital rape. Men can have four wives and concubines as they please. A woman must not go outside her home unaccompanied by her male guardian.

Under Shariah, to bring a claim of rape, the woman must bring four Muslim men of good standing to witness (fat chance of that!). A failure to produce this is an admission to adultery and is punishable by stoning to death. Many Muslim women have been buried up to their necks and stoned to death BECAUSE they were raped!!!

A Muslim parent faces no legal penalty for killing any of his daughters or granddaughters; for this is a 'honor killing.' A Muslim man is permitted to lie to non- Muslims to safeguard himself or to protect Islam. Islamic doctrine permits the marriage to prepubescent girls, ie. arranged marriage. The girls are sold. This is common slavery. This is also child rape!!!

Gender inequality is the norm in Muslim culture and is mandated in the Quran. In Europe right now, honor killing takes place regularly and is ignored by the police in many areas....as the Muslims have taken over the neighborhoods. These areas are impenetrable by non-Muslims. It is only a matter of time until this becomes more widespread in America, unless men can be men and start caring enough to stand up and put a stop to this! I mean, have you ever seen Arab or Persian women? So many are beautiful!... But that is beside the point.

Islamic countries are less developed than other countries because their governments are completely based on the teachings of the Quran and they live by Shariah law. Then again, are they *really* governments? As I've said before, the Quran reads like it was written by a nine year-old, and its suggested way of life is not one that would promote the curiosity necessary for innovation. As I've also said, the men do not fully mature, leaving them 'little boys' even when they are grown men. So it's natural that they take 'little girls' for slaves, because they are not mature enough to relate to a fully mature woman. The backbone of this is the suppression and veiling of their women. This is why Muslim men will see women in typical western clothing, think they are whores and feel free to sexually assault them.

Most Muslim men do not even look to the Quran but just hear what their Imams tell them. They are still living in the sixth century and have been absent during the rest of the world's progress- be it social or scientific. Muslim men are developmentally challenged in the world because of their culture and their holy book's teachings. They do not think with the sophistication of any common westerner. Think about it: tell me they do not act like cavemen, dragging women by the hair? These are the people that our scriptures refer to as a people that "know not the meaning of peace."

Why do you think they want the end of capitalism? They are claiming to want democracy---but do they? The spiritual leader for the Muslim Brotherhood is Yusuf al Qaradawi, who says suicide bombing is a legitimate form of 'self' defense. His show attracts 40 million viewers a week broadcast on Al Jazeera television. He also advocates using the 'children bomb'. Just like communists, he states that "the right of the collective supersedes the right of the individual." His TV show is called 'Shariah and Life.' He is the chairman of the American Islamic University in Michigan, which has 50 chapters in the US. Please think about this.

Other Muslim Brotherhood representatives have said,"A nation that does not excel at the industry of death does not deserve life." Iranians in 2009 said, "We love death more than you love life," Referencing the West, 84 percent of common Egyptians believe apostates from Islam should be killed. 82 percent believe stoning (to death) is suitable punishment for adultery. 77 percent permit cutting off the hands for theft (no way for repentance!). 49 percent support Hamas, the Sunni Islamic organization in Palestine who wants the total obliteration of Israel. 49 percent of Al Jazeera's viewers say they believe Osama bin Laden to be a virtuous man. The Obama administration is fine with sitting at the table with these people and working things out. Why?

Organizations like CAIR (founded in 1994 and is the stepchild of Hamas) have been trying to infiltrate our media, and even wikipedia has been letting Muslims enter their ideas into their search engine. So anytime your children are seeking something on the internet they can likely find some entries that convey their philosophies.

Cowards kill women. Cowards kill children. Muslim extremists are not extremists. If you read the Quran, you will see many passages that advocate the killing of innocents, Jews, 'people of the book' and women. Children are used for shields in combat and even taught to kill themselves. Muslims kill themselves to kill others.

Christians are currently being killed *en masse* in Egypt (where twenty one were slaughtered on New Year's Day) and in Iraq. Slaughtered---in their churches---for worshipping God. Tell me, how can you slouch in your easy chair, enjoy a ball game while eating pizza, and ignore this? America really needs a lobotomy. People only care about themselves. You see- this is what happens when people become complacent.

How has this stupid, primitive, Cro-Magnon, Neanderthal religion been allowed to thrive in the world? Why haven't the rest of the world's religions come together and declared that Islam is not to be recognized as a valid religion? The rest of the world's religions are all about peace and harmony. Muslims are people that kill innocents. They are doing this all over the world! Why hasn't a coalition of nations come together and gone into these countries and taken their women and what little else they have, and left them there to die in the desert- like Mohammed did to the people he robbed in Arabia? This is *the only thing* we should be doing in these countries! Seriously, if I had the ability to get together a large enough group of men (?) well-armed enough, I would do just that. Take their women and little girls. Leave the boys; they have already been infected. I mean, where are the f**king men? Are you guys busy watching football, getting wasted at some local club trying to get laid or playing with your video games? Pussies! All of you. Yeah, I mean you!

What's worse is the video games that you play kill everybody involved, and sometimes even feed you stupid propaganda. Have you seen the new Xbox game, "Homefront?" It promotes a scenario where the U.S. economy collapses, and you (the video game player) must fight off millions of Korean-led communist invaders in San Francisco in the year 2027. Well guess what? Do you think somebody wants to ready you for this? Maybe the Bilderberg group?

Look, I have to say this. ANYTIME men who do not know the God of Abraham (no, Islam is not one of these, no matter what they say) live in a way that they are not held accountable BY WOMEN there will be only violence. Women ARE here to "tame the beast." This is what the suppression of women is all about: to not allow them to do this. Education would help too, but most Muslim men simply don't want to become educated. The ones that do just take Islamic studies (amongst other things), but don't seem to care enough to study other more sophisticated cultures. Sociopaths want violence. God gave us women to love....so these men hate them.

The fact that they sell their girls for money tells all. Love is meaningless in this culture. The girls and boys never fall in love. The girls are sold to older men and become servants. Sickening.

There is a readiness to resort to violence anytime a Muslim man's wants are not met---and that's a product of how they're raised. Not showing aggression when provoked or criticized is seen as a lack of courage or a lack of ability to protect his honor, and his social status will decline as a result. Westerners are brought up to handle criticism with an open ear. 'Maybe they're right,' a non-prideful western man might think. Using the criticism constructively makes one wiser. In Muslim culture, criticism=insult, and is to be treated with hostility. So they never grow up. As a result of this, Muslim men are plagued with low self-esteem. This is what happens when your perceived 'honor' is the only thing holding you up in your society. Real honor is highly esteemed in western culture, too, but 'honor' means 'honesty' in the West. Muslim men are encouraged to lie when the need arises. The two definitions of 'honor' are totally different. As a result, introspection is almost absent in Muslim culture.

Look, this is a religion that states that anyone who chooses to abandon the faith and go somewhere else must be assassinated. Any religion that believes that apostates must be killed has just admitted there's something drastically wrong with it. And that they don't believe their religion will stand up to the other religions if evaluated. The same with anyone that says anything but praise for that lying, pedophile, murderer Mohammed. And you guys actually *debate* with these people? We should be telling them their hateful religion will not be tolerated in this country! Instead we gracefully genuflect before them, seeking harmony and, instead of co-existing, our acceptance of them. Why? Can't you see they're just stupid, misogynistic, arrogant haters of all that is good on the Earth?

Tell me, why do even men that are not only Christian but Americans, who care about our country, still refer to Islam as a viable religion? Maybe you have children- I understand- and you're afraid for them. Or you're a coward and are afraid *OF* them. I do not have children and have a little more anger than you (perhaps righteous indignation). Because of my love for women, I am protective of them.

We pander to them. We engage them in dialogue about what to do about the way they feel in our society and even cater to them. Hell hath no fury in our society like one labeled an 'Islamaphobe.'

Y'know something, I do not hate Muslims. Some Muslims are wonderful individuals. Muslims are people. People are flawed and make mistakes. Lord knows, I am the king of bad decisions. I repent of these and try to do better. I, however, AM an Islamaphobe! I think Islam is the *dumbest* religion I have ever heard about. Ignorant, dumbshit men trying to build a world around their own little penises. Do you think, maybe these Muslim men have the smallest dicks in the world? Maybe this explains why they want to cover their women in stifling face coverings in the heat of the desert. "Don't look at my property, she will probably want you." Maybe that's why they do clitorectomies. Why decent men anywhere will tolerate this religion of imbeciles among us is a mystery to me. I hate Islam because it is *stupid*...and I have *no tolerance* for STUPIDITY!!!

Why are we so diplomatic with them? Are they just as diplomatic with us?

They want the extermination of the Jews. And the Christians. They want to make Shariah law the rule of our world and will stop at nothing to get this. This is a religion that mandates the slaughtering of millions of innocent people just trying to go to work to support their families! Look, I am truly sorry for the vitriol but think about it..... or are you busy? Doing what? Oh, I see...playing with your X-box, but (trust me!) they WILL take that! Does *that* speak to you?

I'll tell you- I know what has happened. You numbskulls have been pampered and set up for this. Pampered by a new society that allows you to walk through life expecting a fun and pleasant time, every day of your life, all day long. This is why you're such shitty employees. This new society came in during the sixties and has become our way of life. Personal responsibility means nothing anymore. Honesty is obsolete. Men these days don't seem to believe in anything but themselves. Guys...there WILL be a PRICE to pay for this! Do not be fooled! Or maybe you don't care...they just interrupt your television baseball game anyway. Yeah, I understand...the Dodgers now lead the Giants in the all-time series by a count of 1,089-1,074. Sorry to interrupt that all-important Game #2,178! I *really* understand!

You know, the communist ideology you've been fed is also a philosophy that wants the slaughter of innocents. Stalin starved to death fifty million of his subjects. Mao did the same to seventy million. Can't anyone see that the decadent, hedonistic way of life that has been given you by the communist party, stealthily brought in and offered to you, leads to the eventual death of innocents, and maybe even you? Sure it doesn't look like that right now, but are you unable to see anything for what it will become? Can you only see what is in your face right now? Are you really that STUPID??!!

Okay, I'm a little harsh. I'm like that. Look- I was a stupid rock musician and I'm going to admit something to you so you can beat me up a little. I was responsible for the death of two little children. I had abortions with two of my girlfriends during the eighties. I have never cried about this and I don't know why. I have begged the Lord's forgiveness and I believe I have gotten this. I'm *so* sorry I deprived two little children from ever getting the life they were given. I don't deserve anything. I, too, am a murderer; I am sorry. I repent of this and swear it will never happen again.

My point was that Islam, as a religion, should not be tolerated at all by decent men everywhere. I mean…look at the way they fight. Plant a bomb somewhere and then run away and watch people blow up. In war they construct IED's, bury them, and run away. Wait for the carnage. Kill themselves and others, thinking they will go to paradise and be given seventy two virgins as a reward. They're just LITTLE GIRLS with beards!

They're not getting their virgins- but a burning hell instead. Many years ago black people were taken from their homeland and forced to be slaves on plantations. They were eventually freed by people that saw the injustice. They now enjoy educational opportunities and as a result- careers, have bountiful black churches and we wave hello to them at the coffee shop, but we still *whine about them*. So why don't we care about the millions of Muslim girls who, as young as six years old, are enslaved to older Muslim men? These women are slaves too- and have been for generations!

The Ayatollah Khomeini (Iran's ultimate Islamic spiritual authority) says he channeled the spirit of the twelfth Imam who has climbed out of the well he fell into in the 10th century, and for him

to return there must be a bloodbath all over the world! They really DO want to do this!

Look, I have a solution as to how we can stop this genocide in our country and eventually all over the world. The problem is, I don't see any men that are man enough to do it. This is because YOU ARE ALL PAMPERED LITTLE PUSSIES! You should be ashamed of yourselves!

Okay, here it is. It is simple. Just decide that upon even one attempted terrorist attack on American soil in the future and Muslims everywhere will be tracked down and deported.

I know this would be next to impossible to implement- and this is okay. We wouldn't need to be completely successful, as they would just go underground anyway. But they would definitely stop killing innocents, and this would be well worth it. Some might say, "Wouldn't this make them mad and then they'd retaliate?" This person doesn't deserve a response, but I'm going to give one anyway. They are *already doing* that! You NEVER trade liberties for temporary security. At that point you deserve neither!

Look, if you suck up to the bully on the playground, does he, then, treat you with respect, or does he, then, begin to take your lunch money? Believe me these men *are* little children and they will be like this.

My solution would definitely work. It is foolproof, really. I just think Americans are too diplomatic for something like this anymore. Oh, I forgot, the *pansy-assed* Obama administration is in the White House right now and they like Muslim culture and religion because it is anti-American. And American men are too busy slobbering over ball games to care! Again, you should be ashamed of yourselves!

But I say, do not engage with people that kill innocents. Do not talk to them. In Hollywood movies, I always see our good guy walking up to the bad murderer and giving him a mouthful of tough sounding words before deciding to beat him up. I learned in my martial arts training and boxing to not be a man of many words. If I am going to do something, I simply need to do it. Talking about it just wastes time- time spent on an idiot. I do not want to engage people that murder innocents. I want to put them out. The same thing with people who believe in the doctrines of those who murder innocents- they are just as guilty. They promote their way of thinking. This includes men like Dr. Zuhdi Jasser, the well-meaning Muslim apologist that regularly appears on Fox news. I'm quite sure he is well intentioned but the fact is, this is still ISLAM. I really have to question the *intelligence* of anyone who believes devoutly in Islam!

I guess they have to, or fear for their lives!

Wafa Sultan, author of "A God who Hates," spoke on the Bill O'Reilly show, explaining how Muslim women who are raped cannot express it without four Muslim men that would say it happened. Without that she would be condemned to stoning to death for adultery. For the purpose of balance, O'Reilly had an opposing view: Portland, Oregon's Harris Zafar, the Ahmadiyya Muslim community spokesman. He said, "I feel sorry for Miss Sultan. She has clearly experienced a brutality in Syria and other nations and blames Islam for it, while true Islam (as taught by the holy Quran and the prophet Mohammed) is a tolerant and humane faith."

Then O'Reilly said they had done some extensive research into the Quran and paraphrased a verse: "...Men are the protectors and maintainers of women because Allah has given one more strength than the other and support them from their means. As to these women who are disloyal and commit ill conduct, admonish them, refuse to share their beds and beat them." Bill then said, "If that's in the Quran, you are going to have psychopaths and sociopaths take this and act upon it- are you not?"

Mr. Zafar replied, "This verse talks about the power and guardianship a man has over the woman, as the man is the head of the household and is responsible for the protection and sustenance of the family which includes the wife/mother as well." (...I say, answer the f**king question!!)

Then Bill said, "Five sentences later it says, 'as for those women from whom you fear rebellion, (if someone disagrees with you) admonish them, banish them and scourge them.' So you've got 'beat them' and 'scourge them' in the Quran, you know this is going to be used by people that are ignorant and sadistic."

Zafar replied, "You have to take the whole Quran in its entirety to understand, it's rebellion and that causes chaos not only in the family but in the society as a whole and nowhere does it say to beat your wife, it's just the escalation process." (A confusing bunch of words mixed with lies, Bill just quoted the Quran and it *did* say beat her!) Then Bill said, "You're familiar with the Hadith, right? This is book 8, No. 3432, it says flat out, 'The prophet Mohammed says raping a captive, married woman is permissible.' What's that?"

Zafar replied, "That's not a valid Hadith, there are so many Hadith that have been used and misused or even made up and that's why there are books of authenticity, and what the prophet *did* say is, 'Their treatment of women, and when it comes to the allegation of a woman who is raped, that she needs four witnesses to prove she was raped, that's just the complete opposite of what the Quran says. Chapter 24 verse 5 says, 'If someone accuses a chaste woman of having extramarital affairs and cannot bring forth four witnesses, they can be accused of slander. I mean if a woman has to bring four witnesses, I mean where's the justice in that?" (Again, I say answer the question. O'Reilly asked about Mohammed, regarding the scripture saying that it is permissible to rape a married captive woman!). LIARS!

Do you think Mr. Zafar is ignorant, confused, or in denial? Is it perhaps a little bit of all three? He can't even answer the questions asked! I'm just giving you this to illustrate how Muslim men are not able to defend their holy book or their belief system as a whole.

You know something I think is funny- hilarious, really... The very fact that there is such a thing as a Quranic scholar. This totally cracks my sides! Boy, I bet they feel sooo smart and knowledgeable. Read the Quran for yourself. You would think a grade-schooler wrote it. About a hundred pages in, you will end up saying, "if I read 'Lo, but Allah is most merciful' one more time I'm going to throw this book away." Look, this is what I would say to any willing Muslim. I would ask them to read me their favorite three full pages out of their Quran, whatever spoke to them. Then I would read them another three full pages from our Bible, namely, the Sermon on the Mount. Then I would ask them which one spoke to them with the most authority.

I need you to know that peaceful, moderate Muslims do exist and are genuinely good people that just want to support their families like you. I have one Muslim friend- and he is one of the best men I have ever known. He was the only one to keep in contact with me after I moved up to Washington state. I stayed with him for two weeks and he *did* try to introduce me to his faith. I understand: he believes in something, and if it was what he thought it was, it would have been a good thing.

But there is a problem with this. They will proselytize, just like my friend did, while ignoring some of the terrible stuff in their holy book. The underlying motive is still to want Shariah to be the law of the world. This is what Imam Rauf, who is the man behind the ground zero mosque, is doing right now. Touring our beautiful country and speaking on how Islam is good for everybody and we should let him build their victory mosque there. They say the mosque is a multi-faith center, but they do not say they will allow Christian worship there. Donald Trump offered to buy the Ground Zero building (soon to be a mosque) for the price they paid plus 5 percent more and they declined. Why would they? They want to announce their victory- even though there was no fight. Isn't it sick to build a Muslim worship center on top of where thousands of innocent citizens were slaughtered by Muslims? To these pantywaists this is a victory.

And I say you're all pantywaists too, for not standing up to them!

As I write Rep. Peter King (NY) is holding hearings on the rapid threat of home grown terror. At least there's one man in the bunch! He also wants to find out how cooperative the Muslim community has been. Outside, groups like CAIR (Council on American Islamic Relations), the unindicted co-conspirators in the Holy Land Foundation trial, (the largest terror funding case in US history) are protesting. Why? Do they blatantly love terror plots planned by American citizens? And why is CAIR the primary voice for Muslim Americans? Many others are out there protesting with them. People are waiving signs, saying Mr. King is Islamophobic. These are white Americans that *think they're fighting racism*. They say Mr. King is demonizing the Muslim community. What he is doing is not giving in to the political correctness that led to the Fort Hood massacre. He doesn't want bombs planted to kill innocents, so he is Islamophobic? Where the f**k are peoples' brains?

MUSLIMS... are demonizing their *own* community!

When political correctness causes Americans to protest over hearings done to protect *them*, why isn't anybody asking why? So it's worse to be called an 'Islamophobe' than to have innocents killed in the streets?!!! Do you know that since 9/11, 161 Americans have planned terror attacks? 126 terror indictments...and ALL of them committed by Muslims...

Never underestimate the stupidity of the American public!!!

Trying to be fair, Rep. King allowed Muslim representative Keith Ellison to testify during the hearings and Ellison started tearfully blubbering about a Muslim who was also killed in the 9/11 attack named Mohammed Salman Hamdami, in a way that was shamefully transparent. Have you ever seen someone try unsuccessfully to cry? This was really over the top. It really doesn't matter anyway, as the Muslims are clear that they will kill anybody, even their own, to further the cause of Allah. Hell- they strap bombs to themselves- and their children!

Now Peter King is getting threats from overseas. King wants to show how the Muslim community is not helping stop the recruitment of terrorists here in the US, and also how CAIR is conspiring with Al Qaeda in recruiting them. A study by the Center for Security Policy, headed by Frank Gaffney, found that three quarters of the mosques in the US actively seek to teach Shariah law, with its mandate to militant action and jihad. The other quarter are the minority. But we need to learn to be more tolerant?!

Now, because the Obama administration has actually brought CIA counterterrorism experts up on charges for DOING WHAT THEY WERE INSTRUCTED TO DO, they will now not be interrogating terror suspects unless they were captured in Iraq or Afghanistan. This obviously makes us less safe, as we are leaving out potentially 80 percent (give or take a few) of the terror population by applying this rule. And now that the Obama administration is in place we can no longer use enhanced interrogation techniques like waterboarding as this is torture, even though it has been proven that these very approaches were what led to Osama bin Laden's discovery in Pakistan and many others. I mean these men are accused of slaughtering innocents and we don't want to make them uncomfortable?! President Obama does not love or care about you.

Anjem Choudary calls Americans 'the biggest criminals in the world today' and said 'the flag of Islam will fly over the White House.' He planned a failed rally on March 3rd. He says the event is a 'call for Shariah in America.' The event was organized by the Islamic Thinkers society. Hmmm... Islamic thinkers. You're kidding...right?

Sheikh Yusuf al Qaradawi says, "O Allah take this oppressive tyrannical band of people, this oppressive Jewish Zionist band and do not spare a single one of them. Count their numbers and kill them down to the last one." He has been banned from entering the US and was denied a visa to enter Britain for medical treatment.

These men hate the Jews and Israel so much that the Arabs who live in what was Palestine are not allowed citizenship into other Arab countries, because they want them continually at war with the Jewish people. Why would they want that?

Tell me, when the Jews, in 1948 moved into the Palestinian terrain and built (actually re-built) their nation there, the whole area began to blossom. Their agricultural abilities were more developed than the Arabs living there and they even seemed to have a power greater than that helping them (God). They were much more advanced technologically and showed more foresight in their development of the land and they had a more rewarding culture than the Arabs. Now, at this time the Arabs living there had a decision to make. They could welcome their new neighbors and learn from them (the intelligent and mature thing to do) or they could hate them and desire to kill them (the childish and unintelligent thing to do). Well, like I've been saying...

Look, have you ever wondered why Muslims that attack the US do not use weapons that they designed?...*because they don't design anything!* Why? They live in a stifling world dictated to them by the Quran and the Hadith. Their world does not create an environment that gives birth to creativity. So they use OUR cell phones, drive OUR cars and use OUR technology to try to bring us back into the sixth century with them! I think Islam is ugly because it just displays the worst part of manhood possible. I am at war with this stupid belief system because YOU are, shamefully, too cowardly or preoccupied to do so!

You, clearly, *do not...* love women as I do.

Their countries are impoverished because one half of their population does not contribute to the economy. If a country is poor, everyone must work- if they are healthy. It has gotten that way here now. Can you make it by yourself? Do you need your wife to work also? Do you see the direction we are going? Why is this?

Because you are all such pansy-assed, pampered wannabes that you're letting it go this way! You pussies don't deserve to have women love you!

Do you know why I'm talking to you this way? I want you guys to become defensive enough of your masculinity to stand up and join me and DO SOMETHING!

Now, look at the slogan that the Muslim brotherhood expounds:..."Allah is our objective, the Prophet is our leader, the Quran is our law, Jihad is our way and dying in the way of Allah is our highest hope." Sound like some good people you want living next to you, huh?

Recidivism among Muslim men convicted of terrorist acts after their release is at 81 percent. 81 percent of them return to terrorist activities after being incarcerated in the United States. Do you ever think about why these people are so comfortable in American prisons like Guantanamo Bay, where you or I would hate life? It's because this world is much more comfortable to them than they would even have at home in Afghanistan. The same situation regarding women is present- women are largely absent- they have cable TV, all their boys around them, and free meals. I will, again, refer to the underlying homosexuality in Muslim belief even if it (?) is not sexual. They, simply, prefer to be around boys because they have such disdain for women. Seems kinda homo to me...

When Muslims are in the minority and perceive vulnerability, they will agree to most anything and be conciliatory towards other religions and cultures. But the moment they sense superiority in numbers, a ruthlessness sets in. They begin to oppress all the minority religious groups, rape women that dress in typical western attire and totally disregard any agreements they made during their time of weakness. LIARS!

Now, all over America, Muslims are playing the 'religion card' and claiming to be victimized by white Americans that just can't understand their religion of peace. They're making this a civil rights issue. LIARS!

In some European countries they have been banning the hijab for women because terrorists dress in them to sneak into places to bomb. They have taken over neighborhoods to the extent that law enforcement cannot do their duty. Europe's response: the banning of building more mosques. So Muslims are saying these nations will pay for not integrating with them enough!...MUSLIMS are the ones who will not integrate!!! They claim that this is the reason for their terror campaigns. LIARS!

The Quran was written in two stages. The first part was written when Muhammad was living in Mecca, Arabia and his following was sparse. These passages are used to support Islam as being a 'religion of peace, love and tolerance.' They avoid references to the second and largest part of the Quran, the part written when Muhammad had moved his headquarters to Medina, Arabia and he had increased in strength. Then came the inflammatory passages. So the Quran is not sequential as other religious books of all types are (like the Holy Bible) to try to hide this painful fact. As per Shariah law and Quranic mandate, Muslims are *permitted to lie* to protect themselves or further Islam. This is the reason why non-Muslim women (who marry Muslim men) are faced with a nightmare in the transformation that occurs after marriage vows are exchanged. The men are given license to appease their prospective wives with promises they have no intention of keeping. LIARS!

Look, can you see why I have such disdain for men in general? I realize that these are not American men. But remember what I've already said about American men? I think American men without knowledge of the truth are increasingly becoming more like their Muslim counterparts. It's still very subtle- but if you look for similarities, they will be found. I watched the riots in Libya and

Egypt and noticed that it was really, all men. Of course it was- it looked like the footage I saw in downtown Los Angeles of cars broken into and on fire after the Lakers won a basketball championship in June 2010. Same thing in some parts of San Francisco after the Giants won the World Series. In time these same men will be raping women in the streets after their teams win! Part of why I'm writing this book is to slap you guys into waking up. I'd like to BEAT some sense into you because you like tipping a car after a team in your city wins a trophy, which *you* had nothing to do with. Or would you just go whine to the police? Pussies! You homo's only care about your cock & balls buddies and ignore the women who love you. 'Cause they don't play your stupid ball games! The *degree* of your stupidness...almost...fascinates me.

Increasingly, American-born Muslim men are lured, via the internet, into terrorist activities. Even though they are born here and have all the advantages our country offers, they are lured into this hatred and turn on their adopted country. For what? Does the promise of seventy two virgins really make one want to kill innocents? I mean every one of them could have a wonderful wife and live in comfort here. Anwar al Awlaki is one of these. He was born in New Mexico and then migrated to San Diego, where he was taken into custody for loitering around a schoolyard (probably seeking a bride). Then he was busted three times soliciting prostitutes. He is one of Al Qaeda's spiritual leaders! What would happen if one of OUR spiritual leaders did this? He is also the man behind many of the attempted bombings of 2009 and 2010, like the Fort Hood massacre, the botched Times Square bombing and was even inspirational in the 9/11 attacks.

I mean, Osama bin Laden has now been found and killed but Awlaki has actually been the inspiration for many attacks and remains at large (as of this writing). It really doesn't matter as their cause will be alive as long as Islam is still in the world and seducing the 'not so intelligent,' or 'slow,' or uneducated, as that is its function. And speaking of cowards killing women, it was reported that when bin Laden was about to be shot he grabbed his wife and pushed her toward the Navy Seal who had his gun drawn. F**king coward mother f**ker!!!

What would you do in a situation in which there was gunfire and a woman present? 'I' would stand in front of her! That is the noble thing to do.

But not these animals, nooo, women are shields. Hundreds of people went to the streets in support of bin Laden and burned an effigy that was supposed to represent the US and stomped on it. There were also reports of US flags being burned. They are rioting in the streets over the US coming into their country and killing a mass murderer that slaughtered 3000 of our citizens. Not extremists...common citizens... Muslims.

Now there have been two suicide bombings in Pakistan that were said to be by the Taliban by a spokes person for the Pakistani Taliban to the Associated Press in a phone call killing 80 people, mostly young men finishing months of training in the police dept. on the way home with gifts for their families. There will be more. Their hero is now dead. Their celebrity hero and deeply religious leader that had a large stash of porn in his place, while his wives labored over him. Hypocrites! They condemn the US for its decadence....LIARS!

While Pakistan has been secretly harboring bin Laden FOR 6 years and lying about it, our country has been giving Pakistan 20 (b)illion dollars in aid since 2001, some of which was for counterterrorism. 3 billion annually to help keep us safe! LIARS!

But regarding their assassination of women, I think this just appeals to their sense of 'machismo' and toughness. What's tough about killing women or planting a bomb and watching innocent people die? I guess to them it is not manly to have a loving wife and good children and provide for them. That is not angry enough. But when they live here in America, what are they angry about?

They can have so much more than they could over in Saudi Arabia or Iraq... as I've been saying, IT'S THE RELIGION, STUPID!!!

Look, the Baha'I religion, the Hindu, the Buddhist, the Jewish and the Christian religion tell their followers to be truthful. Why is Islam the only religion in THE WORLD to excuse dishonesty?...Because...they...are...LIARS! LIARS!

I'm telling you right now what these people (excuse me, men) want. They want their Caliphate back. The last Caliphate the Muslims had was also the largest: it was the Ottoman Empire, which lasted from 1571 to 1924, when the Turks (who were not so overtly Muslim) regained power and ended the Caliphate. At its zenith, the Empire spanned all of North Africa, as far east as Indonesia and as far north as Spain. It has been 87 years; they want it back. They are right now preparing all of Europe for their new Caliphate and unless Europeans grow 'a pair,' quickly they will succumb and a new version of the Ottoman Caliphate will emerge, ruling with terror over their subjects.

"Jihad is the Way" is part of a five volume work called, 'The laws of Da'wa,' written by Mustafa Mashhur, the reported leader of the Muslim Brotherhood. The book includes writings that say that their mission is the "global conquest of Islam and reestablishing the Islamic caliphate." It says, "The Islamic ummah can regain its power and be liberated and assume its rightful position, which was intended by Allah, as the most exalted nation among men, as the leaders of humanity."

I personally do not want to spread this religion around. You need to know that these people not only were brought up with this religion, but are really trapped in it by the threat of death to apostates. The Muslims that *do*, in secret, think their religion is flawed, dare not speak up for fear of retaliation from the true followers. Think about it. How can *we* 'grow a pair' and do something about this?

There is only one thing to do. We, men (?), need to organize and make way for apostates from Islam to be in a sort of 'witness protection' program and given new identities. There are a couple of these organizations already (one is leaveislamsafely.com), but they are not well-known and have little funding. Maybe we can take the funding to protect the 'spotted fish owl squirrel' and direct it to a more helpful cause. What do you say?

Islam threatens the entire world, and I can't believe there are not enough men in the world to combat this. We need to do this for our very lives. We need to do this for the GIRLS...! In the name of Jesus we need to do this just because of our decency and love.

So, what did I say to do? To take power in our own country, first, which means *weed out all the communist sociopaths*, THROW THEM INTO PRISON and then tell the Muslims that no more killing will be tolerated- or they have to go. Trust me, they, then, will police themselves. The second thing was to set up exit routes for people that want to leave Islam. Trust me: there will be a mass exodus. The truly good decent people who are trapped in Muslim Shariah law will unite and leave. Pretty much all the women will go. All that will be left is a bunch of little girls with beards looking at each other and wondering if they should kill each other or maybe......?

Remember please, whatever you compromise to keep, you will lose.

Chapter 14

The Stupidity of Communislamic Belief

Unfortunately most people, everywhere, are lazy thinkers. Physically lazy, I would understand-but just thinking? I think people reject thinking because it necessitates some degree of research. To come away with the right view on something, one needs to first sift through all the wrong stuff, as it is more abundant. This is where the rub comes. Now we have to compare. It's easier to just turn on the television. Y'know the sociopaths see people as sheep--and I seem to agree. I don't like it. I definitely wish more people would learn to think for themselves, but for some reason I think this is *not* going to happen.

There are people that notice this in other humans, whom are sociopathic. They seem to despise others; they see themselves as superior to most people. They want to elevate themselves above the rest to a position of power, exercising control and using others to serve themselves. *These* are stupid people, and are very misguided. They see anyone who believes in a God of any kind as backwards and primitive. But isn't it kind of unintelligent not to see some order in the universe higher than oneself? Do these people really think they are incapable of making mistakes? Anyone who is a thinker of any order knows this is stupid. But you know who is *really* stupid? Their followers.

Just look at any communist country- past or present. A tiny elite (and masses of the 'great unwashed') living under government rule, or kingship. Look at China, the USSR, Cuba, Cambodia or

North Vietnam. In these cases, when their regimes came to power, one of the first things they did was sequester off all the free thinkers into reeducation camps (or simply kill them). That would help reduce their population down to a manageable level. In the case of the USSR and China, this was done by just redirecting food supplies elsewhere, thus starving a whole segment of their populations. If you will notice something else about communist countries, they are all extremely poor- except China- and that is because we buy their goods. This is because the lack of a taxable working middle class deprives them of the kind of resources needed for a prosperous nation. They really don't care how most of their populations live- as long as they themselves are sitting in palaces.

One thing I have noticed about communists are their ability to 'eat their own' when the need arises. No honor among thieves, I guess. I have not witnessed the revolutions firsthand that led any of these countries into communism, but I am seeing it in my own and have witnessed the 'throwing under the bus' of our own commie elite when faced with obstacles. The White House was so quick to let go of Shirley Sherrod, Van Jones and Rod Blagojevich when the going got tough. Juan Williams, a progressive who works on Fox news frequently, was fired for saying that he got nervous when he was flying and saw Muslims in traditional garb boarding the plane. It really was not only that, but the fact that he was working with Fox, the only conservative cable station. Fox always balances their opinion shows with someone from the other side and Juan was one of these. They should have been grateful.

I guess my problem is motivation. What motivates one to side with a group in which there is no honor and no security? One has to want what these people are after pretty bad to put oneself in that position. You have to believe you will be putting yourself in a position to fully benefit from it. The people that support this must think they will become immune to being 'thrown under the bus' in order to do this. Or their motivation (subliminal or not) is the same godlessness and hatred that the sociopaths have. They want a world with no accountability.

Michael Moore (the filmmaker that made "Sicko") went to Cuba, and was given the 'privileged' tour of a hospital. He concluded that their healthcare was better than the US and is now saying that wealthy Americans' money is not theirs; it should be taken from them. He says we've allowed the vast majority of cash to be concentrated into the hands of a few people. Moore has always complained about this.

Here's what's new: he says they're not circulating that cash. *This is because companies are unsure of what their tax burden will be under the Obama administration.* Also, he says "they're sitting on the money, using it for their own, putting it someplace else with no interest in helping you with your life. We've allowed them to take that and that it's not theirs, it's a national resource, that's ours." So *other people's* money is a national resource? It's these people that employ Americans! Communist sociopaths want to take these people down, because they want people unemployed and dependent.

Michael Moore was in Wisconsin during the March 2011 protests, saying that the Governor is robbing the middle class. You know what he is also doing? Suing his production company (middle class), he made 21 million but needs another 2.7. He wouldn't even hire union workers (lower/middle class) to work on his films himself. You see, this is what sociopaths are like. Hypocrites, all of them!

So who the hell is President Obama anyway? What does he believe in? Well...the answers to this are very eloquently put by Dinesh D'Souza in"The Roots of Obama's Rage." Absolutely a must read for anyone who wants to know what President Obama is all about. Barack Hussein Obama (aka. Barry Soetoro), attended Reverend Wright's church in Chicago for twenty years. Wright expounds an anti-American, anti-Anglo philosophy known as Black

Liberation Theology. After being exposed as the hate slinging pastor who has had a good relationship with the President, Rev. Wright was too, thrown 'under the bus' by Obama because he'd lose too much support. Liberation theology is quite anti-Christian, and communist in nature. It tells the lie that freedom from authority will create freedom for all (when it actually does the opposite). With people dwelling on the Earth in their normal sinful fashion, this will NEVER be the case. All of our New Testament saints lived under Roman rule, and even Jesus' arrival didn't change that. Jesus' redemption was a spiritual one, and our simple acceptance of this will manifest itself in the next life.

Barack, or Barry, is an anti-colonialist, meaning he believes that one country should not occupy another. He has no problem; however, with having communists occupy any country. His father was a Marxist, fighting for the Socialist liberation of Kenya. Barry also is a Marxist and has admitted this, saying that in college he and friends would "sit in our rooms and smoke cigarettes and discuss Marxist philosophy."

When President Obama first came into the White House, one of the first things he did was to go to Egypt (interesting, eh?) and tell the people there, who were primarily young men out of work, that he wanted to help them acquire their own form of government. So look at what is happening there now. Civil unrest is now ousting their dictator, Hosni Mubarak- the one who held to the Camp David Accord treaties with the US and Israel. Nothing good about a dictator, I know, but now the Muslim Brotherhood is poised as the ones to come in and 'fix' the problem. Trust me...there is a reason for this.

If anyone has educated yourselves in Marxism, you will first notice that in Karl Marx's and Fredreich Engel's book 'The Communist Manifesto,' the word 'proletariat' comes up at least three times on any of the twenty pages or so. The 'proletariat' is the underdog- the less fortunate. They are used to bring the aspiring leader to power. Actually they say pro-le-ta-ri-at which is five syllables. I would say un-der-dog which is three. So I guess they're two-fifths smarter than me. Wow, maybe they should be rulers!

The Manifesto, when taken at face value, is simply a framework for 'community organization.' It is intriguing that Obama was a community organizer before becoming President, with many beliefs and actions which emulated those in the Manifesto.

The aforementioned Richard Cloward and Francis Fox Piven, communist educators in the sixties, advocated the collapse of the American system from within by getting as many people on the welfare rolls as possible, and to spend as much money on anything possible, like social aid programs, which also will make people dependent on the state. It will then bankrupt the country, creating dependents to serve them. When the economy is successfully collapsed and the rioting that results happens, the sociopaths simply come in with the solution. If you look at almost any of the wasteful spending of this administration you will see exactly this in action. They are hitting us where it hurts: financially. They want us bankrupt. President Obama, after passing the extension of the Bush tax cuts, is now trying to reinstate his original plan to overtax the wealthiest Americans, even though they are the ones paying the bulk of American taxes already and are the ones that employ the citizens. How much taxes are the poor paying? Almost none.

Saul Alinsky's books on how to stage sit-ins and protest groups rallied the students of the sixties with his communist ideology. Known as the father of modern radicalism, his book, "Rules for Radicals" is the handbook for protest. You can see Alinsky's principles in action during the ACORN protests that created our current housing crisis. Interestingly enough, his book is prefaced with a statement that says, "At least Lucifer won his own kingdom." Please think about that. After Glenn Beck pointed that out, they are removing that paragraph from the beginning of the book in new copies. A definite point to ponder...

President Obama also lived in Indonesia during his high school years. Indonesia is perhaps the largest Muslim country in the world. Barry has an enduring kinship with the Muslim faith. I do not personally think he is a secret Muslim or anything like that anymore than I believe he's a Christian; I believe he is a sociopath. Sociopaths do not worship anything. They are totally *self*-centered. His wife and Valerie Jarrett spent time in Chicago wrangling money out of hospitals. Those two are quite the pair.

For a people to live without God to guide them, they must naturally cling to each other to survive. They need to exchange their freedom for some security. This is where unions (and secret societies) come in. The union makes sure their members have job security and adequate benefits. The unions and their members are the ones who actually usher in the new police state and cause the riots to come about. The current administration is so over-regulating and taxing the private sector job creators (rich people) so much that they have to cut costs by not hiring new employees. This also will collapse the economy, which will start the riots. The union folk will not sit in the palaces, and they know it. But they will not have to compete for job security, which to them is worth it. 'Useful (proletariat) idiots!'

The stupidity, or, more accurately, short-sightedness of these people is just in that they have gone from valuable to expendable. What is intelligent about this? The state can dispose of you at any time. I think some feel that they were the ones to 'bring it in' so they are immune to finding themselves 'under the bus.' Time and again this proves not to be true. So it really is true that to give up your liberty for temporary security, you end up deserving neither. In a communist society, it is only the elite who truly benefit. Plus, the country will become poorer, as a lack of a taxable middle class will soon make their government unable to keep their promises. Everybody loses except the elite.

Something I really wonder is what people like Nancy Pelosi and Harry Reid think they're going to get out of bringing socialism to America? I mean...they're 70, for Christ's sakes. Shouldn't they be living their golden years? Maybe they just want to go down in history as the ones that brought down America....go out with a geriatric thud!

I'm just looking for motivation. I'm not finding it.

Now I can see the motivation in what is seen as radical Islam. They actually do believe in something. What they believe in, though, is flawed down to its very basic tenants. The very fact that anyone who leaves the faith and speaks out against Mohammed should be killed should raise red flags to anyone with the ability to understand even basic principals of human interaction. This is stated clearly because the founder(s) of the religion didn't think the religion would hold up under scrutiny. I mean, isn't it obvious? But these very precepts in the religion are the things that keep people from leaving the religion. Now that's suffocating...and cheap!

They are just now beginning to debate, in some Islamic countries, whether or not to let their women go to school. This is being met with fierce opposition. Now there are supposed 'moderate Muslims' who have educated women in their society. They often work for pro-Muslim groups advocating Allah for all- but you must know that these women are still beholden to the demands of their men. Ladies like Daisy Kahn, the wife of Imam Rauf, touts the empowerment of women in Islam, but you need to understand that in these more primitive, (Islamic) cultures there is a distinct class system. They are in the privileged class and have only known entitlement; they are self-centered enough to not care about their sisters, and sociopathic enough to act like they do (much like rich kids). Islam breeds selfishness; it's part of the culture.

The common denominator I'm seeing in both of these is education. The sociopaths think people are basically stupid, and they go out of their way to help make them that way. These sociopaths have brought in a totally hedonistic lifestyle for Americans, and then, upon seeing how stupid they have come to behave, decide they need to decree what's best for them. The Islamic environment is different in that the bulk of the people are already uneducated. Your typical Arabic, Somalian, or Egyptian hasn't the education of a third grader in the United States, England or even Japan. They believe anything their Imams say to them.

In Islam, human life is also worth nothing. They, too, will eat their own. Strap bombs to yourself in the name of Allah. A man says you went outside your home and spoke to a man not in your immediate family; therefore you must be killed.

More recently, women in Afghanistan have been killing themselves because of their sordid lives. They have even been lighting themselves on fire (something called self-immolation). Do you know how painful it is to accidentally touch the burner on a stove or a lit cigarette? Then imagine pouring gasoline on yourself and lighting yourself on fire! Unbelievable! What causes someone to do something like this? They obviously feel absolutely no self-worth. There is no love in their existence. They were bought as a child to be a wife and a servant. To these women, this is the only life they know. Their mothers and sisters suffered the same. This is their lot in life. Shameful- not for them, but the men who enslave them! This has nothing to do with God. I noticed that most of them were not dead, but hospitalized from their burns. I can't help but wonder if this self-immolation is to make themselves unattractive so their old disgusting captors will leave them alone.

The communists (at least) can see another way of life and choose not to accept it. They want us to be slaves to the ruling class. The communist leaders need to lie to the people in order for them to go along with their program. In Islam, they grow up that way and know nothing else. So women in Afghanistan kill themselves and Cubans risk their lives getting on inner tubes to Florida trying to escape their oppression. Yeah, communislam is great!

I want you to think about Guantanamo Bay one more time. This is the place where terrorists are detained awaiting trial. President Obama wants to close the facility. Why? Because Gitmo detainees want to bring down capitalism and any free society. So does Obama. There's a kinship there. Obama does not want his wife to wear the hajib (and I'm sure she would not), but he wants to move Gitmo detainees to a prison in Illinois where they will proselytize in the prison system. He wants them tried in US federal courts so they will have lawyers who might be able to exonerate them. He wants them Mirandized, so they won't have to speak and incriminate themselves. The more converts to Islam in America, the weaker we are. This is one of the main places new converts to Islam come from. Islam really appeals to the macho sensibilities of prison inmates. Really, young men of all stripes can be sucked into this stupidity quite easily, thanks to our acceptance of the hedonistic lifestyle that our media expounds daily and disenfranchised young men's anger.

Thursday May 12th 2011. Two men of Moroccan and Algerian nationalities that have lived in the US since the early nineties have been arrested and are going to court for an alleged terror plot to blow up an NYC synagogue. They stated that Muslims are treated like 'dogs' in the world and that they needed to come against the Jews as a result. Well, are Muslims treated like 'dogs?' The US is currently over in Libya helping the rebels overthrow Muammar Gaddafi and are now entertaining the idea of helping rebels do the same in Syria. I say bullshit!! They're treated like royalty! These men just are MUSLIMS and full of hatred for their brothers and especially their sisters! LIARS!

The United States was at war with communism for most of the twentieth century. This century it's at war with what is called radical Islam. But we have been devaluing our brothers and sisters since the sixties, because we have been welcoming in communist (and Islamic) sociopaths and listening to them- to the point of excusing Islamic Sharia law in some parts of the country. Dearborn, MI, is almost an Islamic state right now. Liberals all over love the idea of becoming a communislamic state. Anything to rid themselves of capitalism and God.

I need to say this...ALL the wars we are in-in the Middle East are INTENTIONALLY-- to help the Muslims establish their caliphate! Is this OK with you?

In Illinois recently, there was a conference held on the Khalifa, or the Caliphate, which is an agenda that demands Islamic world domination. They were saying that democracy and capitalism is dead. Revolutionary communist groups like "Organizing for America" were there. The rallying cry for a king and a subordinate class is in full swing here and abroad. Whether it is Islamic or communist, they want freedom gone from our world. In the attempted rally by SHARIA4AMERICA the rallying cry was "Communism is dead, capitalism is dying, Islam is the solution." Interesting...communism, to them...*dead?!* Right.

Both the communists and the Islamic people want Israel to go. But there is a scripture that says, "I will bless those that bless you and curse those that curse you" in the Hebraic Talmud. (Genesis 12:3) This is evidenced in the way America was prospered because of our love for Israel and in the way Islamic countries have lived in poverty. This is also evidenced in the way that now, with the Obama administration, we have decided Israel is not our friend and why we are now in decline. Think about this, please....

On February 6, 2011, President Obama was interviewed by Bill O' Reilly on Fox news. Bill asked President Obama if he thought that the Muslim Brotherhood was a problem in the Egyptian revolt. He successfully deflected the question and moved on. Now, why would he do that? Wikileaks later released a headline that read, "Egypt protests: America's secret backing for rebel leaders behind uprising." Obama gave his 'thumbs up' to the Egyptian protesters, claiming they wanted a true democracy.

Now, Iranian citizens have been risking their lives in protest over their dictatorial leaders (probably because of the success of the Egyptian and Algerian uprisings)- and the White House is absolutely silent. Why would the US be partial to an Iranian dictator over an Egyptian one? Answer: Egyptian Hosni Mubarak supported the aforementioned 'Camp David Accords' truce with Israel. His 'coziness' with the United States would eventually lead to instability in his country. The same thing for Yemen and Saudi Arabia which now have their own riots going on.

Just weeks after the Egyptian uprisings, protests broke out in Libya over dictator Mummar al Qaddafi. He was also given the silent treatment by the White House. 'Alinskyite' Secretary of State Hillary Clinton denounced the dictator, but she is in too diplomatic of a position with the other governments to be silent. Why is the White House silent? Because the Libyan dictator is the one that ran Osama Bin Laden out of his country. It is obvious that someone wants these terrorists to prosper. Obama doesn't condemn Qaddafi, but says the bloodshed is outrageous. Do you remember Qaddafi at the United Nations meeting? One of his translators had to leave and couldn't take it anymore when he rambled on about how he didn't get his egg rolls with his Chinese food? This man is the leader of a country! Amazing....

The White House has finally decided to tell Gaddafi he must go because of so much outrage from human rights advocates and because he has encouraged his military to fire on civilian protestors. They have frozen Gaddafi and his son's assets in America. These (men) are just Islamic anyway, saying they want freedom when they actually are still living under Shariah law and abusing their women, selling little girls as slaves. Al Qaeda is urging the rebels to overthrow Gaddafi (and our President has us, ironically, helping them), but I say who cares? Let them kill each other. Hell, ship arms to both sides, a nightmare will ensue for about two weeks and then suddenly, a great C-A-L-M will come over the land...

The women will be safe as the men blow each other up.

Y'know, I am mandated by my Lord and Savior to love every one of my brothers, including the Muslim men that enslave little girls and kill them. Sorry... I just love women so much that I can't bring myself to this level of spiritual maturity yet. I hope someday I can.

Here's one other forgotten fact: Libya only commands 2 percent of the world's oil supply anyway, so it's not like we have any vested interest there.

But (go figure) we're supplying the Libyan rebels with weapons. The Washington Examiner says jihadis who fought against us in Iraq and Afghanistan now enjoy American support in Libya. Evidence is emerging that the United States' forces are waging war in Libya on behalf of rebels whose ranks include these same jihadis. The Britain Daily Telegraph also says the leader of the US-supported rebel forces in Libya, Abdel Hakim Al-Hasidi, went to Afghanistan in 2002 to fight against the US-led foreign invasion. *All these regime changes* have led to an international increase in hostility towards Israel and the US. WE ARE IN LIBYA HELPING PEOPLE THAT WANT TO KILL AMERICANS!!

And as of this writing the White House says we need to intervene into the Syrian conflict there. They want to oust their dictatorial leader President Bashar al Assad. Hugo Chavez of Venezuela says the US is getting involved so we can seize the country's resources. Don't believe it, we are helping them to do the same thing as we have done in Egypt and Libya, which is make the way for the Muslim caliphate and it's leaders!

Look, all Middle Eastern dictators are now coming under fire for a reason. What do you think that reason is? Think about this. If most of the dictators end up being ousted, who is going to replace them? Well, the Muslim Brotherhood would be likely, or Al Qaeda, who support the uprising in Libya and the brotherhood. Or perhaps there's a global influence here- and someone with much bigger aspirations is going to take control. Maybe some kind of a global leader?

Here's something else to think about. The Book of Revelation in the Bible speaks of the Antichrist and the things that lead up to his coming. Muslims have him prophesized as well; they call him the "Mahdi." The duplicity in both of these are astounding. In the Hadith, which is essentially Muhammad's 'musings' on eternity, the return of the 12th Imam and the 'washing of the world in blood' needs to occur for "Mahdi" to be revealed. But in both the Hadith and the book of Revelation, the Mahdi/Antichrist kills both Jews and

Christians, rules for 7 yrs, makes peace with Israel and breaks the treaty (LIARS!), gains a global seat on the temple mount in Jerusalem, kills and beheads non-believers and develops the 'mark of the beast,' which is an skin-implanted identification for the exchange of currency. Are you aware that it is getting so hostile towards Christians *and* Jews all over the world that the US and Israel are close to being the only two countries where they can be treated fairly and be safe?

Following Egypt and Libya, the US later helped Ivory Coast president-elect Alassane Ouattara, who is a Muslim, take power from the former president, Laurent Gbagbo, who is a Christian. Gbagbo is afraid the new president will round up all his supporters and kill them, and has refused to cede his seat. Supporters of Outtara have been taking people out of their cars, lighting them on fire and now beheading them. Incredibly, President Obama- is supporting this (albeit quietly). In April 2011, French and US forces began to try to force Gbagbo from power. After a week of fighting, French and Ivorian forces arrested Gbogbo. This came after hundreds of innocent citizens were killed. Outtara is said to be the democratically-elected candidate, but we all know how North African elections are (kinda like Florida in 2000). If Outtara truly IS democratically elected then Gbagbo should go. But anytime Muslims are in power, Christians need to fear for their lives!

Two Google Vice Presidents have now been exposed as having part in instigating revolution in Egypt. Taxpayers are also funding the National Labor Relations Board (NLRB). They use Google to advertise for 'How to start a union." Do you know that those vice presidents helped create an Egyptian "union" of sorts, which spearheaded the Cairo uprising? Facebook is a fabulous modern way to bring proletariat unions together. What next- the same here?

The aforementioned Code Pink rallied with the Egyptians, and also tried to keep the protests in Wisconsin going. What they want is for this revolution to spread to America. Revolution and protesting is becoming contagious. Greece is seeing it already. So is Britain. So is Wisconsin and Ohio. Soon, baby, soon...revolution will be coming to a place near you.

Oil prices will be one of the next things that sets people off all over the US. The turmoil all over the Middle East is affecting oil prices here at home. This will soon be (if not by the time you've read this) the thing that not only shatters our economy, but also causes citizens to revolt. I really want you to know that this is all orchestrated by people who want things to become like this. Revolution is good for them. 'Democratic revolution,' they call it. Real democracy means that the people govern themselves (which can be *only* be done if they follow Jesus Christ). They want a king.

Their democratic revolution is something else. People who do not live by Jesus' teaching cannot govern themselves; there will simply be chaos. So the communist sociopaths will come in with the solution to it. This will be a 'top down' form of leadership that will simply tell the people what to do. Just look at our current 'nanny state' and tell me this isn't happening already.

I still can't see why President Obama hasn't been brought up on charges of treason. There are so many things he has done that could make for his impeachment. The fact that he hasn't says something I've been saying all along. He is where he is because God wants him here. Undisciplined people (ie. most of our citizens) need structure, and soon....they'll get it.

I know people living here in the United States- who have children, even- who want nothing more that to see America fail. And this is the very country that has given them a stable life and granted them real happiness. Why do they want to see us fall apart? Most of these people are in my age group. I'm 54 and grew up in the seventies and I understand. For whatever reason, they think that the rich corporations are out to screw them, so they want to see revolution. Against what? The establishment? The establishment that provided for them? Weird. I just think they grew up with the idea of bringing down the establishment and cannot see past this. Hmmm, kind of like growing up Muslim. An inability to see outside of your own mindset. It's how you grew up. What a shame.

You know the aforementioned Van Jones (Obama's green czar), before Glenn Beck played tapes of him admitting he was communist and they threw him 'under the bus,' once said to an audience, "Rise up and feel your anger."

I say different. Rise up and show your love. This is the only thing that will *really* sway people. It's the true love that is only found in a changed heart that lives to be like Jesus Christ. If we fight against them, it's just enemy against enemy. Us against them.

This means nothing. Hearts haven't changed. We are asked to make people want to be like us- not to crush them.

Think about this: the banality of the emotions that drive our leaders and their followers. Stupid people, or misguided people, need someone else to rule over them or they will be lost. These people reject God because they don't want to make choices. But choices are all we have to define ourselves. We can choose to be good as we can and to love God and each other- or we can choose to love evil. Free people will never succumb to slavery. People already enslaved in their minds will go willingly into servitude. I am making my choice to be free. Damn the torpedoes!

I want to make a point here. Communism is a force to seduce intelligent, manipulative, godless people into hatefulness by appealing to their supposed superiority. Real intelligent people would never believe in something as dumb as God! The rest of the people need to be subdued- or killed- because they are just too stupid.

Islam is a religious belief system designed to fool the less intelligent. They need something to look to for guidance. They are so primitive in their thinking that Islam appeals to them. It makes them feel they are being godly even though they are just barbaric.

Lucifer offers something for everybody. Notice that every form of religion is works-based (my deeds make me righteous) except true Christianity, which is faith-based. Think about this please.

The Christian faith is one that is for the very intelligent *and* the intellectually challenged, as it is simply the TRUTH.

I want you to think about something here. Look, if all comes to pass like the Communislamists want, what will happen? Some people on Earth will cease to be, because they are *in the way*. Who is this? Who will be gone?

Who do you think? Jews and Christians. Islam is here as a force to eradicate the Jewish people and communism is the force to enslave the rest of the 'lay' population and rid the world of Christians. Well, what's so special about these two groups that the whole world wants to be free of them? Answer: it's not them; it's who they worship. Will you please think about that?

But there will be a great deception before this can happen- a false peace. The Bible says that a rebuilt temple (with a *singular leader* claiming unity and peace for all- the 'man of lawlessness') will be a major sign of the end times prior to the return of Jesus. He will be charismatic and will hold the whole world under his sway. World Net Daily published an article in late 2010, saying, "What Muslim leader wants the temple rebuilt?" Author Joel Richardson says Jewish Sanhedrin leaders and a prominent Islamic teacher are trying to do just that. "Out of a sense of collective responsibility for world peace and all humanity, peace of all nations will be accomplished through the building of the house of God. Let us love and respect each other. All humanity is one family. Let us establish a house of prayer in his name."

The powers that are trying to do this want to bring Jerusalem under international control. They want an interfaith house of worship, and subsequent peace. Christianity needs to be brought into this for it to work. So there must be some kind of deception.

Rick Warren is an evangelical (Christian) leader who spoke at the largest society of Muslim leaders in the US. He did not try to tell them of Jesus' redemption but to convene with them. He is on the board of directors of British Prime Minister Tony Blair's faith foundation. This foundation is meant to unify the world's religions. This is to establish that all religions are pathways to God. Much of this effort is to bring Christians and Muslims together. The Chrislamic movement, also known as the 'emerging church.' I call this compromise. The Bible is clear in that it says Christians are not to participate in others' religious ceremonies and that Jesus alone is the way (to eternal life with him). Tony Campolo, a liberal evangelical leader (and others), have said that interfaith is the way. Pope John Paul II, the Dalai Lama and other religious leaders have said that the Holy Spirit is present in all- whether they are Christian or not. Pope Benedict issued his charity and truth statement on July 6th, saying "there is a real need for a true world political authority. In the face of unrelenting growth of global interdependence there's a strongly felt need, even in the face of a global recession, for a reform of the United Nations organization, regulated by law," bent

on globalization (I personally don't believe he said all that but had help, it would be far too much for him to remember).

The coming Maitreya (the word that some use to describe the future world leader) is the large bright star that will be visible to all throughout the world and is the Christ to Christians, the Imam Madi to Muslims, Krishna to Hindus, the Messiah to Jews and the Maitreya Buddha to Buddhists. Although not using the name 'Maitreya,' he will appear on a major U.S. television station and perhaps throughout all digital outlets in the world. (He might even appear on "Dancing with the Stars.")

"Therefore if any man shall say unto you, 'Behold, there is the Christ', or 'there he is,' do not believe *him.* For there will arise false Christs and false prophets and shall show great signs and wonders and so much that if it were possible they shall deceive even the elect."

Matthew 24: 23-24-

"He shall neither regard the God of his fathers nor the desire of women nor regard any god; for he shall exalt himself above them all."

Daniel 11:37

I'm going to ask you something. What kind of man does communism make you into? Look at them. Hateful spineless sissies!

What kind of man does Islam make you if it really takes hold? A hateful animal. What kind of man will you be if you see something greater than yourself and accept Jesus' redemption? Loving, kind, fair and trustworthy. Think about it.

Communism is the opposite of truth. That's why they lie. Islam is the opposite of love. That's why they hate. They both are the opposite of truth and love. Remember, the truth has no agenda. Love never lies.

Oprah Winfrey tells us there are many ways to heaven. Jesus tells us, "I am the way, the truth and the life and *no one comes to the Father* BUT THROUGH ME."

III. ON GOVERNMENT & MEDIA

Chapter 15

Nanny State Motherf**kers!

That's exactly what proceeds from my mouth every time I get into the car and realize I have to strap myself in like a mummy just to drive to the coffee shop, the gym or the market. I just can't stand having to wear seat belts! Part of my anger is just knowing I'm mandated to. If I still rode motorcycles I would be just as angry at having to put on a helmet. Who the *hell* is the government to tell me I have to protect myself? What have I done to make them think I'm stupid? I am an adult and can make decisions for myself.

As I've said elsewhere, sociopaths first make people into childish simpletons *and then* start treating them like children. The making of Americans into children has been done through their television sets. You are all Homer Simpsons. People of no wisdom. Just like the show you can't stop watching, you are "Lost." Living from one sound byte to the next. Do you know what ADD is? Television watching. Do you know where a lot of promiscuity comes from? Your internet. Why are you so distracted? There's usually stupid music coming from the trees and the rocks. Well, there might as well be- it's coming from every storefront, every restaurant, every outdoor mall, walkway, every coffee shop, every supermarket. And, what a shock: every household!

Even the gym I work out in has television sets all over the floor *and in the bathrooms!* Watching TV all the time tends to depersonalize other people. Just look at how people drive anymore. They'll cut you off in a second and run you over if you are not careful. People who only think of themselves do things like this.

In case you forgot (ADD), I'm a musician. I love music. Music is my life and has been as long as I can remember. But the thing is, you can't please everybody's taste in music. So, what do they do? Play sort of middle of the road muzak that NOBODY likes!... Brilliant.

Just who are 'they' anyway? People hell bent on transferring your money into their bank accounts. They play uplifting, breezy, well...shopping music, I mean muzak. Coffee shops used to play sort of lesbian folksinger music. Now I've noticed they play middle of the road 'pop' rock. I liked the lesbian folk stuff better. It was more relaxing. Maybe they want you more wound up to buy more coffee!

The Cheesecake Factory used to play cool jazz to make the place romantic. Now they play the same music the coffee shop does. Maybe Christopher Cross will be the only music allowed at some point.

What I'm saying is.... Is there ANYWHERE you can go to think anymore?

You know, I hate to say this, but I think this is not some communist plot to make us distracted, but just a natural outgrowth of capitalism. Its crony capitalism that perverts the free market for their own gain and is capitalism infected with greed- greed that has been brought in by the decline in values. Now that *was* done by the communists. It is just idol worship because it is self-worship. All this distraction is just companies or corporations trying to make you feel like buying something. Look, capitalism is the only fair way to let a society thrive, but there is an ugly side to it. And it always goes back to man's sinful nature and self servitude.

So, on that thought, since Dick Clark brought in the "single" to the radio and helped companies make millions by spawning "playlists" that get every song eventually "played off the air," is he a communist? Thanks a lot, New Year's Rockin' Eve!!

Human society is not supposed to be perfect. It is not supposed to keep things like greed and hatred in check. It is this flaw in our way of life that exposes things like this. Otherwise you would not see them. Life will not be perfect until our Savior comes. God wants His people perfect for Himself and it is their going through this imperfect world and standing firm that teaches them to be the kind of people He wants, anyway. We are to be in the world- but not of it.

People who want your money will not let you think. They want you distracted so you will be more likely to 'impulse buy.' I mean, Times Square is partially beautiful because of all the video advertising signs. The Las Vegas strip hotel videoboards are fun to drive past, too. But too much of that is just plain irritating.

So what does this have to do with nannystate mutha's? Well I think they feed this distraction with much manipulative stuff to mold you. Look at any advertising on television. What isn't just dumb is really asinine. Do you go 'cuckoo' for Cocoa Puffs? Do you want to yell through a bullhorn for Men's Warehouse? Do you talk to geckos?

Look, they really *do* think you are stupid. In Florida recently an unemployment agency launched a 'Cape-A-Bility' challenge to its 'Everyday Superheroes' campaign. They ordered 6,000 capes to hand out to the jobless. The gimmick had a cartoon villain, "Dr. Evil Unemployment.' They spent $14,000 on the capes. Couldn't that have employed someone?

Just see for a minute how we all have come to believe we are our possessions. I am my car. My stereo. My dog. My job is my life. Young people everywhere need to have the new kind of Nikes or coat. This is their identity. Canon cameras say, "Image is everything." You can see what drives this. This mindset says what you have is who you are, not the kind of person you are. If you are an honest reliable person, doesn't this say much more?

Have you noticed that people with pets don't learn how to teach them anything anymore? They go to work and let their dogs bark all day long. If you dare try to talk to them about this, they immediately become defensive and very angry. This is their Beloved Little Fluffy you are talking about! Everyone else just smiles adoringly on their walks when they are out pooping the little thing, why cant you? He's just an animal. He can't help it.

I say, where the f**k is your brain? It didn't even occur to you that I might be over in my own apartment trying to write or just think, for crying out loud! Yes animals are just animals. They need to be trained. If you don't have the time to train your dog don't get one. I really think so many girls in the cities just get a dog for a companion because men are unreliable.

Jeeesus...sometimes I just need to reflect on a previous conversation or maybe even invent one for my own amusement. When I walk anywhere I hear something coming out of a car a business or walkway or another apartment.

How about people that blast their wonderful musical taste at a million decibels out of their houses (or especially apartments)? People really act like little children these days, totally oblivious to the needs of anyone but themselves. I really think the sociopaths have done just what they set out to do. They have made Americans into little dependent children who have no idea what is good for them. They need slavery; it will teach them some respect!

I read that a study was done and it came away with the opinion that twenty-five percent of the American population wants authoritarian rule. Do you believe this? I would be really surprised to find this is true, but then again......?

I really think too many people find it hard to make their own choices. I really think they want 'daddy' to come along and tell them what to do. Maybe I should have called this chapter "daddy state" huh? Most people these days don't even have the attention span to take this in. I seriously believe that most Americans would do much better under an authoritarian government. They just don't seem to care enough about other people. One day, I was waiting outside the bathroom at my coffee shop for, like, 15 minutes for someone to come out...and they came out with the newspaper! Public bathroom, coffee shop, helloooooooo??????

You know who does act like this? Homer Simpson. Is that what you want to be like? I don't. I am a man and I try to act like one. I try to be a man of few words. I would rather listen . . . for opportunities. Just kidding! To find out more about you. You are important to me. I love you or else I wouldn't be writing this book. Believe me- I would rather be writing music.

So when they have you distracted with the greedy capitalists' American Bandstand repetitive music and acting like an idiot....now they have you where they want you. First they infected the capitalists with greed. They then begin to start telling you what they think you should be doing, or eating, or driving. Get it?

What's different about kids these days is that they are killing themselves when they are bullied (especially cyber-bullied). I was not only bullied, but beaten badly, by jocks and ranchers' kids when I was in junior high. I'm stronger for this. Why are kids these days so feeble as to commit suicide over something like cyber-bullying? Because their parents are feeble, so that's what they learn. And let's not forget that cyber-bullying= isolationism. Being alone sometimes is good, as you can think. But isolated?

President Obama has had a meeting in March 2011 about the bullying problem. But the rest of the month, he spent most of his time on other 'important' activities: acknowledging Women's History Month for the first time, playing multiple rounds of golf, hosting a Stevie Wonder concert at the White House, and attending NCAA 'March Madness' basketball games (to make sure his 'bracket' is filled out correctly! Which it was...he picked the winner). In the meantime, there's rioting in several states in the country, Japan is in a nuclear crisis, there are wars in four theaters and a looming financial meltdown. Do you know why he is like this when there's so much going on? BECAUSE YOU ARE!!! *You elected him!* He, therefore, is a direct representation of you! He doesn't care because you don't!... Sometimes Americans make me sick.

If you want things to change, get on the "Tea Party" train. Attend Town Hall meetings. Become part of Freedomworks. Join the 9/12 project. Go to www.teapartypatriots.org or www.theteaparty.net and start a revolution that's actually needed!

The American political machine has finally gotten most of us to think like selfish idiots. Almost everyone seems to go through life with an attitude of 'more for me- even if it means less for you' approach to living life. Tell me, where is the love in this?

We, as Americans, were a people that used to actually love one another. Families helping other families. Young people really wanted to be like their parents. Our parents were our role models. Now our parents are our adversaries. How did this happen? The sixties generation (yes mine!) told us not to trust anyone over thirty. We knew better. So, if we knew better, why is the country like it is right now? Just look at the faces of people on the street. Why are people so unhappy? Because things are not going well. Young people are pitted against their parents. Parents, now, see their offspring as rebellious and burdensome.

Have you noticed that the government wants you single? I mean it; they want you to think that a relationship is a waste of time. People are untrustworthy. But first... they help make them that way by telling them they should have freedom to choose (anything!). Why would they want you single? Because a strong family is anathema to their desires for control over you. A solid relationship is just that. Solid. You are more committed to your significant other (*and* hopefully to God) than their manipulations.

After the horrible Gabrielle Giffords shooting in Arizona, hateful rhetoric came spilling out from everywhere. So Washington insiders decided that any symbols or words and even gestures that suggested any kind of violence had to be met with some kind of punishment. Even a little schoolboy who made a pistol kind of gesture at school was suspended! No more Cowboys and Indians!

After just one lady walked into a fountain at a mall (and wanted to sue the mall) while she was texting, Arkansas, New York and Michigan have made it unlawful to walk and text! Talk about 'nanny state!'

At the coffee shop I go to (yes, I'm talking about that again!) they used to have this really good toilet. This thing would flush *anything!* Now they have replaced it with a toilet that clogs up from any idiot putting a paper towel in it and then they close down the bathroom for the day because they don't know how to fix it. They put in one of the new High Efficiency (green) Toilets that only use 1.6 gallons per flush. What good is it if it is out of order?

How about the new, compact fluorescent light bulbs that don't last even though they are promoted as lasting much longer than the standard ones we all had? Not only that, but they don't even light up the room enough to read! Both the toilets and the bulbs are the energy and water conservation models. But new government regulation mandates we use them! I say *get off my back* you nanny state motherf**kers, give me something that works first before you start mandating I use it!

I know they won't mandate the use of hybrid cars, even though they work. I wonder why...? By the way, the Masters' golf tournament is brought to you by Exxon Mobil....

New York City has issued a ban on trans fats. Mayor Bloomberg has issued a statement saying that their police force is too busy to give smoking tickets to people smoking outside of restaurants (within close distance from the doorways). So the answer was to let citizens go ahead and perform arrests on smokers. Los Angeles has banned new fast food restaurants and liquor stores in poor areas. San Francisco is regulating pretty much everything. I'm not kidding; just look it up! You will be amazed. I mean the amount of water in doggy bowls! They almost passed a bill making spanking your child a crime that was punishable by a one year sentence in jail. Not spanking them will make them like I was, and trust me...you don't want that! Smoking anywhere is the worst. No, they want you healthy. For.......what....?

Why do they care if I'm healthy or not? Look, they're not planning to make you their sex slaves... yet. Right now it's just preparatory work. At some point they're going to make their move, their takeover of everything-- and it will be global. Right now they're just laying their foundation, and getting you ready.

Our government, the European governments and the global elite want you and I to be young, healthy, beautiful and stupid. Young is evidenced by the health care laws being passed that target the elderly for dismissal because they are not productive anymore. Another reason for this focus on the elderly is the fact that these older people do remember when the United States was a decent place where God was revered and people helped one another. *They need this generation to go so nobody will be alive that remembers this!* Healthy can be excused, but making it unlawful not to be? Trust me: when they are finished with their program they will be using a eugenics plan to cleanse the world of any *races* they deem unfit to be here. They want their young, healthy and beautiful people to...? What do you think? Why do they want you stupid? C'mon...

You must see that the world government (and its elites) want you to be dependent on them. So they need to get you where it hurts. This is your money. You may or may not feel it yet but global currencies are falling fast. China has overtaken the United States in the value of its currency. What kind of country is China? Totally repressive. The dollar *is* going to be replaced as the world currency. Then what? How does this affect you? America will fall to become just another nation state and soon will be answering to global regulations and laws. You and I will be impoverished to the point of dependency. Once you are dependent on them they can have their way with you.

They really just want control. Most of these laws are unenforceable. They're just enough regulation that law enforcement can act indiscriminately. Al Gore said *government* was "like grandparents in the sense that grandparents perform a nurturing role." What!?... He also told a high school full of kids that they know things their parents didn't. So to realize this and follow what they were being taught. Think about that.

Do you know where all this is going to lead? Listen to me ...dress codes. For you. Yeah, you! It's been done before. In Mao Tse-tung's China, pretty much all the people had a same colored jump suit to wear. In Islam what do you see? Okay, don't say it can't happen here- it certainly can. Remember they don't want you to be equal; they want you to all be alike. They're doing a pretty good job of making you all alike right now. What do all American males do with their hair? Buzz it off. Why? 'Cause that's what men look like right now. Why do soooo many women dye their hair blonde? See what I mean? Now we both know Madison Avenue plays a big role in this. Here in Beverly Hills, their lips are succulent, juicy, and....botox-y fuuull. And their bosoms....

But, tell me, do you think Madison Avenue is not affected by the sociopaths? I beg to differ. The big department stores are owned by corporations. Corporations want all people to be alike too. Their motivation is similar to the sociopaths. Their motive is to extract your money. The communist sociopaths want to extract your soul. They both want your obedience. So you've lost your soul and now they are able to tell you whether to poop or not. Is their mission not accomplished? They own you. You will be beholden to them for everything. Maybe they will have you wearing grey jumpsuits. Maybe nothing at all. (Stop fantasizing!) You will amount to nothing. They want you stupid, needy and dependent on them.

Many of us are just that. In Detroit in 2009, it was rumored that President Obama was giving away money to the poor, which turned out not to be true. But the people that lined up in wait for the free money were a reflection on the state of the uneducated. One of a group of black women was questioned as to why they were there and she replied, "I'm here for some money." The reporter then asked, "From who?" "Obama," she replied. He then asked where he got the money. She replied, "I don't know, his stash, we love Obama," at which point the rest started chanting, "Obama, Obama, Obama."

These people are obviously not educated enough to see what's going on and believe anything told to them. They are totally dependent on welfare to survive. They sit in front of their indoctrination boxes and eat cheese puffs. This is not the way the newly freed slaves wanted to be and not the way any intelligent, educated person in America wants to be. But they want people like this: needy, dependent and indoctrinated by their entertainment. Look, I personally do NOT want this for myself and neither should you.

Where do you draw the line? I draw it pretty close to home. Your rights end where my nose begins. Got it?

You know I really am a libertarian. I really believe anything should be legal that does not hurt somebody else. Yes...this means heroin, sex clubs, prostitution, even polygamy! The government is not the answer to ANYTHING! I believe we should all be free enough to *show* who we are. All this legal interference and regulation just keeps us from showing our true colors. It's like hiding. I believe this is to show how good we are when God already knows who we are. We are not going to *prove* ourselves to him or each other! Look, communities should be the ones that dictate what happens in them; not the federal government. If one community does things one way and another a different way, the good or evil will be evidenced in the success of the community. This is just and fair.

Even many Christians seem to think they're here to tell other people how to live their lives. Shame on them, you lead by example! Let people show who they really are!

Look, I also need you to know that the time will come when being anything other than blonde or white will be punishable by extermination. Don't say it can't happen, look, what did Hitler do? Being Jewish was punishable by execution. I still haven't figured out how Julie Banderas (who is Cher, on alternate days) and Kimberly Guilfoyle have managed to evade the Fox news dyed blonde mandate. But eugenics *was* and *is* part of the communist agenda. Remember: watch anything the sociopaths do for where it is going- not just for what it looks like now. Have you noticed a lack of any definition of just what the 'New World Order' really is? What does it look like? Who will be leading?

Look, now is a time of war and so it is a time for warriors.

Say no to these nanny state mother f**kers! Take your freedom back.

Chapter 16

"School's Out"

So what did you learn in school? Well, it depends on how old you are. When I was in grade school, we were still taught that America was exceptional- and we were fortunate to be here. We were taught that the United States was the most charitable nation on Earth- and we were. But then again, it was the sixties, and the communists had just gotten involved in our colleges. College students were protesting all over the country.

Not the case in Auburn, CA. I do remember a couple of my teachers would expound philosophies that smacked of 'hippie' kind of values. One said that being naked was the preferred way of all peoples unencumbered by church morals. I immediately developed a powerful crush on her. Later I would hang out at nude beaches near Santa Barbara, CA. Amazing, the influence teachers have!

Its true- my generation grew up with everything. We were ripe for rebellion, for rebellion's sakes. Rage against the machine. At that time we called it the establishment. It wasn't so openly against capitalism then. Maybe that would have been too direct. They needed subtlety then. Their program was in its infancy. It was all about how bad the war in Vietnam was. I dropped out of high school to sell pot and meth because I could make money and it was more fun. I later needed to go back for the GED exam when I decided to go to college.

I learned guitar by playing Crosby, Stills, Nash, and Young (Neil's solo stuff as well), along with Bob Dylan's songs. Later I learned all of Carlos Santana's solos. I learned piano by studying

Ravel's piano pieces and Tori Amos's songs. All of these have strong anti-Christian leanings. Tori, actually, is an ambivalent, guilt-ridden Catholic. Ravel was likely gay. Crosby, Stills, Nash and Young wrote some of the 60's 'revolution' anthems. All these are and were brilliant. It's all in the music, baby. Music moves people. I once read that someone said, "give me a peoples' music and I have the people." I really believe this. The sixties and seventies had the best music I have ever heard! Genius everywhere! And sooo communist. Today's music is much less creative.

MIDI technology drum machines and rapping have dumbed today's music down.

Anyway, I am shocked at what our kids are learning now. The communist and the Islamic 'machine' have been involved long enough to have rewritten most all of the textbooks. In schools now it's considered factual that Mohammed DID go to paradise on the mount in Jerusalem. Jesus was 'repudiated' to have been born of a virgin. Evolution is a proven fact- even though it has been disproved. All this is simply communislamics indoctrinating your children and you. How does it feel to be thought of as so stupid that they can tell you anything- and you will just accept it?

I was sitting outside at the coffee shop I go to and heard a couple talking about economic issues and heard the guy say, "Look we can't use nineteenth century economic policies to fix twenty-first century problems." Really? So is our economic situation right now better or worse than then? Wasn't our Constitution written in 1776? Maybe we can.

It has been established that kids in private Catholic schools are outperforming their public school counterparts. An interesting part of this is that in Catholic school there are no teachers' unions. Also, teachers choose to be where they are, instead of being assigned to a post. Kids that are taught to behave seem to learn more. Amazing! There's a new study out which says students don't really learn anything in the first two years of college. Almost all of them cannot decipher fact from opinion. Boy, isn't THAT right where the progressives want you? Young, healthy and STUPID!

Fox news correspondent Jesse Watters went to Columbia University to interview students on what they thought about the 'Muslim' problem. Some answers were: "Define Muslim," "I wouldn't call it a Muslim problem because there are terrorists in all religions, yes- even Christian terrorists," "It's not really about Islam; it's been going on throughout history," and finally, "Fox News is just as nutty as the Muslim extremists."

In early 2011, anchor John Stossel interviewed people on the street in NYC. Some of them were college-aged. He asked them about the most important current events in the world today. Their answers were "Prince William's wedding to Kate Middleton," "Lady Gaga" and "Charlie Sheen." He also put three pictures up in front of these people: Joe Biden, Nancy Pelosi and 'The Situation' from MTV's sad-sap reality show, "Jersey Shore." Guess which person out of the three they knew? Enough said.

There was a report just out that said that only 22 percent of eighth graders passed a basic civics test in the country! So millions of young Americans will be unprepared to be informed enough to manage their society. So who will? Communists. I guess it shouldn't surprise anyone that Michelle Rhee of StudentsFirst is saying that 82 percent of schools in the US are failing in proficiency. Georgia, California and New York spend *three times* more on prison inmates than on education. South Korean students are far outperforming their American counterparts. Why?

Pavlovian and Skinnerian behavior (and thought) control is the new model for education. Do not question where information comes from or what it is supposed to elicit in your knowledge or behavior. Just answer the questions the way you are supposed to. Echo the ideas of your educator. No 'two sides' to the story. Only the ideas of the socialists are tolerated. Hegelian philosophies now are the norm in the classroom. The students don't even know that these philosophies just mean that the common man is squashed into the state. They think they are being empowered, much like some privileged female Muslims say Islam is empowering for women.

Colombia University students yelled "racist" at a student who was a former Army staff sergeant that was given the Purple Heart after being shot 11 times in   Iraq. Anthony Maschek said, "It doesn't matter how you feel about the war, it doesn't matter how you feel about fighting, there are bad men out there plotting to kill you." Students laughed and jeered. This is the school that invited Mahmoud Ahmadinejad to speak. This is the man who says that the Twelfth Imam is managing the revolution now and that the final move has begun to destroy America, Israel and the influence of western powers.

The University of Florida is now hosting terrorists and forcibly removing people who question them. An incident took place in November 2009. The question that ACT for America representative Randy McDaniels was asking was a pointed question about Islamic Law. It was based on facts sited from a book called 'Reliance of the Traveler,' the classic manual of Islamic sacred law Umdat al-Salik, which is considered a 'valuable and important work' and is a legal reference for use by Islamic scholars (?). McDaniels asked if the council endorses the laws in the book which call for the stoning and execution of apostates who leave Islam and non-Muslims. McDaniels asked his questions in a calm manner and then, as he sat and listened, he was forcibly removed from the event.

The person he asked the question of was Jamal Badawi, who is an unindicted co-conspirator in terrorist activities and is a member of the board of directors of the Muslim brotherhood in the United States, a Hamas front group. He was listed as co-conspirator in the Holy Land Foundation trial; also known as the largest terrorism fundraising trial in American history. On February 25, 2011 UCF hosted radical Sirhaj Wahaji, another unindicted co-conspirator in the 1993 World Trade Center bombing. Wahaji testified on behalf of Omar Abdel Rahman, known as the 'blind sheikh.'

In Tucson, police were asked to restore order at a local school board meeting. School officials suggested that teaching children that trying to reclaim land for Mexico is a bit questionable. Not enough to cancel the class, however, just questionable enough to see to it that the class is an elective and not mandatory. Also taught in this class is that Thanksgiving is the day that the dominant white culture celebrated the beginning of genocide. As a result of this class NOT being mandatory, the students chained themselves to desks and basically rioted, screaming "What do we do? Fight back. Our education's under attack." Riot police were called in when this happened a second time. Journalist Mike Shaw who lives in Tucson talked to a woman who was a former community organizer and a democrat and part of a non-partisan group to look into this curriculum. She said "This program has been hijacked by 'social justice.' One of the groups other members, a former teacher, described the kind of teaching that is going on now in the class, "The same kind of teaching that's being done right now in Nicaragua and other communist controlled countries, it's Marxist driven, its all about opposition to capitalism, it's all about the class struggle, and it's all about looking at *everything* through the lens of race." The kids are part of a youth group and are being coached by a local professor. They are also getting help from local community organizers. A picture taken at the protest showed Ward Churchill the former University of Colorado professor who was fired after his comments saying that the innocent victims of 9/11 were little Eichmann's (referring to the Nazi organizer). This man was fired for teaching things like this to college students and now he is rounding up high school students and teaching them how to hate America. I have Glenn Beck to thank for this very revealing story. Glenn has posted the curriculum on his website. Trust me, everybody now in school, be it high school or college is being indoctrinated by communists and Islam! *They are now making foot soldiers out of your children!!!*

The week that Osama bin Laden was shot by Navy Seals the number five search on Google was Osama bin Laden. Most of the searches were done by people 24 or under asking why was he killed and why does it matter? A new Yale study says 57 percent of teens understand that global warming is caused by humans! Children are not allowed to fail in our schools anymore. Public schools do not teach morals and neither do parents. The National Education Association (the largest labor union in the US) is far too politically active. The board of education controls what is taught and they are subject to pressure by special interest groups (Islam, social justice groups). Academics have been pushed aside for the political agenda. Family values are not taught anymore. They discourage parent/teacher involvement. The aforementioned are complaints made by concerned teachers! The Bush administration's 'No child left behind' policy is not allowing them to fail, giving no incentive to do better. History is being taught in dates, the date of this battle or that election, but not much about the events themselves resulting in children never learning the LESSONS taught by historical events. Ethics are not being taught and kids see things simply in the light of 'does it make money?' and this is enough. Teachers are given a curriculum and cannot teach with their individual approaches. Naturalist philosophies devalue individuals. Honor, self reliance and discipline are not taught or even referenced anymore!

Parents anymore aren't involved as they have other things to do as many are single and many more are just busy (doing?). The government is making stupid young adults so they can steal their freedoms right from under them!

It appears that the socialists have decided that the preamble to our Constitution is not good enough. They have now inserted a passage into it that is to be chanted by students that says, "The Peoples' basic needs must be met in a country. Needs for housing, education, transportation and health care overseen by our government." These words are being chanted by school children and are part of a program called "Building Fluency through Practice and Performance." Mind you that THE ORIGINAL preamble said "We the People of the United States, in order to form a more perfect union, establish Justice, insure tranquility, provide for the common defense, promote the general welfare and secure the blessings of liberty to ourselves and our posterity, do ordain and establish this Constitution for the United States of America." So housing, education, transportation and health care are our rights? Isn't this just what the communist regimes of Castro's Cuba and Stalin's USSR promised? Oh, by the way-- is that what they delivered?

Anne Graham, Billy Graham's daughter said "For years we've been telling God to get out of our schools, to get out of our government and to get out of our lives. And being the gentleman He is, I believe He has calmly backed out. How can we expect God to give us His blessing and His protection if we demand He leave us alone?"

Home schooling is a better answer than this. However the powers that are dominating our education systems are now beginning to infringe on our ability to even choose that for our children. Recently, a mother in New Hampshire was told by a judge that she was 'too Christian' to home school. This is what's coming. Soon this will be illegal!

Maybe this is because Saul Alinsky's 'Rules for Radicals' is not mandatory reading for high school students who are home schooled, like it is in most public schools. Our kids need to know how to handcuff themselves to the door of a bank, or stage sit-in's in high traffic areas!

I talked to a guy outside the coffee shop the other day about where education is going and he said, "We are going to be communicating with space aliens soon and they will teach us what we need to know." ...Wow (deadpan), I guess we should just wait for them... then. Jeeesus! Look, (readthisrealfast) WE WILL NEVER SEE SPACE ALIENS! I know, I read the back of the book. There's no mention of this. That book is our Bible.

However, it might be possible that the sociopaths might use holograms or something to stage an alien invasion in their attempt to bring mankind under their rule. This would be a natural way for them to invoke fear into the masses. Really, though, NASA is the biggest waste of money and time I can think of. Well, I guess for floating spacecraft around the world it makes sense. I mean we do need satellites for lots of reasons. This is how we monitor aircraft coming in or out of any area- even the weather. But not for going to other planets! With all of our technology and so much evil in the world, we are not going to be around that long. We need to use these resources for fixing our problems here on earth. Side note: what did Neil Armstrong's landing really do for *anybody?*

Now let's talk about teachers' unions for a minute. Do you know that no matter how bad a teacher is, they cannot be fired? Three years and you have a job for life? Seriously, it takes an act of God to get a teacher fired. Usually, when they commit some wrongdoing, they just put them into 'blue rooms' where they collect full pay and do nothing. Carpenters and iron workers' taxes go up (even when they are out of work) to pay the teachers pensions. Their lobbying is so powerful that in some states like California, the state is going bankrupt because of the teachers' unions and the pensions they are awarded. They are so exorbitant that they burden the states into insolvency. When a state is bankrupt they will seek a bailout from the Federal government, which will then make them beholden to the Feds. States' rights will be lost. This is right where they want you. There was a 2010 movie accurately depicting the deplorable conditions in our schools called 'Waiting for Superman" and I suggest you see it.

Harlem NYC, according to the Wall Street Journal 22 schools are failing. Their students are failing English and math (only 3% perform at grade level English) and they need to be shut down. But the NAACP and the United Federation of Teachers have filed a suit against the Department of Education to prohibit 17 charter schools from gaining traction in the district. The NAACP and a teachers union. Mmmm...isn't the NAACP for the ADVANCEMENT of colored people? Is this going to advance these kids or keep them in the ghetto forever to be used as stupid pawns for the democratic party? My African American friends, do these people love you? Do they even LIKE you? Or are you being lied to and used?

The NEA's (National Education Association) top retiring lawyer Bob Chanin spoke at their meeting in July 2009, saying, "Despite what some among us would like to believe, it is not because of our creative ideas, it is not because of the merit of our positions, it is not because we care about children and its not because we have a vision of a great public school for every child. NEA and its affiliates are effective advocates because we have power. And we have power because there are more than 3.2 million people who are willing to pay us hundreds of millions of dollars in dues each year because they believe that we are the unions that can most effectively represent them, the unions that can protect their rights and advance their interests as education employees."... 'School's out!'

This really is all about *collecting union dues and gaining power.*

Just look at the classrooms now. They are overcrowded and the teachers are usually terrible at what they do. Look, anyone not held to account for job performance will become lazy and not put all their effort into their work. There are exceptions. These must be applauded; for they are doing what parents really should be doing.

You know, we could blame the teachers for all the communist bullshit they teach your children but I think teachers teach what they know. They know what *they* have been taught. I really don't think most of them even realize they are teaching dependent society philosophies because these ideas are brought in- in such a sly, insidious manner that it seems really nice and caring. I think if many of them realized what they were doing, they would be appalled. Sociopaths are cunning and deceitful.

Even in the area of faith, we now have collective salvation, which stems from communism-not Christianity. Think about that. Collective anything. Tell me, do you really want to be nothing other than one of many in a collective? No individual worth aside from being just one of many. This is what President Obama speaks about. His salvation is dependent on the collective. This is part of Liberation Theology, which is directly communist. That's what they are teaching now and they are painting it with all this fluff about kindness, people working together and protecting the Earth. These things sound noble and all but I'm sorry, I AM worth something and this Earth was created and it was for me to grow and mature on and become what God has always wanted me to be.

Look no one can force you to believe these things. But if you don't see something bigger than yourself (ie. God), then you *can* do anything. If you can do anything, that means ANYTHING- whether or not it is considered 'good' by one group or not. This kind of relativity is what they were beginning to teach when I was in school. This ideology has evolved into a postmodern, 'for the greater good' collectivism. Your individuality does not exist; you are just part of the collective. This is exactly where they want you: 'Less for me, more for Mother Earth.' A zombie like obedient little dumbshit willing to do or be anything requested of you by your 'worshipped' leader.

If you research people, you will find that the very proponents of this philosophy do not adhere to it themselves. This is because it is not for them. *It's for you!...* Al Gore is an unabashed meat eater. His "An Inconvenient Truth" has been proven to be a pack of lies-yet still they go ahead and hold a global warming summit. Look they're not giving up on this because it's the best thing they have

got going. It all just sounds sooo noble, doesn't it? We need to care for our Earth. They really just want control over you.

The biggest problem here is that parents, since the sixties, just aren't doing their job. They're not parenting the way they used to. They have rejected the parenting of their youth and the new model is less restrictive and more freedom-oriented (so they think). Sounds good, but is it? Should kids be given freedom before they know right from wrong? I was, as soon as I went to live with my father. Look how that turned out. I ended up beating up my dad! Deplorable!

I wouldn't wish that on anybody. It has taken years to undo what I was allowed to do to myself. But first parents need to know right from wrong themselves. They are the same as pet owners who don't want to train their pet; they just want a companion. They torment their neighbors.

So the result is that kids have to learn life's lessons the way I did, through the 'school of hard knocks,' if they even learn this way. They have to, because their parents don't have wisdom to pass down to them. They are both like ships without sails: directionless, subject to whatever happens to them. What a shame. It's truly heartbreaking. If they *do* know more than their parents- it's about dependency!

The parents aren't doing their job- so who is? The school and its liberal teachers, who are pawns of the government. The government and the media now raise your kids. Marxists use quite a bit of foresight. They know to start with the schools. When someone decided to go to school to become a teacher in the sixties, it was a noble thing. But the sociopaths had already gone into the colleges and were teaching there. So socialist ideology was what they were taught. Not their fault...but still, this has infected ALL of our institutions of learning in America. No learning environment is free from this. Pretty much everyone is being duped into believing they will be the beneficiaries of the 'top down, government knows all' world, and the philosophies they have been fed- often without knowing it. None of them will be beneficiaries. They are fooling everyone! They will be reduced to serfs just obeying their king. Remember, all of this originates in one place. This place is a place of no God.

I want to imply something here...that all the media hype towards Prince William's Royal Wedding on April 29, 2011 to Kate Middleton (although I acknowledge we've seen it before) could be a preparation of sorts. We will have a king at some point and he will want worship because he will be handed royalty. Just something to ponder.

Many Christians have said there will be a great awakening just before the end comes. I can find nothing that says this in our scriptures- however I still believe this to be true. I'm just seeing people tired of the same old bullshit they have been fed for years and yearn for something solid to hold onto. It *is* in our scriptures, however, that there will be a great apostasy and many will turn from God. Wheat from the chaff.

Take note of something if you are in school. Everything we are taught says the same thing in one way or in another. There is no God. No definite right or wrong. Well what does this produce? It produces Jared Lee Loughner, the 22 year old that shot Gabrielle Giffords and 19 others, including a nine year old girl. Tell me, just what will Kevin Jennings produce? Remember, he is Obama's 'safe schools' czar and advocates the North American Man Boy Love Association. This is the guy that thinks your fourteen year olds need to ponder whether to spit or swallow and need to be taught how to take a fist in their rectums.

What I'm saying is...you must believe in something larger than yourself; that is a creator of goodness, or else you are doomed. Period. There is only one. Look, do I come off to you as some Christian 'goody two shoes' trying to make you be good like me? Do I talk like that??!!

Jesus said, "If one strikes you on the cheek, turn to him the other also." Sorry, I am *not* the perfect Christian. I am trying. Sorry, if you strike me on the cheek you WILL lose all your teeth! I'm working on this. (Note: this is just for guys. For girls, I will just get out of her way.) You know one thing I have learned from reading my Bible? I do not fear death- *at all*. How many people can say that? *I know where I am going.* I have no idea how I will die and I don't particularly care. I have a feeling it won't be pretty. I have dealt blows to the sports fans and the communists, gay community, and the Islamics. I might turn out to be the most hated man in

America. I don't care, I must do this. I have been given much; much is expected of me--and I realize this.

In times prior to Jesus, when a generation was bankrupt of goodness, God would slay them or give them into slavery. It looks like the latter for this generation. Jesus compares this world to a vineyard in a parable, with God as the vineyard owner. When those who are put in charge of the vineyard continually mistreat (and kill) others who are sent by the owner to be involved in the up keeping (including His own son), the vineyard owner eventually says, "Enough." He wipes out the keepers and gives the vineyard to others.

I just don't want to see this for you. I know some of you and love you and I want the best for you. But you all have been re-educated to believe all these stupid things that devalue you as human beings. You are worth so much. You really are loved. Love is really unconditional. Don't believe what you are taught by smug, arrogant fools. They do not love you. I do. God does. Jesus died for you. How much love........?

Chapter 17

Is There Nothing to Fear but Fear Itself?

There's so much to fear. Our economy is collapsing. Our children are subconsciously indoctrinated in the ways of communism. Our government is trying to take our freedoms. We are at war with Islamic societies that are trying to turn us to Shariah law. The European Union (and many wealthy businessmen) are trying to get us to submit to international laws. Our current government is dismantling our defense systems...so we are vulnerable. There really is so much to fear. So much is out of our control.

It seems that the people in power want us to be afraid. Why? Because people in fear act irrationally. Irrational people make hasty decisions. People will give up their freedoms for temporary security if the sociopathic leaders are convincing enough to convince them that they will be the long term solution.

This will eventually lead to a dependent society. Dependent people are ripe for the plucking. Then in comes the government, with its fear already imposed, to the rescue. They want submission. Fearful people will submit to them. The word "Islam" means "submission." Communism *is* submission. Both of these (religions) want authority so they have subjects to manipulate and use. They will stop at nothing. They want to rule the world.

Just a reminder: Man CANNOT rule over himself because he is flawed. His personal desires get in the way. His lust for power, material gain and adulation make him incapable of self rule. God must be his leader. The United States was not an experiment in self rule, because our founders had a profound devotion to God. They read the scriptures and followed their teachings. The people that are saying that the   American founders were deists and didn't believe in true Christianity are LYING!

America is the last bastion of freedom in the world. The first truly free society. That's why they want to bring us down. I really believe they would like us to be bombed. I mean, they would just love all the chaos. Then at our weakest moment they would step in with the solution. They also want to take our guns. Historically, when communists get the power to take a peoples' arms, that's when the bloodbath begins. It is looking like this might not be necessary as Mexico has decided that they want to sue our gun manufacturers over all the guns that end up in their country, thus, shutting down that industry. Bring us down they must if they want their utopia. Fear is their tool. They want you to be afraid so you will submit. They always divide to conquer. These against those. Always finding their proletariat, they pit us against them and cause a rift between peoples and then exploit their what?

Fear. Fear of oppression from the ones that are free. The free peoples are always singled out as the oppressors. So ironic that both the communists and the Muslims want to oppress others and use fear of oppression as their tool to coerce people into submission. LIARS!

Our Director of National Intelligence James Clapper described the Muslim brotherhood as a secular organization. Then CIA director Leon Panetta said he is getting his information from the media. Well I feel safe now- don't you?

Right now, in America, race is the main dividing factor, as it has been in other countries. Uneducated blacks, Latinos, whoever, always finding the ones at the bottom, and then pitting them against those that are free or just wealthy enough to warrant opposition. Then starts the fear campaign.

You know what's kept full fledged civil wars from happening already? The grace of God, manifested in God's people. Take them out of the picture, and then....

Until then, what's needed is for us to educate our people as to what the Communislamists want to do. We are not running educational advertisements that state what they are doing. This is the only way we can stop this rift between our peoples. We keep campaigning against certain candidates while avoiding telling people what is actually happening. Why do we do this? Are we *also* being politically correct? We need to start running advertising that informs people just what they are facing. We need to stop being politically correct and start being more blunt about what we are trying to say, without invoking fear as a tool to manipulate them.

We need to tell people how they use entertainment figures such as comedians to instill fear. Also how they use screenwriters to paint pictures that support their agenda.

I have been a personal trainer for many screenwriters and know firsthand that most of them are gay. Gay people are basically countercultural, which means anti-capitalist, anti-family and pro free society (translates, servants to their lust). This is reflected in their screenplays. Just watch any modern sitcoms and what kind of plots they write. Watch the new MTV hit 'skins.' It really is child pornography. And the promotion of drugs and booze with minors? Sadly, Bravo's "The Real Housewives of New Jersey" had a Times Square wedding episode...with two of the HOUSEWIVES on the show! Deplorable!

They are turning our society and our country around to where sex, even with *kids,* is more acceptable than *faith*! I am saying that our media figures have transformed our society and our people are getting all their information from THIS media. They work through our popular media more than the news, because that is what people watch. Our media is full of free thinkers. Nothing wrong with free thinking but when it is entirely one-sided, he or she is no longer free. Any dissent is quickly dismissed. Even attacked.

Kids having sex and doing drugs is okay, but Jesus gets a sneer. What has happened to us?

Fear is used for submission. The more afraid you are, the easier it is to make you submit to their desires. Screenplays are used to seduce you and instill fear. Seducing you is done by creating scenarios in which decadence is acceptable. Many lovers and a lust for violence will seduce one into thinking this is normal life. If you watch enough movies and television shows that promote this way of life, you will begin to behave this way. Fear is instilled by telling people that the people who are living for their children are the enemy. Real threat, huh? Those *darned* families!

So families are the enemy. People raising their children are a threat to *their* way of life. They want you to believe they are a threat to *your* way of life. They are succeeding. Why? YOUR addiction to THEIR media. This is what has to stop. Why are we watching their television shows and movies? There are other things to watch. There are also other things to do. We can do other things besides watch their propagandistic programs. Be creative. Educate your children and make it fun. Use the Bible. Do not pacify your children by sitting them in front of the television! After a while, television begins to define reality. This is scary!

It would be different if moviemakers were of the mindset that they would make movies that would prop good people up instead of tear them down. They used to. Watch almost any old movies and good people are respected, while bad people are maligned. Look at how many movies now make heroes out of organized crime figures! Part of the problem in today's moviemaking is that if they did that they wouldn't sell nearly as much in tickets-- and that's OUR fault.

Hollywood anymore is always so anti-big business. Why? They ARE a big business! For one thing, the people that make these movies are not the same people who act in them. The coffee shop I go to is one that attracts a lot of film industry folks. They come in, in groups, and discuss their latest projects and act so important about what they do. I mean, you gotta see these people. They are almost always real goofy individuals. I call them 'movie nerds.' Most all of them are gay. The others consist of guys and some girls and are flagrantly bisexual. Watch shows like 'Californication' and tell me that seduction isn't a tool Hollywood uses to coerce you into a hedonistic way of life. Look at television shows like 'Shameless' and the worldview it expounds. A drunk of a father and his hopeless family. These are used to portray a typical American family. The sad thing is that it has now *become* really typical. This is what they have done to you and I. How sorry is it that they actually can manipulate us in this way.

The two tools used to manipulate you and your children are fear and seduction. Fear is used to cause you to panic and make rash decisions. Seduction is used to prompt desire and cause you to make rash decisions. All these things come to you through your television.

You should pray, think hard and talk to rational, God-fearing people before making important decisions.

"The fear of the Lord is the beginning of wisdom."

One must remember that the basic tenants of communist belief are to rid the world of the accountability that comes with a belief in a power greater than oneself, namely God. This is their enemy. They want total control. This can be seen in the bills they pass that restrict food and monetary resources and limit personal responsibility. Personal responsibility is given to the state. What used to be done by acts of war are now done by monetary collapse and the aforementioned panic. They want you to need them. In time you will. This is why you need to be prepared. Your children will be living under their rule. If you are afraid, how are your children going to respond? You need to stand your ground and not be worried for yourself or yours. You need to know what you believe in. We all need to be prepared to stand when our world is disassembled.

The crazy thing with these sociopaths is that they will eventually use the Muslims' faith against them just like the Christians' "God." And don't worry...they're already in the process of manipulating them as well. They are just using the Muslims as 'useful idiots' anyway, for the hatred that is inbred into their belief system. Ok... but the point is, GOD IS UNDER ATTACK.

They are attempting to fill our minds with their propaganda. Their values. Their hedonism. This is what they want. These are THEIR screenwriters. What they want you to have is the celebrity worship that they seduce you with. They want you to want to be Johnny Depp and Angelina Jolie. They want you to want to be a man or woman who follows your own desires. Love their idols and you love them. You worship what you pursue. All this is worship. That's why I said, know what you believe in. Follow what you believe in. Believe it or not you already are.

If you are learning what they are teaching through their media, you are one with them. If you live according to their teaching, you are one *of* them. Then their screenwriters are YOUR gods. Your children will (and maybe already are) worshipping their gods. Children or not, you have friends that are worshipping their idols. Learn how to talk to people about what you believe in. If you are truthful you cannot be swayed. Do not succumb to their scare tactics. You will be taken care of.

If you are not afraid, people will wonder why. Then you can tell them how you know where you are going and why you are not fearful. Tell them you have a place man has not seen nor heard prepared for you. Then they will listen. Remember, if you fear, you are denying your Lord and...you will be like them. They will be living in fear. You will not. They will want what you have and then you can tell them about Christ's redemption and how the others will perish. Invite them with you and they will cling to you. Then tell them to cling to your God and not to fear. Believers in Jesus Christ are the only people on the planet promised eternal life. There really *is* nothing to fear but fear itself.

Chapter 18

Media Bias and Mudslingers

Why do you suppose all the things I've told you are hidden from most peoples' eyes? Well for one thing, it's your complacency. You don't perceive that you need to know. This IS going to bite you in the ass at some point. Why isn't our media covering these things? Good question. Unfortunately, I think I have the answer. Most newscasters and celebrities have the same worldview as the communists. I'm telling you, when all the countries are brought in under the umbrella of the one world government and destabilized to the point of poverty for all, even the media figures will prove to be nothing more than 'useful idiots' themselves.

News reporters, by necessity, need to do quite a bit of reporting on celebrities. No matter how humble their beginnings (and most of them didn't really come from impoverished beginnings), as soon as one acquires all the wealth they need and are widely admired by the population, something happens. They soon begin to think (instead of thank) that they're somehow special and deserve admiration. I can see why, because they are worshipped. As soon as this mindset sets in, they seem to think all those 'little people' out there who worship them so much, are not really deserving of anything. Thankful--aren't they?

This mindset is typical when a child actor hits their post-adolescence. They think the world revolves around them. This actually is quite typical of any adolescent. What I think is that Americans just don't grow up anymore. This is because they don't have to get knocked down and get back up and try again. This is what entitlements do. It is struggle that brings you to maturity. If you haven't yet reached adulthood, no matter what age you are, you are going to fall privy to anything which makes you feel special. You have not learned humility. You might be fifty-five years old, but you are nothing more than a spoiled little brat.

So why are these people in a position of leadership? Who put them there?... You! Yeah, *you* put these people in a position in which others look up to them and, yes, worship them. So what is it exactly that they know that you don't? Nothing! Then why do we still look up to them? Because they're successful. Success really is the American dream. I guess my point is that we have come to worship the success and not WHAT brought them there. Do you think Bernie Madoff is worth modeling yourself after because he was successful?

Look...I don't mean to cast stones at another's art but when rappers after their second album start acting in movies or guys like Arnold Schwarzenegger become famous actors, you gotta wonder what it takes to become an actor. I know that world; I live in it. Tell me: if you can lie, then can you act? Yes, what I'm saying is that I do not think there's much real talent that goes into acting at its best. *At it's best!* I think *you* can do it just as well as Mel Gibson and Natalie Portman. Think about that before you gaze up in adoration to your fave star. They have the money to have perfect teeth, Perfect hair. Perfect bodies. Perfect lives. OTHERWISE THEY WOULD LOOK JUST LIKE YOU. They are not smarter than you.

And why the f**k is anybody listening to what actors say about political things? This is not their area of expertise. Most of them are spoiled little brats who happen to have a soapbox to just babble communist bullshit. This should be obvious in the way Sean Penn is now Hugo Chavez's new butt buddy, down in Venezuela openly endorsing the despot.

So what has happened to investigative journalism? In years gone by, journalists would investigate politicians' behaviors and identify corruption. They seemed to relish in exposing wrongdoing. When the journalist is just as bad personally as the politicians, then we get no real news. They just seem to cater to left wing politicians or left wing politically motivated celebrities and do what they want them to anymore. They're nothing more than highly paid ass kissers. So how did this happen?

Well, this is what happens when liberal views get combined with atheism. Since they're only living for this life, reporters cater only to celebrities and politicians. And this affords them some celebrity status themselves. Just look at Katie Couric. Yes, the girl who thinks the bigotry against Muslims is one of the most disturbing stories this year. We know she is a celebrity; she is one of them. I don't know if she started out that way, but it is obvious in the way she tries to make Sarah Palin out to be something terrible. Palin is just a mom and a decent politician who cares about the welfare of her country. She and others make her out to be something other than a caring person because she didn't *abort* her developmentally disabled son. Real awful...isn't she? But Sheryl Crow is okay and just wants us all to use one sheet of toilet paper. Now *she* deserves worship!

Look people, whether you agree with me or not, Sarah Palin is the only great candidate for president right now. Herman Cain is good but weak on some issues (he believes Obama has mismanaged the budget because he has surrounded himself with the wrong people). Cain is the ex-CEO of Godfather's pizza and knows how to run a business (the United States) and was a Fed chairman in Kansas city. Some people don't know a communist when they see one (or possibly he knows but it would not be beneficial to say it right now, but on the Glenn Beck show he admitted he saw intent). But he believes in Jesus and credits him for his recovery from stage 4 cancer and for the direction his life has taken. Mitt Romney IS a communist like Obama is. He designed the communist health care bill in Massachusetts. He also unabashedly believes in man made climate change (and thus, in taxation for carbon emissions). This *is* a communist ploy to sink the American ship, damn it! Recently 2400 pages of emails were made available to the public from Sarah Palin and the New York Times, Washington Post and the League of Women Voters went berserk! I mean they were wetting their pants over the chance to find some wrongdoing by Governor Palin! Why do you suppose this is? Because she IS the one that could upset their apple cart! She is the most intelligent and aware person out there and if you don't vote for her (or if she doesn't run) in the 2012 elections then you deserve everything that comes upon you!!! It's Palin or Cain or... Happy poverty!!

Rock stars are always choosing causes that end up wrong. The first Live Aid concert could have killed as many Africans as it saved, by encouraging Ethiopia's Marxist dictator Mengistu Haile Mariam in his 'land reform' program that caused the famine in the first place. The money raised was distributed among non-governmental organizations- some of which were resettlement programs that displaced millions of people and killed between 50,000 and 100,000.

Fourteen years ago, Peter Jennings forced then-ABC News reporter Peter Collins to insert into a story language which cast a positive light on the communist Sandinista thugs of Nicaragua, praising their efforts to create "an unselfish society" and success in "land reform." And, sure enough, they're still around in force today.

Janeane Garofalo considers anyone who takes part in the Tea Parties or voted against President Obama as racist, as does Jimmy Carter. Anyone who knows anything about the "Tea Party" knows that racism is absolutely forbidden in their rallies. They have sent people home who come with signs that can be construed as racist. The "Tea Party" wants to stop the wild White House spending of their children's futures and want to lower-not increase- taxes and the federal deficit.

Rosie O'Donnell said on national television that Christians are much more dangerous than radical Islamic terrorists! I mean, do Christians strap bombs to themselves and blow up innocents or mutilate their wives genitals so they won't desire anyone else?!! Do they take hostages, behead them, and display it on the Web? What news does she read? Socialism Today? Maybe she watches Al Jazeera! I could see USSR red communist garb fitting well on her...

The Washington Post's Greg Sargent (who they pay to be an objective reporter) went onto Twitter saying, "Dear union 'thugs' will you please get violent in Wisconsin already." Mmmm...'thugs,' he even says. He also insists that the "Tea Party" people want to reverse abolition, women's suffrage laws and civil rights... Huh?

On March 14, 2011, Time Magazine released an article titled "Dead man Walker," after Wisconsin Governor Scott Walker and seventeen Republican senators were given death threats by email. What is it they want to see?

And there's been other "activity" in Wisconsin as well. Democratic state representative Gordon Hintz first received a municipal citation in February 2011 connected to prostitution by visiting a massage (brothel) parlor. Later that month, he was in the news again for telling a female Republican state representative that she is "f**king dead!" Hintz made the statement to Michelle Litjens for her vote on the budget repair bill that would curtail union powers in the state. So a man who feels the need to hire prostitutes tells an attractive state Assemblywoman that she is "f**king dead" for her vote on legislation. Shows real character...again... look at the people...

Senator Sherrod Brown is calling Jim DeMint and Governor Scott Walker 'Nazis.' He says, "As a nation, I look back in history and some of the worst governments we've ever had, you know one of the first things they did? They went after the trade unions. Hitler didn't want unions, Stalin didn't want unions and Egyptian president

Hosni Mubarak ...didn't want independent unions." Then what was Stalin's "workers of the world unite?" These people spout off this bullshit thinking you won't even check to see if they're correct or not. Unfortunately, you don't. You just hear it and nod your head like good little robots.

He has, since, apologized. But in Mein Kampf, Hitler wrote, "As things stand today, trade unions cannot be dispensed with. On the contrary,... they are among the important institutions of the nation's economic life." Hitler also supported universal healthcare, animal welfare laws, minimum wage and gun control. Trade unions are the way communists sociopaths gain power. Think about this.

Just look at how the whole global warming hoax was supported by journalists. The scientists who supported the misinformation managed to keep the scientists that did not support it from getting their work published. They had the positions of power with the science magazines. Now (unless you watch Fox news) did you hear about their leaked emails that made it clear they were lying? Of course not. That's real good investigative journalism- isn't it?

The UN Secretary General Ban Ki-Moon has asked for Hollywood's support for the global warming agenda to be publicly presented to Americans. Ted Turner (Jane Fonda's husband) has set up an office to facilitate this. His message: make global warming a hot issue. "I need your support," he told entertainment industry insiders during a daylong forum that focused on recent heat waves, floods, fires and drought which *some* scientists link to man-made climate change. "Animate these stories, set them to music, give them life and together we can have a blockbuster impact on the world," he said. Dan Hassid, a Walt Disney vice president who was in the audience, said the UN climate change effort "...feels like an early step. How do you make it marketable, palatable and engaging without preaching?" So this is what our media is doing to help. Sweet!

The reading of the Constitution aloud in Congress was decried by Joy Behar in January 2011, as she said "this Constitution-loving getting out of hand." Can you believe this? An American talk show host not agreeing with the decision to read our Constitution? Isn't it from our Constitution that we get our freedoms? Why does she want our Constitution de-emphasized? Does she not want freedom? Joy Behar and Whoopi Goldberg also walked off the set of their popular ABC gossip show "The View" in October 2011, when Fox News' Bill O' Reilly said Muslims killed us on 911. This is because he didn't say Muslim 'extremists,' and also said we have a Muslim problem. Do Katie Couric and Joy Behar secretly want to have their genitals mutilated, wear face and body coverings and serve an older Muslim man? Or do they want that for *you?* Look, you gotta wonder exactly what they're thinking when they're saying and doing things like this! They're taking the "it's all good" approach. Is it *really?*

I want you to take note of the fact that, when people of communist ideology encounter people that do not want a communist environment for their home and express this, they immediately become like schoolchildren and attack like wolves, viciously slandering anyone who will dare expose their manipulations. Just look at the previous examples I have given you. Progressive bloggers keep attacking conservative people like Glenn Beck and Sarah Palin with references to their use of "Nazi" tactics. Isn't it ironic that the people attacking are *really* the ones who are trying to create the same kind of society that Hitler did!!! Sometimes unaware of it themselves! Useful idiots.

I want you to look at how the attempted murder of Rep. Gabrielle Giffords by a lone lunatic, Jared Lee Loughner riled up the progressives. Immediately after her hospitalization, pundits like Paul Krugman said it was due to the teachings of Rush Limbaugh, Sarah Palin and Glenn Beck that the murders occurred. Illinois Senator Dick Durbin blamed the "Tea Party" and Sarah Palin. A nine-year-old girl, Christina Green, was killed there and these people used it as a platform for their hateful vitriol.

I'm telling you these sociopath bastards have absolutely no shame whatsoever! Jane Fonda, the hateful communist who garnered much popularity in the sixties (and Ted Turner's wife), said the attacks by Loughner on Rep. Giffords were done because of Sarah Palin's rhetoric. This woman actually gave a stealthily received note about soldiers still being held in Vietnam (POW's) back to the Vietnamese rather than to US officials! Do you know what those men suffered because she slid the Vietcong a note they thought would lead to their freedom? Three were killed...and a Colonel was brutally beaten.

You thought that Fonda had learned. 22 years ago in a Barbara Walters interview, she apologized to all the families about what happened in Vietnam. I guess, in this case, once a commie sociopath, always a commie sociopath. She had the *audacity* to say that about Sarah Palin! You see, any chance they have, they become like attack dogs. People who are truthful about what they say don't need to bring *this kind* of attention to themselves. And they certainly don't need to use that kind of hateful vitriol.

President Obama went to Tucson and addressed the Giffords attack, and its effect on our society. It actually was a very good speech, and even though it was a time of mourning, the college kids there cheered very inappropriately. Also, it was painfully obvious that Obama was campaigning for his 2012 re-election run. He just was very cold toward the actual killing, and the media blitz actually made it seem like he cared- even though we who were

watching could tell why he was there. What's a tireless opportunist to do?

I know- wait until he is campaigning for re-election and his poll numbers are down and *then* tell the armed forces its time to go ahead and go in and take Osama bin Laden even though he has known his whereabouts since last august and it is May 2011! This will definitely help Mr. Obama's re-election campaign tremendously!

Both the aforementioned Saul Alinsky and Rahm Emanuel, President Obama's ex-chief of staff (and George Clooney's effeminate doppelganger), have said, "Let no crisis go to waste." This means the obvious: be 'on it' when there is a crisis and use it to your advantage. The fact is that Obama's policies and programs have not been living up to their promises. This is always the case when communists try to take power. They cannot possibly make good on their promises, but this time it is happening ahead of schedule. Their policies are not producing-- and they are panicking. They have come so far and they may be losing it. People are waking up.

Look at how Juan Williams was not allowed to have his own opinion, and was subsequently fired from NPR. These people will not tolerate any opposing views at all. Now NPR President and CEO Vivian Schiller has resigned, following an incident where then NPR fundraiser Ron Schiller was videotaped slamming conservatives, the "Tea Party," and questioning whether NPR needs federal funds during a lunch with men posing as part of a Muslim organization (actually James O'Keefe's friends). Schiller told the phony Muslims what (he thought) they wanted to hear for $ for NPR: that the "Tea Party" people are anti-intellectual, gun-toting racists. This is another sting put together by O'Keefe--and was brilliant! I really do admire this kid, he's got balls. We definitely could use more like him. O'Keefe engineered a media firestorm that was necessary, as those two leaders of NPR were totally corrupt. It's nice to see the media work for truth- for once!

Both NPR and PBS have been government-funded communist propaganda tools for long enough now and need to be privately funded.

Al Jazeera, the Middle Eastern cable news channel that Bush-era Defense Secretary Donald Rumsfeld called 'vicious, inaccurate and inexcusable,' has become a White House favorite lately. Hillary Clinton recently praised it as 'real news' in her Senate testimony.

Officials tell Obama that when they go down the hallway at the State Department Al Jazeera is "on virtually every TV and computer." They say 'it doesn't have commercials (no capitalism?) and nobody is arguing on it' (no honest debate?). This is the station that Yusuf al Qaradawi, the man who says suicide bombing is a legitimate form of self defense is on...People,... just what the f**k has happened to us??!! These are the government officials *you* elected into office!

Isn't it interesting that once someone reaches celebrity status using the tools given them by a democratic society and a republic that favors entrepreneurialism, they immediately turn on their host, like some sort of cancer? Human pride is a beautiful thing- isn't it? All of a sudden their celebrity is not enough. They need to elevate themselves up even more, even to the necessity of seeing their admirers as worthless! I really think this is just what happens when Godless people find fame. They are never satisfied with how 'big' they have become. They need to be *even bigger!* Even if it means pushing everyone else down to elevate themselves. Childlike.

This is what I mean when I say Americans don't grow up anymore. I really think this is the root of the problem! What do spoiled children do when they become adolescents? Beat up mom. This is what Americans do that become successful. Beat up the country that fed them. Shamefull.

Most of the time these days you will notice that actors, politicians and musicians have not come from humble beginnings; they have had parents who paved the way for their success. It's not unusual for wealthy music (or movie industry) kids to grow up feeling that they are special, and common people are somehow inferior. Not so much with reporters and columnists. They come from commonplace beginnings and now are offered positions of notoriety through their reporting and opinion-sharing. With these positions come a certain amount of fame. At this point they think they are special and deserve some adulation themselves. The famous, notorious, cutting-edge journalist.   Just follow the party line, do just what everyone else is doing, kiss some ass and regurgitate what all the rest are saying and now you are cutting-edge... Wow!... Quite the innovator!

Could you believe the early 2011 media rage following Charlie Sheen around and listening to his incoherent rantings? Look, OUR WORLD IS MELTING... and this is what we hear about. Stupids! You call yourselves journalists- shame on you.

Isn't it interesting that during the sixties and seventies the government was what we all railed against, you know, the machine, and now we all want the government to come in and take control of everything? What happened here? Well for one thing, we now have a progressive administration in place- and MANY more progressive citizens.

IT'S IMPORTANT TO REMEMBER this is *not* what we had in mind when we all rallied against the Vietnam War. Some obviously did, but they were the ones stirring us all up. The rest of us just wanted peace. *We didn't know what they were building!* We didn't know we could be used as 'useful idiots' to bring them to power. Most of our current media figures are either 'useful idiots' themselves or are one with them and want the rest of us subordinated. It's one way or the other.

It's true; some people just want peace and harmony, want us to be kind to animals and to not destroy 'Mother Earth.' I know this and just wish these people would open themselves up to the voice of reason and realize that the Earth will never be free from strife as long as Islam still exists and sociopaths are in the world (they always will be). The world is not supposed to be peaceful without God- it cannot be. People are flawed, which means self-serving and desiring of things beyond the scope of their needs. This naturally leads to an 'I want some of what he has for me' mindset and eventually leads to thievery, and sometimes murder. This is human.

We will not build a utopia here on Earth with our own hands. Even Christians who have accepted and read God's word are not immune to all the same human groping for self-worth, self satisfaction and self-self-selfishness!!

There will be a great apostasy in the latter days, which will come in the form of a great world leader/teacher that will be able to sway "even the elect" into thinking he is the Messiah. He will be able to do this, because in the midst of great turmoil he will make a peace treaty with Israel and many nations for seven years. This world leader will be so charismatic, almost everyone will follow him. This man WILL be possessed by Lucifer himself. Do not be swayed. He will cause all to need to use his currency...which is one that will be capable of being implanted into our bodies. This is the "mark of the beast," spoken of in the Bible's book of Revelation. The technology is already being developed in different places around the world, most notably Florida.

Newsweek's Evan Thomas said, following Obama's June 2009 Cairo speech, on MSNBC, that the President is "greater" than any "small" idea like America. He compares him to another recent president- and to the Almighty: "Reagan was all about America...Obama is 'We are above that now.' We're not just parochial, we're not just chauvinistic, and we're not just provincial. We stand for something- I mean in a way Obama's standing above the country, above-above the world, he's sort of... God..."

Yeah, he is. The one who won his first election for Illinois State Senate by getting all of his opponents thrown off the ballot on technicalities. Now he is...God. Wow! America really *is* the land of opportunity!

In a fallen world, the closest place you can go to find truth is Fox news. They always offer a balance to their opinions with a view from the other side, for honest debate. All you will have to deal with is a lot of dyed blonde newscasters (like Christian television) and denture adhesive commercials. Find a liberal station (which is pretty much all the others) that will offer this kind of unbiased coverage. You won't. No more investigating, just fame seeking journalists. I'm sure they are invited to all the right parties and are guests on all the right talk shows. Celebrity status is so rewarding! Let's see what right winger we can bash and gain some more notoriety. Let's follow somebody around and see what kind of dirt we can justify inventing on them. Anything will do. Just sling some mud. Kinda like apes, don't you think? It's clear that some of the people involved in Fox News believe in God-THAT'S THE DIFFERENCE!

There's no socialist/communist/homosexual /feminist /environmentalist agenda at Fox News. They're not perfect, I have problems with them as well- but at the moment they are the only place to go for the TRUTH. Andrew Breitbart, the right-opinioned

website owner and author has expressed an interest in starting a new network and I wish I could help...!!!

In early 2011, outside the Fox News building, there were protesters chanting and waving signs saying that Fox News lies. A Fox representative named Jesse Waters went out and talked with some of the protesters, asking them exactly where Fox had lied. One man answered "too many." When asked again, he said, "I read." Great answer. You see, these people do not even find out what they are protesting about! They just listen to people around them and regurgitate the horseshit fed them.

It's just like Glenn Beck is saying: they want you *uninformed, unaware and afraid!* Beck says that the George Soros-funded 'Media Matters' has 87 people assigned just to debunking what he says? None of them have been able to refute ANYTHING Glenn has said because he always uses the peoples' own quotes in his statements.

Local TV stations' reporters tried to search "Tea Party" candidate Joe Miller's campaign crew's backgrounds for pedophiles.

Union leaders encouraged members to vote for Alaskan senator Lisa Murkowski as she had an "in" with the union appropriations committee and this would ensure the leaders keeping their jobs. Sarah Palin said her write-in campaign was backed by liberal union thugs. She was only the second Senator (Strom Thurmond in 1954) to win a seat on the Senate via write-in votes. She is a Republican.

What needs to be done is some investigative reporting on the journalists who make a living slinging mud on the only people who are trying to set things right. Now that would make someone reputable for doing the right thing. James O'Keefe was doing just this. James recently made headlines for setting up a girl journalist, a CNN reporter, in a way that would be considered to be entrapment of sorts. This is playing their game and I think just belittles his 'position.' He (and a beauty named Hannah Giles) successfully exposed the ACORN people for their corruption, but after this he became, maybe, a bit full of himself and succumbed to the same thing as the journalist he tried to 'punk.' This is a shame- and something we all need to be on the alert for. This can happen to anyone. It just shouldn't happen to those of us who are trying to lead by example, that's all. He's young. Much of his work is brilliant- it's just unfortunate that in order to get to the truth about the sociopaths, he often has to manipulate scenarios so much himself.

Glenn Beck is sure that we "Tea Partiers" are more numerous and surround them. I'm not so sure about that. Even in rural areas, the communist machine of the sixties is alive and well. Just look at the voter polls. Even in states like Wisconsin the liberal progressive (which is actually regressive) voters are still there. Labor unions seem to be largely responsible for getting them to think like this. It's just that conservatives vote more than the liberals. Maybe they're too lethargic from their bong hits. Just talk to random people you meet on the street. Most all of them don't know what is really going on and think like liberals. I really think 'they' are more numerous than us. This is why God is not blessing this country anymore. If we were more numerous than the hateful ones, He would still bless us the way He has in the past.

Even look at our lawmakers. I mean...Cass Sunstein? Will someone please tell me what Nancy Pelosi is good for? I know: starving Samoans of Starkist tuna...and serving herself. Good Lord, Jon Stewart's comedy show the 'Daily Show' is actually affecting White House policy on 911 emergency responders' compensations, after they became ill during their service.

One thing that makes my case is the fact that the Republican party is just as corrupt as the Democratic party. The communists, during the sixties, targeted the Democratic Party to hijack, because it was already the most left-leaning- and now there are few Democrat-elects who are not communists (at least the 'lay' variety). Most of the old school Republicans are just self-serving 'corruptocrats', spoiled by the benefits of high level government work.

Our new breed of Republicans are sooo much different than these: the ones who came in with the 'Tea Party.' Sarah Palin, Michelle Bachman, Chris Christie, Bobby Jindal and the rest can be the solution. Anyone that now goes into politics who wants to be part of the solution must know they will be attacked over and over again, and their personal life WILL be exposed! The people who want a dependent class want it BAD. "We will pole vault in, we'll climb fences, we'll parachute in," is what Nancy Pelosi said. Many have echoed that "the ends justify the means (*scary!*)." They are vicious. One who walks into this needs to know that their life must be clean as a whistle- and even then, there will be things that are invented about them. This is why I'm trying to come clean about everything ahead of time. The real reason I'm as candid as I am is the fact that I need to be real with you. I love you and cannot be dishonest with you. In cases like this one should not try too hard to defend themselves, but to simply maintain their dignity and stand for what they believe in. When people see that kind of mudslinging, they know something's wrong.

Our job is to lead by example. If we fight with their tools we are no better than them. We need to be loving, and not seeking ill for someone. We need to love those who persecute us (that will really piss them off). We are instructed to do this. We need to defend ourselves- yes- but that's all. We need to remember that we are all sinful and make mistakes. We are not better than the ones who persecute us. But we are trying to be the ones that show what God has done in us. Then through us, He can reach others if we behave with the dignity He bestowed upon us. This is by being truthful and loving in this hateful world, and preferring to give than to receive, (listen to your own words here, Cliff). Those given much will love much. To those given much- much will be required.

It's a lot to ask to stand up to hateful people, but look at what you have been promised. If you have accepted Christ as your Savior, you are given everything.

IV.   ON THE TRUTH SETTING YOU FREE

Chapter 19

Greater is Their Condemnation

Those who teach the flock the ways of evil, purposely or negligently misleading them, will suffer greater condemnation. Judging from this paraphrased scripture, it sounds like if one wants to go into ministry one must really know what they're going to teach. People go into ministry for a variety of reasons. One is a hereditary one: ie. your father was a minister and you grew up in the church. This can be a good reason or a bad one. For anyone to lead, one must really feel called to do it. Heredity by itself is not a good reason. For one thing, you need to feel equipped. A fundamental knowledge of the scriptures is not good enough. Can you sway people? Do people listen to you? These attributes are good- although not necessary. They simply help. If you are a churchgoer, have you ever gone to a church and heard a grand and very emotional sermon that affected the parishioners greatly but heard something in it that bothered you? I have.

I was living in Hollywood, CA working as a personal trainer while writing classical music in 1995. I felt empty. I was addicted to studying music and had nothing else going on in my life. I decided to make a dramatic change. I packed up my musical gear and left for Tacoma, WA with my mother and her entourage who were in town for a believer's convention. Before we went north, we had to actually *go* to the convention. What I saw there sickened me- and still does. This big rich evangelist singing karaoke to Willie Nelson with Christian lyrics and saying "sow that seed to meet that need" and getting all these believing people to run up to his feet, with fistfuls of cash and throw it at him. I'm so surprised I ever became a Christian. The kind of preaching I was witnessing was the "Word of Faith" ministries that began in the thirties with Oral Roberts and has been taken up by many since. Their messages have been affectionately referred to as the "Prosperity" gospel. There is nothing Biblical about one's faith correlating to an increase in personal income. It does appear to me that these pastors are robbing their faithful, but it is not my job to judge them; the Lord will do this. It's true, nations have prospered that have followed Christ and so have the individuals in them, but to sell Christ as a path to prosperity is in complete opposition to His message. Our reward will come in the next life.

I just didn't like the way the preaching was done. It was taught that praying using scripture was the only way to pray powerfully (insane) and everybody was encouraged to become an instant 'prophet' and prophesy continually. Talking in tongues was done at all times and although I really *did* see many that seemed very faithful I just couldn't help thinking this was the gospel for the simple, something that I couldn't relate to. I mean I pray in tongues occasionally when I know something needs to be said and I can't articulate it. Also the 'falling out' in the spirit seemed fake and I hated participating in helping people from falling down when it was obvious they were just pretending. My family took me to a 'healing convention' with Benny Hinn and this was really over the top! Maybe he really does heal lines of cripples in wheelchairs at the touch of his hand I just don't know if it's real. The music didn't help either. It was usually stupid simple little clap along's saying things like "we will fight you Satan and not retreat, we'll stomp you Satan under our feet." I realize not all these churches played music that was this inane but this whole branch of Christianity just seemed wrong for me. I was reading the scriptures and saw none of this in them.

Anyways, I continued on up to Washington and my mother bought me a Bible: I read all of it in three months. This is still my main Bible. I fell in love with the words I was reading and was aghast at what I had been missing all these years. I had started working in construction and also took over as the music minister at my mother's home fellowship church. I had big muscles and long hair and Mom decided I was right for her youth ministry too. I objected, as I had no toleration for noisy children and love the adult world I live in. This was done without even asking me if I was interested. I understood that it was a small church- but this really bothered me. I soon left and moved to Seattle.

My mother was 'saved' in 1982- and immediately began evangelizing in concordance to the "Prosperity" message. Later on, this bothered me. I think people need to mature in anything before going into teaching. At least with biblical scriptures, if you adhere to them, you really can't go wrong. But my mother was immature in teaching that 'prosperity' can come with acceptance of Jesus Christ, which is completely unbiblical. Maturity, in any endeavor, has nothing to do with age. Maturity is getting to know your subject so well that you lose the youthful ambition that naturally comes in with a little knowledge. My mother started evangelizing early after her conversion. She needed more time to mature, and made some decisions that were self-serving. I do know she loves the Lord and taught the good news of Christ's redemption.

I need to be clear about something. My mother was and is a great orator and pastor. My feelings about the way I feel pastors should be teaching stems from her. Hers was the only church I have been to in which the pastor demanded accountability from the flock. Flawed as I believe her theology is, I have to respect the way she insisted her congregation be rigorously honest with both themselves and others. If you were lying to yourself, she would expose it, lovingly. This, I believe is the single most important thing anyone going into ministry should be able to do.

Since then I have been to many churches and have found most of them good, but not great. So what do I want to see? Accountability. Virtually all churches/pastors seem to recite a simple message from the scriptures and then describe what is good about being good. I hear this---and feel empty. I want someone to say to me, "Are you truthful in all things?" I want to hear, "Do you return evil for evil?"

I want to be challenged. Why do, seemingly, no pastors do this? The answer is painfully obvious: money. Scare people away and church revenue declines. So what is going to make church leaders hold their flocks responsible for who they are? 70 percent of born-again Christians commit adultery. THIS is why we need accountability in our churches! We are to be the city set on a hill, shining our light to those lost and in darkness.

Church leaders are supposed to be paid for their services. This is also scriptural. But for them to challenge their flock, will it take publicly known crises on a global scale? I don't know. But I also don't think most church goers know what we are up against these days. Christians and our Jewish brothers are about to be persecuted like hasn't been seen in America in our lifetime. We need to know that the Jews are God's chosen and have their own covenant with him. Throughout history, they have continuously overcome insurmountable adversities. Do you think that was all based off of their own merit? Hardly. They are our brothers and sisters. They have their covenant; we Christians have ours. There is no requirement for them to covert to Christianity.

Do you know who is not helping? The Westboro Baptist Church in Florida. These weird fanatics have protested at soldiers' funerals, causing much grief to the mourners, just to cast the "You're all going to hell" bullshit at people who are already hurting. They say the army's tolerance of homosexuals is unholy. What do you suppose God thinks about their harassment of the mourning relatives of fallen soldiers? The scripture already says homosexuals will not enter into the Kingdom of Heaven...what more do they want?

I'll tell you who else is not helping: Jim Wallis, President Obama's new pastor. This man teaches 'social justice' as a way of bringing forth Christ's message. This means that the government needs to be Christ's tool to bring the needy and elderly their needs instead of Christian charity. Jesus said, "Assuredly, I say to you, in as much as you did it to one of the least of these, you did it to me." Social justice is nothing more than communist redistribution of wealth. Taking from working people and giving it to those not working. We are to give out of our love- not a government mandate. This is how we show them that we care. Anything else is not *us* willfully doing this, but is just communism taking hold and hijacking Christ's message. The taxes never go to the needy anyway and always just make the corruptocrats richer. Jesus also said, "Beware: for false prophets will rise from among you."

One more: Shariah4America was going to hold a rally that was cancelled and a group of (perhaps) well-meaning Christians showed up and ended up taunting a Muslim man who was on the street praying. They shouted him down with chants of 'Jesus, Jesus" and threw crosses on the ground... This is a wonderful way to convert anyone to... ISLAM! Stupids, you've successfully pushed the cause of your Lord all the way back to the tenth century. Maybe we can force them to convert at gunpoint? Brain death! We are told to "love our adversaries!" Let *them* be the ones that do this kind of shit!

The problem is when people see these things, they think, "the church is hateful-there is no God." Or in the case of Catholic priests' illicit behavior, "the church is corrupt-there is no God," rather than, "these people do not know God like they think they do." We need to know we are being watched. How we behave *is* an accurate reflection of what kind of people we are. We are to represent our faith just like Jesus.

In our scriptures, the book of Revelation goes through seven churches that were present when they were written, that most biblical historians agree are also churches that have evolved over the last couple of millennium. Two of these churches were condemned by our Lord. One was the Church of Sardis, which historians agree was the church of the reformation. Christ said the church was dead. This is not good. The other one is the Church of Laodicia. Christ said this church was neither cold nor hot. Historians agree this is the church of the latter (these) days. Christ said he would spit this church out of his mouth! He was repulsed! He described their opinion of themselves: "You say I am rich and have need of nothing" but you are "wretched and miserable, poor, blind and naked." It is clear that Jesus is more disgusted with unclean holiness than he even is with the wicked.

What does this say to a pastor that gives a simple little sermon and then lets their flock go their way, unable to have the tools to cope during the hardest time the church is going to have? In the late nineties I was studying to be a pastor myself but after going to a church that started out very faithful, I changed my mind. I had returned to my mother's church with the intention of moving to Seattle.

After moving to Tacoma, I found work as a trainer in Seattle and found a beautiful church, founded by a pastor in the late sixties who welcomed in the 'hippies' and built the church from that. The music was good and the people were so nice and worshipful. Being a musician, I hated the music at my mother's church (the dumbest music I have ever heard!) and longed for intelligent songwriting and lyricism. I loved this church. But after a few years, the church started changing. The pastor had a daughter who was a semi-pro basketball player and the sermons started including all kinds of sports references. This angered me and so I decided this was not the church for me. I decided that pastoring the faithful just wasn't my calling.

I met my wife in Seattle and we went to this church for a while, but then just stopped. We got tired of the church crowd, and I haven't returned. We have been back in Los Angeles for eight years and have not sought a church, as we have been busy recording and

just living and dealing with Hollywood life. I would like to return to church but can't stomach the same old non-message and church crowd. I do, however, pray every day. I think if I return to church, it might be a black church. I just find them much more spirit-filled. I'm not sure Angie, my wife, would like this much though, as she knows black women like me.

I have a real problem with the church crowd. I really don't like being around them very much. I swear sometimes, when I think it makes my point as emphatically as I want and this offends their saintly little sensibilities. Peter, when aware he had renounced his Lord three times, began cursing. Paul says in our scriptures, "Let no filthiness proceed from your lips." Okay, try "Look at that skirt she's wearing, she looks so fat in it." And "Yeah, he thinks he's all that because he has big muscles, I'll bet he has a little dick." I have heard both these things from Christians and trust me, in our Lord's eyes, this is filthiness.

And tell me the truth: do you *really* clap your hands when you hear music you like? I don't know anybody who does! The men act like pussies, the women like prisses. They don't integrate as much as would really be beneficial. They watch Christian television, listen to Christian music and spend all their time with fellow Christians. They don't learn enough about the people around them. Our Lord said we should be "Wise as serpents but harmless as doves." What part of 'wise as serpents' don't you understand? Christ also said, "Go into the world and make disciples of all nations." Which means go INTO THE WORLD! We are to be in the world- but not *of it.* Why do you think Christians get sick or contract diseases like everyone else? In the world. However, we cannot make a difference if we are not in it. I personally believe Christians should be part of the environment in which they live. They should be the ones that are honest and loving in this hateful world. They are no good for anyone when sequestered off in their little Christian communities. What good is a Christian that cannot convey his or her faith because they only communicate in little 'Christian slogans?' This appears stupid and simple-minded, *because it is!* Relate to the community around you! Christians have made Jesus repulsive (why do you think he said he will spit you out his mouth). Christians can be so anti-intellectual because they believe intellectuals have been the cause of all that's wrong. I personally think communism is stupid and *very anti- intellectual,* even though it was created by supposed intellectuals.

Look, I also know many Christians who insist that we not drink alcohol. This is ignorant and stupid because it sequesters us from learning how to make day-to-day choices. Aren't we being "in the world, but not of it" when we have a deep discussion over a beer with a buddy? Why reject an opportunity to help a friend for fear of being seen having a drink in a bar? Is there anything wrong with enjoying the taste of an alcoholic beverage? Doesn't that sound kinda Muslim? Why do you think Muslims do not drink? Answer: they need to elevate themselves above the other people so they appear saintly. Why do Christians do the same? TO ELEVATE THEMSELVES ABOVE THE OTHERS TO APPEAR SAINTLY! What was

Jesus' final beverage of choice on Earth? I'll give you a hint: it wasn't grape juice! The same word for wine as used in the bible for drunkards is used for the wine at the last supper.

And let's not forget that our Savior ate with tax collectors and associated with asses and prostitutes (not interchangeable)!

Look people, we are SUPPOSED to learn how to do things and show restraint. This is the whole idea (and the problem I have with Alcoholics Anonymous)! We are supposed to be able to have sex with our wives, and not bed hop. We are supposed to be able to drink, but use restraint. We are supposed to learn to be wise with money, but not be selfish and greedy. This is how our Lord molds us into the kind of people He wants us to be. It's all about choices. Muslims and communists eliminate choices- and if we do the same, we are like them. We are here to become people that CAN make the right choices- and this can only happen if we are free to make them. If we say, 'no, we do not do that,' where are the choices made? Choices are momentary, like, "am I going to have *another* drink?" If one is free to choose, he or she can then make Spirit-led decisions that are Christ-like.

We are told we must be the light in this dark world. We are to be truthful when those around us are dishonest. We are told to love our brothers and sisters when they are hateful. We are told to stand out for this. To lead by example. Not to avoid saying cusswords or drink alcohol. Not to be better that everyone, BECAUSE WE'RE NOT.

Many Christians are very entrepreneurial. This is fine...as long as they are honest. The advertising world can be difficult. I found it difficult when the gym business turned and my boss, the owner, mandated that I be a salesman as well as a trainer. I was instructed to tell people that if they could afford a latte every morning they could skip the latte and afford a personal trainer. I had a problem with this. My boss was a Christian. Yet he hired guys to come in and teach us how to 'bleed' the people coming in for as much as we could get from them. He went to one of those 'prosperity' churches. When I left, I never returned to working in gyms. I was very good at what I did- I did not need to resort to conning people out of their money. I think if someone wants a latte they should have one. If they want a trainer, they should have one. If they don't, they shouldn't. I don't want to tell people what to do. I want them to make their own choices. This is healthy.

I love my fellows and think if they want to be dumpy more than they want to exercise, then that's what they should do. I wish they all knew of Christ's redemption- but I'm not going to twist their arms. I will say my piece and encourage them, but then it's up to them.

Another Church mentioned in the seven Churches is the church of Thyatira. This church is known to be the Roman Catholic Church. This church began when Christians were becoming too numerous for the Roman Empire to control. The Catholics were taught to call their priests 'Father.' This is expressly taught in our scriptures as

something anathema to Christianity, as Jesus said not to call anyone 'father' except our Father in Heaven.

Also, praying to mother Mary is not addressing our Savior, but His mother. In our scriptures, Jesus was approached by His mother and brothers outside a house where He was preaching, and He acknowledged the people around him, saying, "You all are my mother and brothers." He did not tell us to bow down before her or pray to her. But he *did* say "No one comes to the Father but through me." And this *does* address not praying to saints and mother Mary. Another thing the Roman Catholic Church has always insisted is that their priests...take a vow of celibacy. This was this was addressed in Timothy in the New Testament, as we "ought not to forbid to marry." This has caused innumerable problems in the Church for centuries, as priests (like all humans) have sexual needs and urges, and eventually these come out. Maybe the same thing that causes them to want priesthood in the first place ends up surfacing and innocent young boys are mishandled by the Clergy. The Catholic Church is going to string me up for this but what about these octogenarian transvestites called the Popes, in their brightly colored gowns! And those stupid crowns! These disgusting old men don't even have anything useful to say, because they can't even remember what they started talking about!

Jesus said to this Church in Revelation: "I Know of your deeds and your love and faith, service, and perseverance and of your works and that your deeds of late are greater than the first, but...you tolerate that woman Jezebel, which calls herself a prophetess and seduces my servants...and I gave her space to repent and she did not." He said he would cast those who committed adultery with her into great tribulation unless they repent of their deeds. He is the one that searches the hearts.

Christ acknowledged this Church for its service and its faith. The Catholic Church has always been known for its charity. They have been a bit misled, but not without the chance of redemption. The Catholic Church has also NOT been very good at teaching their followers to read the scriptures for themselves. They're much too liturgical for that. The old Roman hierarchy wanted to control this, for obvious reasons. Ancient traditions have marred truth, and "greater is the condemnation" of those few elite Clergymen who purposely fogged up the truth, leading literally millions into confusion over history. However, most Catholics I have met have been even better Christians than most evangelicals I have been around. They actually integrate more than most evangelicals. They have been more loving and giving despite not being scripturally taught.

John Boehner, our House Speaker, a republican, comes from a devout Roman Catholic family in Ohio has come under fire from more than 75 professors at Catholic University and other prominent Catholic leaders. Their charges are that Boehner supported the budget Republicans have presented because it will hurt the poor, elderly and vulnerable and has failed to uphold basic Catholic moral teaching. This is because it reduces entitlement spending. I say; this is just Catholics being seduced by communist redistribute the wealth bullshit and has nothing to do with neglecting the poor. The states are bankrupt and the country is the same and it *is* because of massive entitlement spending as dictated by Cloward and Pivin and we *must* stop spending like this or we will live in a dictatorship before you know it! Jesus told us "the poor will always be with you" and he's right. They must be looked after by righteous *Christian charity!* Not the government taking people's money that worked for it and giving it to other people, that's a gift from the government. Communist redistribution of wealth will only benefit the elite and we've seen this already.

There will be a great falling away from the faith in the end times, Jesus tells us, and this is part of it. Things that *sound* noble like this- but are really just dependency creating tools- *will create the falling away.*

I have always had a problem with churches that are very liturgical. It's the processional element and the implied deification of men that goes along with liturgical churches that gets under my skin. Nasty old men dressed in colorful robes leading their procession down the isle. I have always seen real Christianity as an understanding of what the Lord has done for us and having a relationship with him (which is difficult, as all conversations are naturally one-sided). However, I may be full of 'sheevsky' as one cursory read through the book of Revelation, where things are actually taking place in Heaven, and you will not see anything more liturgical than this! It just bothers me when I see old men being

worshipped like they're God or something. Maybe it's just me- and I have something against nasty old men. Yeah- that's probably it.

If believers can separate themselves from this hedonistic world, but still live in it and start thinking spiritually instead of worldly (and their pastors and priests do the same), there will be hope for Christians. We are not better than anyone else; we are repentant. We are forgiven. We have been sinful and remain so. We are to enlighten those who need it. This is done with our charity and by our example. Honest, loving and forgiving as we were forgiven. Remember, Jesus said, "In this life you will see tribulation." You will see this if you are doing the right thing. If you do not, then you should worry. If it's all going real smooth for you in Lucifer's world, what does that mean? Who are you listening to?

So, what is my duty and yours? To spread your knowledge within your circle of influence. Simple.

Chapter 20

The Devil We Know (who are you anyway?)

Newsflash: your thoughts are not always your own. Your brain is a tool you use. Anyone else can use your brain. I can make you feel good. I can make you angry. So your thoughts can be given to you by an outside force. Lucifer hates God. He wants you to also. Saul Alinsky lauded Lucifer for attaining his own kingdom. Saul obviously was listening to Lucifer. You can too. Or not. Your soul is composed of your mind, your will, and your emotions. If you are to be governed by any one of these, which one do you want? Your mind? Not a good idea- given the fact that anyone else can use it. Most people think their mind *is them*, unaware that other people have been using their mind for the last few hours or days. Your emotions? Well, do you want your emotions dictating your actions? Given that emotions are subject to mood changes and other phenomena, this is not beneficial. Okay, let's look at your will. You have a will and a won't. Your will is obviously the most powerful of these. Your will is what dictates whether you will listen to God or listen to Lucifer. Whether you will listen to your heart, or listen to temptation. Listen to your Spirit, or listen to your flesh?

Just as you want a mate who wants to be with you and loves you, so does God. God takes no prisoners. He does not want you captive; he wants you free. Anyone as old as I am will remember the old hippy poster that said, "If you love something, set it free. If it comes back, it's yours, if it does not, it never was." This is why God wants you to be free. He wants you to want Him. This is why God lets you listen to Lucifer. He wants you to choose. Lucifer is cunning. He sometimes will come as an Angel of light. He is

deceitful. God will not trick you. God wants you to love him-
because he loves you.

So how do you know if you are listening to God or the Devil? A
good tree bears good fruit; a bad tree bad fruit. If you think
pleasurable sensations are good fruit, first look at the *potential*
aftermath. That's where you will know who gave you this thought.
That's right- I said "gave you this thought." God gives you
thoughts--and so does Lucifer. Your job is to decide which ones to
follow. Pleasure can be a very good thing. It can also have
disastrous consequences.

Let's think about pain for a minute. None of us like pain, right?
Do you think pain can have good results? Surgery is painful. Can
surgery be good for you? Heartbreak is painful. Can heartbreak ever
be good for you? What if you fell in love with someone who treated
you like dirt? If they left you, you would still be in love with them.
In both these cases, pain does you good.

Jesus said,"In this life you will see tribulation." Why? Because
you are being molded. We are a fallen creation and have been
deceived. The only way we can be made perfect is through

tribulation. Why don't we live in this body forever? EXACTLY. You
have noticed, haven't you, that with life experience comes
maturation. What kind of life experience? River rafting? Going out to
a great club? Not. If you notice, people who are mature are also
able to love much. It's obviously the hardships that make us fully
mature and thus, capable of much love. This world is not always
pleasant because it's not supposed to be. The next one will be. We
are living for the next life.

So are your friends, whether they know it or not. Please do not
let their enemies take this from them. When you remove someone's
choices, you disable the very thing that they will need to bring them
to spiritual fullness. CommunIslam does this. That's why they do
this; it is rebellion against God.

Lucifer is doomed and he knows it. Our scriptures tell us that in the end times Satan comes down to earth "with great wrath, for he knows that he has but a short time." Look at the world right now. Look at almost anywhere in the Middle East. Look at Mexico. Look into what has been happening in Europe for the past few decades. And finally look at what is going on here in the first, genuinely Christian nation. Our schools and our families are being taken over by doctrines of demons, with *our* current government leading the way. This will not be overturned by political means. The battle is a spiritual one and can only be defined in spiritual terms. Unless our country has a truly great awakening, it is doomed.

We are spiritual beings. Believe it or not, none of us are ever going to die. We were created as eternal beings to live with our Savior forever. Some of us have, unfortunately, listened to the voice of the one who has the authority to try to con us out of our inheritance. Do not be conned. They have heeded the voice of hatred. Our scriptures tell us that we become like the God (or gods) we worship. What we follow we worship. We were created to worship. We worship all the time, something...or someone. I urge you to worship the One that bears good fruit.

It is easy to look at the world right now and be afraid. Do not be afraid. Jesus told us, "When you see these things, do not be troubled, as these things must take place." C'mon, you say, the things we are seeing are threatening our very existence! We have to fight them. Well, yes you do. If you don't, more might be lost to the hatred that has overcome the rest. That's the only reason why. It's not for your safety. You are God's own and you will be looked after. Jesus also said, "Even the hairs of your head are numbered."

Let me urge you to do something that is very unnatural: do not fear death. Remember you are eternal. It is difficult, with the distractions all around us, to keep our mind on the eternal, but it is something we must do if we are to face the assault we are going to experience. There will be threats. You will see violence. Even death.

The scriptures tell us that some of us will even be beheaded. Short. Painless. Bring it on. Those victims, we are told, are awarded a very special place in Heaven. They also tell us that in the end times, "Men's hearts will fail them, for the evil that is in the world." Hopefully I can reach some before this happens. I have prayed to the Lord, "Do not let me come before you empty handed." So should you.

The time has come when the dark will become darker and the light will be lighter. Jesus said, "That which is whispered in secret will be shouted from the rooftops." Just look at all the corruption being exposed right now in both the United States and all over the world. Sound like the quote I just told you from Jesus? How about another one? Jesus also said that in the end times the world would see tribulation "such as the world has never seen." Given that the evil we are seeing is now in all corners of the world and really does threaten our very existence, isn't it becoming increasingly clear that we really are living in the end times? I mean look at the technology now. We can communicate both auditory and visually from anywhere, and we can even detonate bombs that can wipe out entire populations. How long can this last, with this capability and this much evil in the world? Sorry, mankind is not going to be here for very much longer.

So is it time to go right away and catch a good football game? Maybe let's go out and find some chicks. Hey, let's go hiking. Do you see where I'm going with this? Look, I have things I want to do too. I write music. I love bodybuilding. This is not to say it isn't good to enjoy any entertainment or stop making love with your spouse or anything. But how much time do you need for these things? There are people around you right now who are confused by all that is going on. They have friends that have listened to the hateful spirits. These 'friends' teach them things that will lead them to an eternal torment. How long is eternity?...Is this okay with you? Please, my friends... do not come before our Lord empty handed.

Most of us know that traditional Christian evangelizing seems kinda lame right now because Jesus has become almost laughable in the public eye. I'm not saying to ignore saying His name, but just to be tactful in the way you present your case. People need to know they are loved first. Love is in short supply these days.

Distortions of the truth are the norm. Satan is the father of lies. Those who listen to the spirits of hatred become liars too. Hatred despises love. Liars hate the truth. If one lies about anything, they can lie about everything. Someone who lies is NOT "basically a good person." They could be, but you already know they are listening to the voice of evil. Do not shun these people; they are lost. Tell them how much freer they would be if they could just be honest. Then tell them about their salvation.

Try to cleanse yourself of lies- any lies. This, in and of itself, will be a testament to others that you are a person they can trust. With trust comes comfort. Then they will listen to you. Remember, deceit by omission is still deceit. People watch what you do. They do not always listen. They don't, because so many people say things that do not convey truth. If you remain truthful, they will start to listen. Be honest in all your dealings. I'm telling you right now that the measure of a man (or woman) is their ability to be faithful to their commitments. If you make a commitment to anyone it is a covenant before God.

So many things are hard to do in this oh so evil world. Almost all business is based on a "get one up on the other guy" approach. Life is hard. As they say, 'its a bitch, and then you die.' But here's the real truth- if you believe in Jesus, then you DON'T die. Being totally honest is hard because the world thrives on deceit. If you are completely honest in all things in this hateful world, will you not be a beacon of light that will shine in the world?

So, who are you anyway?

Are you the voice of reason in this evil world? Or do you say, "Well I gotta just do this one thing." Do you say, "I'll be there for you," or do you say, "If I have the time"? Do you love your friends? God tells us we must even love those who persecute us. This is really hard and I would be lying if I told you that I have mastered this. I can't lie to you. I love you. You haven't persecuted me yet. If you do, I really will try to love you still.

We do not know the day or the hour the Lord will come. Open your eyes and seek the truth. Listen to those who love you. Do not listen to those who have an agenda.

Walk in love and in truth. Be a beacon of light in this dark world. There are people that desperately need you.

Chapter 21

Who the Hell am I, Anyway?

Nobody. Really. Just a guy who has lived many lives and has come away with some gems I'd like to share- that's all. When I say 'many' lives, I mean it. I was born on July 26, 1956, the year "Hound Dog" by Elvis Presley came out. As you know if you've been reading, I grew up in Auburn, CA, lived in town and was beat up on by aggies (the kids studying agriculture) the kids of local ranchers, and jocks. This was because I was a bookworm, with glasses. First I read comic books, mainly Thor (whom I later became) and then I read all of the pop books of the time like "The Greening of America," " Future Shock," "The Electric Kool-Aid Acid Test," "The Pentagon Papers" and even "Doctor Zhivago." This was all in grade school!

My parents split up when I was eleven. I have two sisters. I lived with my mother and sisters for three years, before moving in with my dad. Maybe my identification with women came from this period. From the time I was about fifteen I wanted to be, well, a girl. I just identified with them more than other guys. There has never been a time when I was attracted to men or boys. I was more repulsed than anything, and for the most part- I still am. I loved girls so much I just wanted to be one. Weird...I think so too!

I really identified with glam rockers like Marc Bolan and David Bowie. But when I matured and started playing in rock bands, we were more like the Allman brothers. Drunks and drug addicts. Bikers and tough guys. My father taught me how to box at fourteen, and I went from bookworm to badass right away. I really think it was good for me to get beat up when I was a kid. Most parents these days try to protect their kids from things like this. But this is what made me tougher later. Things don't always happen right away and parents need to realize this. My Dad and I moved from Auburn to Camarillo, in southern California, when I was fifteen so I could be closer to Bay Mare motocross track but I began dropping acid with other like-minded hippies and forgot about dirt bikes. We were listening to Traffic and Blind Faith- picking fights with other drunks around town. I often ended up beating up my friends- something I regret.

I have never dated. I have always either been alone or had a girlfriend. I have always loved tiny breasted, dark-haired or dark skinned girls (or redheads) that are assertive and know who they are. I love an equal. I have rarely ever sought a particular girl but just chose one from those hanging around at the time. Girls always came to me. I grew up at the state hospital my Dad worked at. The hospital's community housing for employees was a wonderful place to meet so many kinds of interesting people. I learned guitar after one of my dad's girlfriends loaned me hers. Pretty soon I met the drug program graduates and played in bands with them. The druggies became my family. I loved them; they were loyal.

I became such a bad alcoholic that frequently I would wake up in my car by the side of the road and not have any idea whether it was dawn or dusk or if I had made it to work. I would just look around the car for some 'hair of the dog' and proceed from there. I was a state employee and we were unionized so I could get away with this behavior. I remember thinking one time that everybody I knew was a bonified alcoholic. So many of the state hospital employees were drunks (especially the ones that lived in the community housing), and not shockingly, most of them were single.

I was kicked out of the band I was playing in about 1978 for not learning jazz and being kind of violent. I had become fat, so I joined a gym and soon became enamored with competitive bodybuilding. Three years in, I began to compete and was very successful at this new endeavor, winning most everything I competed in. I just had the right structure for it, narrow hips and broad shoulders. It was amazing being able to walk out onstage and wink at the audience and flex a thigh and hear the roar. I had played in bands before--but this was intoxicating!

For no particular reason I want to tell you that I have always met the nicest people in the gyms I worked out in. These always became my closest circle of friends. Part of this is because in a gym, the main reason people are there is a positive one. Also they are not there for any work-related thing, and so everybody is coming from such disparate professions that it is always an interesting mix of people. I love the gym and the people there- the energy is wonderful.

I was becoming very well known in the Southern California bodybuilding scene and I was loving life. I was the only thousand pound squatter in the county. I had two wonderful girlfriends during the eighties and played in another band- but then was ousted again- this time for being too much of a drunk. Immediately after that, I would sustain a vertebral injury that would cause the atrophy of some of the muscle groups in my upper body, leaving me with a physique that wasn't competitive at the level I had already achieved. After two drunken driving arrests in 1986 I decided, while sitting in jail, that 'I' was the problem and stopped drinking for 16 years or so. My life focus went more towards music, as I soon put together a studio, and began learning to play other instruments. I started writing and recording with my old friend from the previous band, Mark Hashimoto. The songs I was writing were typical in the lyrical content for any songwriter of the time. My songs frequently changed keys and had modulations usually seen in a more educated songwriter; I had a gift. Finally I was sober enough to really use it!

I went to school in 1980 and got my degree in nursing and psychology. Retrospectively, I noticed a distinct absence of theology anywhere in psychology. I believe at its core psychology is founded on an anti-Christian slant. In school I wrote one of my papers on the sociopathic personality because I have a close relative who is one...and have encountered many since. I must tell you- I worked with patients who were cold blooded killers and trust me- they're NOT fascinating. Their thought processes are usually dull and lifeless. I'm saying this to address America's fascination with serial killers. This is dumb. Stop wasting your time. They are not interesting. My term paper was on reality therapy, because I noticed our patients were treated like nothing had happened, even the day after they would throw a chair and hurt someone. Well-meaning staff did this because they were 'sick.' I didn't think this was the way to prepare them for the real world.

If you read older books (or even watch older movies), you will find that men used to be assertive creatures. Assertive means to be decisive. Contrary to popular belief, it does not mean to be aggressive. Aggressive behavior is someone trying to force a skill that they haven't properly developed. Or they're just ruthless. To be assertively skilled just means to be true to what you know to be the truth, whether or not it makes someone uncomfortable. If you are an assertive person, no one can sway you, because you are acting on the truth.

Have you noticed that assertive skills are obsolete? No one has them anymore (except maybe in New York). People are either timid but backbiting and passive-aggressive or they're aggressive. Sign of the times.

My father was not assertive himself. He was, surprisingly, a coward of sorts. I'm still surprised by this...as he was a good boxer. He was just so afraid of other men it irritated me. I vowed early on not to be like my father. I knew that to survive in this world one needs to develop the resolve necessary to manage others' aggression. When people are aggressive, you need to be able to stand your ground. I've been told numerous times that I'm more like a New Yorker than a Californian in that I am very 'in your face' about things, simply meaning that I am an assertive person. I have my father to thank for that.

My father used to say to me when I was not doing well, "Look at so and so, they're not doing anything like you are." But I decided that I would not ever "compare down" like that. I always compared myself UP to someone who WAS doing something worthwhile. This made me try harder and not make excuses. It still wasn't the best way of thinking as it didn't look to Jesus, but was a step in the right direction.

You know, no matter how bad our parents were, they did the best they knew with what they had. We can hate them or we can love them. I never wanted to be like my father but I did love him. So I wrote a song out of one of my best classical pieces called 'Choices,' that was all about my tortured relationship with my dad. I actually got to recite the lyrics to him before he died in 1995.

I also discovered that I am an individual that is pretty much all 'right brain.' I have a very small analytical side; I am always creating. Most people who get to know me say I am absent whenever we are talking. I am always creating something in my mind. I also make guy friends at times, and some of them expect me to kind of 'boys club' with them, meaning be their pal, talking degradingly about girls or about sports. Sorry, guys- I'm a 'girls club' kind of guy.

Here's something that should tell you volumes about me. ALL bodybuilders choreograph and practice their posing routines for (sometimes), months before a contest to have it right on show day. I have NEVER choreographed or practiced any of my routines. I just walked onstage, listened to my music and let it take me away into my 'zone'- this method ALWAYS got the 'Best Poser' award. I always included some dance or 'breakdance' material and just let it happen. Some of the more uptight (hardcore) guys would criticize me for dancing too much--but I would still win! I am a very good dancer;

why not use it? I think this just means I'm comfortable in my own skin. I make things fun. Sometimes I would be backstage and see how nervous some of my competitors would be. I'd start babbling about my car or some stupid thing (breaking their concentration) and make them so mad that they would start to elbow me once we were onstage. They'd make themselves look like angry assholes and I would just let them and smile at the judges. The judges would like me because I was the 'nice' guy. Don't get me wrong- my physique was worthy of every title I won- but again, I make things fun.

By 1989, I was sick of working six days in a row and started dancing in a club in Ventura, as I was more muscularly developed than most of the other strippers. They called me 'Captain Buns.' I started working private parties soon and a certain group of black girls who really liked me hired me almost weekly. Black girls have always loved me- almost as much as I love them. I was kind of an anomaly in the stripper world, in that I didn't drink or do drugs at the time. Also, I never stayed after and went home with girls. I always had a girlfriend and never cheated on her- that was taboo. Twice I went home with girls when I was in between girlfriends- and that was it.

I was playing in a band at the time that was put together in the gym in Venice and consisted of all bodybuilders. We had a producer and an attorney. So I decided to quit the hospital and move to Los Angeles, which was the bodybuilding and music capital of the world at the time, and work as a stripper. Well, the eighties just ended, and male exotic dancing was going out of fashion. Lucky me. I had moved in with the women's World Champion wrestler I met in Gold's Gym in Venice. Living off my father's handouts, I soon was on the street, as the girl was fed up with me because I was not paying her any attention. She wanted me badly, and I didn't want her *that* way, so she asked me to leave.

I also had a beautiful bodybuilder girlfriend at the time in Venice. She was my kind of girl, pretty, sweet and always was braless, which was really a turn on for me. She had the tiniest little, breasts I'd ever seen (which I really love!) and her ass was nicer and rounder than even the best black girls, and she was giving and loving as well! She talked incessantly but I really liked her. This soon ended because I knew I was about to be living in my car and I didn't want to be a burden to her (even though I really was beginning to love her), so I found myself living in a series of cars. I even tried to return to the state hospital for work, and found there were no open positions. Then in Venice, I had an Italian girlfriend for nine months who had a condo on the beach. This was good, 'cause I was off the street. She even bought me a synthesizer. Then when that ended due to my disinterest, I moved into the Gold's Gym parking lot in Venice, with a bunch of other homeless bodybuilders. I used to make money posing for pictures on the boardwalk with tourists. I'd make $100 a day, and this would do me for the week.

I entered one last bodybuilding contest in 1991. It was at a gay event in Pacific Palisades on the beach and I entered because I heard David Geffen was going to be there. He was the biggest music industry mogul at the time. I wrote my own posing music and hoped he would hear it and see something he liked. I was the only contestant to wear a G-string--and won easily. The other contestants were angry that I had entered because I was pro and they were just strippers, wannabes, and the like.

With male exotic dancing no longer paying anything, and feeling guilty about feeding off my father who was only receiving social security, I began to view my options. I had gotten two agents interested in me by just walking around and looking pretty, and I would occasionally land acting roles. I landed a yogurt commercial, a part in the 1992 MTV Movie Awards, an episode of "Mad about You" and worked for Playboy three times: once on "Playboy after Dark" (among other things). Also, some very reputable photographers spotted me and got me to do some erotic art photography. My pictures have been in art exhibits in galleries.

Working occasionally in gay clubs, I was frequently propositioned for quite a bit of money. I succumbed, and the identification with girls I had began to surface. I liked the way I was looked at. I had an exceptional butt and was even voted 'best ass' at Gold's Gym in Venice by the 'ass crew'- which were all straight guys! In that environment *that* was really saying something (I'm not sure *what,* but something!).

The best bodies in the world gravitate to Gold's in Venice because it's the bodybuilding capital of the world! The girls there have the best asses you will ever find anywhere. So for a couple years I got to be a hot-assed Hollywood chick! How many sexually ambivalent guys get to have that? The only problem with being a 'girl' is that 'guys' start coming around. Gross. I was never effeminate or anything. I just dressed in tights like all the other bodybuilders at the time, had long hair and looked hot. My legs were huge and ripped. My arms were enormous and my body fat stayed at three percent. I remember two bad accidents that happened just because I was walking around in white tights. Mind you- that was then and this is now. At fifty-four I don't think anyone cares what a man's butt looks like. But men and women just stared at me; I loved it.

Then Gold's Gym became annoyed at the old tuna cans littering the parking lot and asked us to leave, so I had to move to the streets in Hollywood. It was here that I wrote a very progressive (!) rock song called 'Survivors' for the band. The song was just an illustration of what it is like to be homeless in America.

I had met the art director for Muscle and Fitness magazine at Venice, training with her boyfriend. Later, in 1992, I ran into her at Hollywood Gold's Gym and she had become single. She and I began seeing each other and began training at kickboxing with a friend from the gym. She got some modeling jobs for me at the magazine so now everyone in the country knew who I was.

Something I would like to set the record straight on is steroids. Steroids have gotten a very bad rap in recent years and some of this is due to a former football legend's denunciation of them. An ailment he acquired that he attributed to his steroid use was actually something acquired from his lifestyle choices. I know, I've been there and come clean. He just wanted his legacy to remain intact and I can't blame him for that. I was around Gold's Gym when he was there and know who he was hanging around with. He just ruined the reputation of some really good strength-enhancing drugs. So I guess its up to whose reputation is more worth protecting: his, or some drugs? Well, I haven't mentioned his name have I? Anabolic steroids...are the single best anti-aging drugs developed ever. Virtually all competitive athletes use them, and they really are helpful. One just needs to use them wisely. I know bodybuilders that stack five drugs and just end up looking puffy. This can be hard on the heart. Too much of anything is not good. They make aging men much more muscular, virile, and are the best thing to pull one out of a training slump. They are really harmless; they're just synthetic versions of hormones we already have.

Life was good until the band broke up in 1992, and then I was lost. Plus, I would spend everything I made. So, in the same time period, to avoid bleeding my father for more money, I began to work as a prostitute. I made sure all my clients wore condoms and I tested regularly for HIV. At one time I had four transsexual girls I was seeing regularly; I loved them! They were all black and every one of them was extremely feminine and beautiful! I liked T-girls so much better than the gay dudes because they were just like girls-they were fun! I GOT TO BE ONE OF THE GIRLS!

This allowed me to rent a room in a condo in West Hollywood in 1993 with a nice gay guy and I was off the street.

It's funny (or not) that the one time I interacted with a guy sexually that was recreational, meaning not for money, I went to my monthly HIV testing--and found myself positive. I immediately quit hustling, denounced all my homosexual activity and managed to get a couple of personal training clients that paid enough to meet my expenses. I just wish I had thought of that earlier! It was uphill from here...but now I was a straight man living with HIV.

I decided that I would not be able to have any more girlfriends for the rest of whatever was left of my life and seeking something to devote myself to I settled upon classical music. I studied piano, orchestration, harmony and counterpoint from books and wrote, composing some surprisingly mature classical pieces right away. I no longer had to 'noodle' on an instrument to write music or listen to someone else's work in order to be inspired. Classical music taught me to compose "in my head." I had not only the song or piece melodically, but had an entire production before I ever touched an instrument!

I also got into Thai boxing with my friend from Gold's Gym in Hollywood who had tried out for my band earlier on. I liked my friend's style of fighting, because he didn't teach any of that pseudo-spiritual 'mumbo jumbo' that most of the other martial arts did. This style of Thai boxing was extremely savage in that most of the blows seemed to target certain bones to be broken. That was just what I needed! Y'know, I am not really a violent guy- in spite of my past. I am usually relaxed and even-tempered. It takes an act of God to make me feel like telling someone off. But I do find it stupid, however, when the legal authorities are called in whenever there is a fight between two grown men. I mean, are we really that unable to fend for ourselves? Men should be able to be men.

I also understand it when men want to keep their firearms. People should, by the rights given us in our Constitution, be able to carry firearms. I neither have nor want any guns; I don't need them. I can take care of myself. Besides, if it is my time to go it's my time. If it's not, there's nothing you can do to change this. This is called FAITH!

After acquiring HIV in 1993, I was searching for some spiritual meaning and started reading Carlos Castaneda books and M. Scott Peck (who made consistent Biblical references while admitting he had never read it). By this time I actually had a good personal training business going but still felt empty.

My mother (and her merry band of Christians) came down to a believer's convention in 1995 when I had moved into my own apartment. I was clearly searching for something; it seemed like my mother had the answer. She did. They offered me a place to stay in Tacoma. They accepted me into their church and I read the Holy Bible in three months. This was encouraged by M. Scott Peck and his inability to read the book he quoted so often. I fell in love with the words I read and gladly accepted the fact that I was not going to die, but was going to live and declare the works of the Lord.

I have a teaching method for reading the Bible for those not familiar with it. First thing is to start with Matthew chapter 5 and read the Sermon on the Mount. This will give you the whole thing in a nutshell. This is also what I would ask a Muslim to read if they were willing. Then read the first two books: Genesis and Exodus. Then go to the New Testament and read it all. It is not very long and can be read in a couple of evenings. After this, read the whole thing from the beginning at your own pace. This approach is to take in what is critical first and then work on a comprehensive knowledge of the text after that. If you do this, it will change you.

My songwriting changed dramatically during this time. My topic matter became more faith-oriented and my classical studies showed- even in my rock music. It was here that I wrote a song that was all acoustic guitars called 'Babylon." This song is about the Babylonian empire and its parallels with the modern world. Most people who hear my music still like this song the most. The vocal melody really is beautiful.

I worked at construction- something I had always hated- at this time. I decided my mother's church was not the place for me and moved to Seattle, and started working at Gold's Gym (I have always had a long standing affinity for Gold's Gyms) and found a new church. I soon moved in with another really beautiful Italian girl named Theresa I met there. I loved living in Seattle, as I write much better on rainy days. That kind of weather is just so inspiring- and I wrote some very good music there. She liked me very much and was relentless in her attempts to persuade me to start something with her. So I broke the news that I had HIV, and to my surprise- she was fine with it. I thought this odd, but girls have always liked me. This lasted about two years. The pressure from her father, and the demands of working on her refurbished houses left me estranged from her. Her father thought I wasn't a real man- being a musician and being Catholic- he hated my church. I moved into her back house and began to write some of the best music I have written to date.

It was here that I began to amass a great many books on Christian theology and was planning to become a pastor at one time. I was reading books that dissected the Christian ethos so minutely; it became very dull. After a while of doing this and going to Calvary Chapel, I decided that becoming a pastor was not for me. I just didn't want to preach to the choir. Telling Christians about Christ may be someone's calling- but it's just not mine. I need to reach the people who need to know Christ's redemption the most. People like me. Lost. This is what Jesus did.

Theresa was a flower person and her yard had every kind of colorful flower around in it you could imagine. One spring morning it was sunny, and there was a thunderstorm going on at the same time. The weather was alternately violent and peaceful. I immediately began writing at my piano. I composed a beautiful classical piece that echoed the weather and called it 'Spring Showers' and recorded it onto a MIDI file. This was a beautiful and very creative time in my life; I was lonely. I wish it were not so, but the really creative periods almost always are the loneliest times.

I have always attracted the hugest guys for friends in the gyms I've trained at. In Venice my friend Paul was a giant monster and got a role on a Sly Stallone movie. In Hollywood my friend Bob, who I scored a movie for, was like six-foot-four and maybe three hundred something. In Seattle, two friends of mine were between three hundred and four hundred pounds- so weird! Most of these guys liked me because of my bodybuilding knowledge. Nice guys, all of them. Paul was one of the homeless guys who actually walked over to my car one night in the Gold's Gym Venice parking lot when I was trying to put a plastic wrapper over my face in an attempt to kill myself. I had hit bottom and just wanted out. I saw him coming and was so embarrassed. I put the plastic away and said "How's it going Paul?" Thanks Paul- I mean it.

Another thing I have always done, especially since I have been made aware of most of the things I talk about in this book, is clash with classic alpha-males. It's really weird; I have absolutely no desire for the alpha-males position but just seem to fall into the position they want without trying. I think this is because I actually have acquired some degree of knowledge about an assortment of things: and this, combined with my physical presence, just sets them off. Alphas desperately want their position of control and just get beside themselves when someone like me is present. They like to be the tough guy, *and* the all-knowing one. They also like being the most attractive and I usually have them there too. Sorry alpha-guys, girls like me. They're so defensive; it just cracks me up. Sometimes they irritate me to the point of wanting to pick on them--and I have to try really hard not to. That would be a terrible way to present the Lord of my life to them. They just can be such passive-aggressive sissies, that's all. Whisperers and backbiters. Wannabes. Instead of trying so hard to be some image in your head, try just being yourself! It's really not that hard.

After four years in Seattle, in 2001 I started slowing down at work at Gold's and didn't know what was happening. I was converting from HIV to AIDS. I had left Theresa's and was renting a room in an apartment north of Seattle. One day, I fell asleep--and didn't wake up. The lady I was renting from called my mother when she couldn't get me up. I was rushed to the hospital. The doctor said to my mother that I probably wouldn't make it through the weekend.

I did, and spent the next four months in a hospice where everyone was gay (which made sense), but I was estranged and felt nobody understood me. I made friends with a couple of the girl volunteers. But the staff started telling them to stop coming by my room and going out on walks with me or they would be in trouble. This was ironic, because that's what they were there for! And, crazier than that, they really had a problem with me being straight and having THEIR disease! After leaving the hospice, I went through a series of sponsored motels and a MAPS house. They had the option to place me in a HOPWA (Housing Opportunities for People with AIDS) program where I could live by myself. My gay social worker decided I was unable to live by myself, even though I showed no signs of any inability to. So they put me in this house with many gay men for 'support,' despite my protests. I had already lived in the motels by myself! I mean, what kind of 'support' would I get from a bunch of giggling gay dudes? They, obviously, wanted me surrounded by them.

I met a girl from an ad in the paper and one evening we were sitting outside in her car kissing, and the next morning the man who ran the house told me I had to leave. I asked why, and he said that kissing girls outside in the driveway was unacceptable. He told me some of the other guys complained that I was groping her (I was). So what! Squeezing titties and kissing. We were two consenting adults! These gay guys poke each other right there in the house and I had to leave for this! Gay people, really tolerant!

You are not what you pretend to be. You are not victims. You really need everyone else to be gay too. Hypocrites!

After this mess, I finally rented a basement room in the home of someone I knew from Gold's Gym in Seattle. I had been so disoriented from being in the hospice and the MAPS house where they were relentless in trying to convince me I was gay. So now I *really* needed a girl in my life. Now, after Theresa, (and the titty girl) I knew I could have a girl. Being alone would not do.

I hate to admit this, but in 2002, I returned to prostitution after renting the basement room. I was receiving Social Security, which paid $500 a month. This wasn't enough to even take care of my basic needs, pay rent and keep a gym membership. I was angry at God, and needed to support myself better- even though it conflicted with my newfound Christian beliefs. I wasn't going to live on $500 a month! I just wish I had realized that this was my time of testing that every Christian called to preach the truth finds themselves in. I had gotten into an escort agency in Seattle that had me (also) seeing women, which, in my eyes at the time, was more acceptable than men. If I had realized that this was my trial period and stayed clean, I'm quite sure the Lord would have provided. I also learned that my AIDS was non-transferable to others, which, based on my behavior, was much testament to the grace of God as anything could be.

I was already dating someone else: a tall, blonde, striking girl. One problem, though: she treated me like dirt. So I roamed the internet for girls, and I eventually found my wife Angie on Match.com. Angie was not my ideal woman because she was pretty, but chubby. But when the blonde would torment me, Angie would be so sweet and reassuring. I felt something there. Angie had a wonderful voice (as she had gone to school for vocal performance) and I wanted to return to the studio to record the music I had been working on all these years. Most of the songwriting I do has always been for female voices, I guess, because I just like being around them. I was falling in love. Angie was the sweetest human I had ever met, and had never even had a boyfriend before and was thirty-eight! Her love was more pure than any I had experienced before. Even my mother said to me when she met Angie that she was so much sweeter than any of the 'models' I had dated before. She has really become part of my family, and I part of hers- something I had never done with any previous relationships. I felt Angie was the very thing I had needed and truly a gift from God. Angie's love for me still leaves me amazed.

Speaking on relationships and dating, I don't know. I've never dated. I can tell you that the single best way to a wonderful and fulfilling relationship is to find someone and befriend them first. Friendship really is the BEST way into a girls panties! No... really, I mean...into her heart. Love is never at first sight. Anything at first sight is something else, which could develop into love. The love I have for Angie could have only come from finding out who she is and admiring that first. At present, Angie and I have been together for nine years- much longer than I have ever been with anyone.

After one year together with Angie, we moved down to my old stomping grounds in Hollywood and began recording with Mark Hashimoto. I had played in bands with Mark in high school and after that. He was one of the ones who ousted me from the band "Sweat" in 1985 because of my substance addiction- he was the one that counseled me about it. Angie's amazing voice really made the songs I had written shine. I really couldn't have found a better vocalist anywhere. We used a form of my previous band name and called ourselves SWET. In a year and a half we had an album called "Hearts on Fire," and although we had a sure fire Barbara Streisand-type hit on it that started out as a piano concerto called "Jerusalem," we were sure the hit would be the rocker "We are Evil." Angie really brought an old song of mine, "Something New," to life and made it a really hard-hitting punchy song- maybe the best on the album. Very 'Heart-' like as Angie sings a lot like Anne Wilson of 'Heart.'

As most of my songs were committed to memory, I had forgotten the verses on a great song I had written at Theresa's, called "Pharisee." So I had to rewrite verses on this song, which addressed the modern Christian church. One of the best written songs I've done, it isn't really flattering towards the church, but is an appeal to return to the real message of what Christ has done.

The following year Mark had voiced that he wanted to do a country or country/rock project, and I had just the songs to do that. So we went in and recorded "Country Fried"- a four song country record. Some VERY *sexy* country songs! We called ourselves "Cowboy Monkeys." One song was "That side of Me": an excellent country rocker in three effortless key changes. It reflected the times when I had been on the street in Hollywood, and my fighting times when I was younger. Another was "My Desire": a song about Angie that reflected her love for me; it's a song that makes me weepy still.

After the country record, I recorded two classical pieces I had stored on MIDI files. One of them was "Spring Showers," mentioned earlier, and another was "Our Time": a piece written in Theresa's backhouse out of pure heartache and loneliness. "Our Time" was an imagined relationship that later materialized in Angie.

I later recorded a record with some of my older dance songs, like "Venice Beach" and "Diamonds and You," with its blistering guitar solo. "Venice Beach" really rocks the house! We now had a dance record, and called it "Dancing with You". After copywriting the songs recorded every year, I would mail packages out to publishers and record labels. The responses were either, "You're an excellent songwriter--just not right for us," or none at all.

So we put together three 'myspace' sites, one for pop/rock and dance music and called it 'Swet'. Another is 'Cowboy Monkeys' for the country recordings, and the last one is 'Clifford James,' which has some of my classical pieces. More to come.

It was good to be back where I called home for so many years and Gold's in Hollywood is probably the best equipped gym anywhere. The only problem is scenery. Don't get me wrong- there are very lovely girls that train there- but they are sooo outnumbered by the gay guys. Everywhere you look there's a guy stretching in some provocative position, to get your attention. It just gets gross after a while. I mean, I understand, I was part of that, years ago, and it's still with me isn't it? It's just that one of the perks of being in the gym environment is getting to see all the little brown yummys in their skimpy little workout outfits just sweating and panting and....!

By the way, one thing I did want to mention is my affinity for marijuana. It really is a 'take it or leave it' kind of thing for me. I quit smoking it in 1977 because it made my assertive abilities disappear, only to resume it when returning to Los Angeles in 2003. Pot is the BEST thing to do for a stressful day; in seconds you're relaxed and even humorous. I am extremely creative when I smoke. Ideas fly right in and sometimes right out. I can't count the times I have had a groundbreaking idea when high, and by the time I get to my phone (to type it in) or get to the guitar I have forgotten what I was doing! But one thing's for sure: pot is the BEST thing for sex anywhere! If you haven't had sex while high on pot, you've really missed something. I'd say pot increases all of your body's sensations tenfold and you feel everything so much more intensely. That means every-thing!

I found a group of HIV-infected heterosexual people online and began to go to meetings and events with Angie in 2004. One thing I learned at one of these meetings is the effect of HIV meds on the waistline. I had noticed that my tiny comma waist wasn't coming back so quickly and they said it is common for the meds to store sub-muscular fat around the abdomen. Damn!

Angie soon got a job at a prominent medical center and I began reading books on politics; I realized I had a mission. 2003 to

2008 was spent in the studio and now I needed to do something else. This new direction was partially due to Mark Hashimoto's death. He was very overweight and this finally caught up with him. Sitting in front of a mixing board working on other people's projects does not keep one in shape. He had a heart attack that was fatal. I wished I had lived closer and could have gotten him into a gym. He was a man I really admired for his honesty. I miss him very much- as good a friend as I've ever had.

I had always been a political creature from early on and read voraciously. Now I had an outlet for this. I went to broadcasting school and decided that politics and faith-related things were going to be my main focus from now on. Most of my songs are faith-based anyway. I wrote several monologues that upon becoming numerous enough, became this book.

So...just who are your star crushes? C'mon--you have them. Mine have been kinda weird. Angela Davis was an early one. To this day girls with afros really drive me wild. Tina Turner was another. Then Cher. When I saw Cher onstage with a rose tattoo on her ass I absolutely had to do the same thing- only mine is a tulip. Yes, that was during my girlie phase. Of course, after that came many more (NOTE: *not* on the same location!). I think some of this is because I just love it when I see tattoos on girls. They're sooo sexy! The more provocative positioning of the tattoo, the better. They're just so addicting! I know, they will look really bad when I am old and wrinkly but I think I am doing a lot to ensure that this never comes. Just how many groups of people will hate me after hearing what this book has to say?

Notice I didn't say reading it? This is because people who have a pre-determined mindset don't want it challenged. They will talk much trash about things they have never opened their minds up to experiencing. If people would just be willing to hear opposing views to their own (except for the Islamic point of view) this would be a better world. Think about all the problems that would vanish with just this one change!

One thing that has never come easy for me is respect. Respect for, well, someone's position for one thing- be it a supervisor, someone's office or any kind of authority. I do realize that an office of any kind gives one the authority to make decisions and that they be followed. Respect for an authority's position is very biblical. Michael, the Archangel, when debating with Satan, did not hurl a reviling accusation, but instead said "The Lord rebuke you." I just have always had no respect for authority. It's a shame, but sometimes it's hard to respect someone when you know you can beat their ass and they are disagreeable anyway. I guess this is the Cro-Magnon in me coming out. It's a natural outgrowth (or a holdover) of the way I was raised; I'm trying to change this.

Even President Obama deserves the respect he has for his office. Believe it or not, God put him there. When people cannot control their own passions there needs to be some discipline imposed from somewhere.

For twenty years, I had been living on the bottom of the world and now I had a purpose. AIDS is no longer killing people because the meds work better now. I am not in denial about having AIDS; I just don't want it to take center stage in my life. I'm supposed to go for blood work every three months, and I wait for, like, a year and a half. It's always the same thing anyway, my T-cell count is 400 to 700 (recently 800) and my viral load (meaning the amount of the virus that is in the blood) registers undetectable. I am told this has something to do with the fact that I exercise regularly and eat healthy. I stopped ejaculating around the time of my conversion, which I think is a gift from God, as this protects Angie. Orgasms have never been that necessary for me anyway, as I have always taken the role of the server rather than the serviced and often neglected my own gratification for the girl's. So I guess if God had to strike someone with something like this- well, I guess I'm your man.

I would like you to know something important. I have had every reason to turn away from the Christian faith there is. I went to churches with one of my girlfriends in the eighties and we would hear speakers who would witness to us and say how great their life had become after having given themselves to Christ. (Look, if your life is running smoothly in Lucifer's world...I think he leaves them alone because they're not a threat to him) My life *got worse*, and has remained such. Almost 22 years since I accepted Jesus and my life has been a living hell! But when I listen to those types of Christians now, I almost have to feel for them. They seem so undeveloped that I fear for them when things go really bad for us- and I know it will go that way. I will stand and they will fall and I can see that. When the Antichrist comes and makes his temporary peace, many of them will gladly succumb and accept him because they will value their peace more than anything else. All they seem to know is complacency and comfort. For temporary security, they will sacrifice their liberties, *and their eternity!*. When Jesus comes to call his own to him, I will be called and they will not, and most of them have been Christians all their lives! Just like 'lay communists,' there are 'lay Christians' too. The biggest misconception about the Christian walk is that it is a cure to worldly problems. Actually, it provides no worldly guarantee of that, but it does promise a spiritual 'advisor,' (the Holy Spirit) who will prompt your heart in day-to-day situations to divert you from troubles. Whether you listen or not is still up to you. Many of us don't as we are all sinful in our desires (I am no exception!).

I also have every reason to lack faith there is. Pretty much all my prayers go unanswered (some things actually have been answered; I prayed for a companion and found Angie *and got an incredible vocalist to boot!*). I just know that my prayers are mostly pleading, but God sees all and I do not. If some of my prayers go unanswered it means that this would interfere with another plan my

Father has for me *or someone else* (the world doesn't revolve around me, waa waa!), and probably wouldn't work the way I think it would anyway. My God is smarter than me. He knows the end from the beginning.

I have understanding, through the school of hard knocks, of right from wrong and I could see how good people were deluded into thinking good things were bad. I also can see why bad things were attractive. I had been there and seen the results of this. I have decided that drugs, with the exception of pot, are useless (and maybe even that!). I think bikers are pussies and none of them can fight. I certainly do not look up to any of them anymore. I currently drink- but watch how much. I set limits. As I have made clear, I have been an alcoholic and know I am prone to abuse. I do not buy the "I am powerless" mantra of Alcoholics Anonymous. I AM NOT POWERLESS! God gave me a will. I am not an alcoholic. I was.

I really do love people and need to communicate the things I have learned to them. When I met Angie, she was someone that always gave people the benefit of the doubt. I soon fixed that. I personally do not give people the benefit of the doubt anymore as I know the sinful nature of man; I often know what they are thinking already. I really am not concerned with what anyone thinks of me at all. I feel that respect is earned, and should be. I am more than ready to earn your respect.

I read once that a renowned Italian general said, "A great man is a man that has mastery over his passions." This has stuck with me ever since. Can you do this? *This is almost impossible for me!* Some passions are good, like music and fitness. So what are the destructive passions I just can't shake? Well, smoking pot has been one (I'm not smoking now- but like Arnold says "I'll be back"). Undressing girls with my eyes is another (and I often go well beyond undressing, and on into a whole lascivious daydream!). Some of this is due to the fact that Angie is quite overweight. I do love her with *all my heart,* but this is hard.... (It is also biblically suggested that God chooses our mates!). I was more than happy to have her when I needed someone!... Jesus says we are sinning when we look on a woman lustfully (*forgive me Father!*). I do not nor have ever cheated on my girlfriends but the *gazing*....God! If I could just stop this! The coffee shop I go to has got to be a hub of the loveliest girls in Los Angeles! And LA is where all the beauties go to be models and actresses! The girls that live in this Beverly Hills neighborhood are *gorgeous* as are the girls that work nearby. I see some of them that are a kind of black and Asian mix (*shivers!*) and Asian or black girls with small breasts make me crazy. And almost any girls with black (or dark brown) hair, and this *is* LA so they're not wearing *anything!* I've befriended many of them and some of them 'hit' on me making it difficult. There are several modeling agencies in nearby high rises and sometimes the shop is full of lots'a little brown (and white) yummy's (And I'm NOT telling you where it is... *it's my little secret...*). Anyway, this doesn't help. So, do you want to know what I'm doing about this? I'm writing this book. Look at the type of man I am portraying as the kind of man we all should be. If I'm going to tell you to live like this, well I certainly better be! Self imposed accountability. Whatever works.

People new to the idea of Christian belief often ask, "Do you hear from God?" I answer no. But I think I do. My mother at church used to come in and say, "I talked to God this morning..." and left me bewildered. I recently asked her how she hears from God and she said she didn't hear words, just prompts. Interesting. Sometimes I do hear words that sound like they're from God. They always turn out to be false in that they never come true, or haven't

yet anyway. I suspect outside interference. I do things I feel I need to do. I agree that this is God talking to me, prompts. Our scriptures tell us this is the Holy Spirit.

Here's a prompt for you. I have AIDS. I am not a victim. I acquired this because I was trying to be something I am not and accept full responsibility. I thought sex with men would be interesting, daring and fun; it really wasn't. Most of it was boring and felt stupid. I definitely wouldn't advise it for someone just wanting to experiment. Find something that actually is fun and interesting.

Something I've noticed in myself is that I'm not thankful enough; I've been given much. I have been attractive and have been given much in the way of talents. Not all people get to have this. I'm always trying to be more. I thank God that He removed my ability to communicate AIDS to others. I think that my musical abilities should have been recognized earlier. I really am at the top of my craft and my songs and music are beautiful! Yet I've never been able to make a living out of it. I'm just not a business-minded person--and this has hurt me. I'm an artist. I did succeed at bodybuilding; I just don't think that was worth anything. All it did was feed my exhibitionistic weirdness. I think I still want that rock star life. Do I really have to give up that dream just because I'm fifty-four?

I have had a hard life. This is probably why I am relatively fearless. I have absolutely no fear of anybody. I am determined to walk through life strong and confident. My life has been a series of mistakes and bad decisions. I have never cared much about money-and I regret this. I will now. Handling money wisely is part of being a responsible adult. Biblically speaking, the money we earn is God's anyways- we should take it seriously. I'm sorry I have done the things I have and will do them no longer. I am a changed man. Whatever the future holds I know it will now be somewhere that I was meant to be from the beginning. I have been prepared for this time. I have been developed into someone tough and loving- a bit hard on others, but also forgiving. I have done shameful and destructive things and regret them. I know how easy it is to be bad and really think you are good. Sorry...none of us are.

We can be forgiven if we ask Jesus to be the Lord of our lives and cleanse us of all our sins . . . and that's what counts. God loves every one of us.

Thank you Jesus for saving my life. I'm sorry I have shamed you. Do not let me come before you empty handed.

Afterword

And Men Loved the Darkness

"And this is the condemnation, that the light has come into the world, and men loved darkness rather than the light because their deeds were evil, for everyone practicing evil hates the light and does not come to the light lest his deeds be exposed." "He who does the truth comes to the light that his deeds may be clearly seen, that they have been done in God."

John 3: 19-22 (New King James)

"But of that day and hour no one knows, not even the angels of heaven, nor the Son, but the Father alone. For the coming of the Son of Man will be just like the days of Noah. For as in those days...they were eating and drinking, marrying and giving in marriage, until the day that Noah entered the ark, and they did not understand until the flood came and took them all away; so will the coming of the Son of Man be."

-Jesus Christ

"You will be hearing of wars and rumors of wars. See that you are not frightened, for *these things* must take place, but *that* is not yet the end. For nation will rise against nation, and kingdom against kingdom, and in various places there will be famines and earthquakes. But all these are merely the beginning of birth pangs."

-Jesus Christ

Let's not forget about what Jesus said about twenty centuries ago regarding earthquakes and famines. In a 15-month span between 2010-March 2011, the world has seen massive earthquakes in Chile, Haiti, Japan, Pakistan and Myanmar, to name a few. Famines have led to uprisings in Egypt and Libya and much of North Africa is hungry including Kenya and the Sahel. Bangladesh and Afghanistan have been in constant famine. Mexico is always starving- that's why they sneak over here to sweat in our fields. Food prices are currently rising to the degree that we will see more famine soon- even in our own country and it will be due to an economic collapse along with severe flooding as well as the EPA restricting planting and harvesting in the most fertile valley, San Joaquin CA, due to the killing of the smelt fish in irrigation lines. As well as burning our food supply in our gas tanks. And with mammoth storms destroying our farmlands Obama has just sent 50,000 metric tons of wheat to his 'we hate America' buddies in Jordan. Somebody wants us desperate. How could Jesus have all this foreknowledge without being the "Son of God?"

Do you know what all these tornadoes and fires and earthquakes are? This really is the time of the end and God wants us all to cry out to him. We are so full of anger and disappointment that we think God has forsaken us. This is what I thought when I left the hospice and found myself having to live on nothing and the way I felt in the Gold's Gym parking lot when I tried to kill myself... This is God's blessing! He LOVES you and does not want to let you go. If he has to do things like this for you to WAKE UP then so be it! WAKE UP!!!

I am going to ask you to think about some things here. In Japan, the elderly are reverently treated and seem to warrant this respect. In the US our seniors are babbling, drooling incoherents for the most part. Do you know why? Because they experience life sitting in front of their indoctrination boxes where it is simply presented to them. Then when they are forced to go somewhere and participate in life they become confused. After the 9.0 quake in March, 2011 that ruined most of Japan, people reached out to help one another. They were calm and thought about what to do next. People would monitor how much water they would buy because they knew there was a limited supply, and many needy people. The Japanese displayed their unity because of their willingness to endure, to persevere, to be steadfast, to respect and honor each other. And the fact is that there is such a thing as SHAME in their culture!

In the United States, self interest rules. In America we have *no shame*. What happened in 1992 when Los Angeles erupted in the Rodney King riots? There was looting, that had nothing to do with the King decision. The police were not stopping them because they lacked personnel. What happened in New Orleans after Hurricane Katrina hit? Looting. Why are Americans so willing to sue their neighbors or businesses over almost anything? Remember what I said in an earlier chapter about Beverly Hills women running into ladies in wheelchairs and pushing strollers? The lady who was walking and texting and fell into the pool in the mall and subsequently wanted to sue the mall? Americans are children and can only see as far as 'more for me right now.'

I noticed that there is a new movie out called 'Arthur.' Hold it,... isn't that an old movie? Yeah, Dudley Moore, remember? It's really one of the stupidest, imbecilic movies ever to grace the silver screen. Why did they decide to do a remake of *this*? It's because they know it will sell. Why do they know it will sell? It's because the Hollywood big shots know you are stupid enough to see it.

I'm going to be honest with you here. I really don't think most of you out there are ready for freedom and would do much better under authoritarian rule. I mean it!!! So many of you cannot control your impulses and act just like children, moseying through life like lemmings, acting on every impulse you have, and really are sheep just heading for the slaughterhouse. You need supervision- or you will hurt others- even yourself!

However, some of you *are* independent thinkers. Just imagine if we had a society full of independent thinkers- oh, wait- wasn't that the America our parents grew up in? Well,.. maybe our parents' parents.

"For when they speak great swelling words of emptiness, they allure through the lusts of the flesh, through lewdness, the ones who have actually escaped from those who live in error.

While they promise them liberty when they themselves are slaves to utter corruption, for a man is the slave of whatever masters him."

2 Peter 2: 18-19

While *your* world is crumbling, you are watching the *dumbest* movies and screaming over your sports teams. This is *insane* and unless you wake up you will *deserve everything that happens to you!* We now have, in the White House, a Marxist president that *you* elected who wants to bring America to her knees and to prep the entire Middle East for a Muslim Brotherhood takeover and the destruction of Israel. This will eventually lead to Shariah law, an Islamic caliphate and a communist takeover of America. We *will* have a dictator. You *will* lose the ability to choose how you live your life.

Also, there is a great financial collapse happening right now under your nose. It's being attempted by multiple perpetrators. The most notable is former SEIU official Stephen Lerner. His decision to destroy JP Morgan, nuke the stock market and weaken Wall Street is potentially creating the conditions necessary for a redistribution of wealth and a change in government creating a dictatorship. This is a plan to destabilize the whole country by organizing "mass mortgage default," causing a collapse of the banks and as a result, the businesses that use them. He has also suggested that students do the same thing regarding their student loans. This would have a devastating effect on our entire economy. This will affect you, because it will affect your employers. If Mr. Lerner fails, there are many others who are trying to do the same thing. ACORN is still active (despite their recent defunding; they just regrouped under different names).

The Pittsburgh Tribune-Review reports that business leaders and Republican politicians accused President Obama of punishing GOP (Republican) states by trying to block Boeing from opening a major aircraft plant in South Carolina. South Carolina is a right to work state (union membership not mandatory) and they want to compel Boeing to open a plant, instead, in Washington State (union mandatory). The National Labor Relations Board has decided that Boeing opening a plant in South Carolina is union busting and retaliating for past strikes at its Puget Sound (Washington) facilities. Senator Jim DeMint said "It is absurd, in this country that represents free enterprise, that one unaccountable, unelected, unconfirmed acting general council can threaten thousands of jobs. This is something you would expect in a third world country. This is thuggery at its worst." *Do you see what I am saying, people?* Unions are ruining our country and our president IS a Marxist/communist and *does* want to bring everyone living in this country to dependence on the state and state run unions, eventually leveling the playing field between ALL countries and place himself in a position of power like has not been seen before. He and many others WANT America to be a third world country and are doing their best to bring us there. They are right now using natural disasters (presumably, conspiracy people insist they already have the technology to manipulate these things see HAARP) to gain control of the worlds food supply so they can simply direct it to wherever they please (food rationing). It is said that Hurricane Katrina was the first trial run of this and if this is so, I would say that the Japanese (another American ally) earthquake could be another. Well hooooray! As of Obama's election we now have a government just like Mexico! If you deny this you are f**king STUPID and have your head up your ass! My dear friends PLEASE pull your head out of your ass and wake up! You will not be able to *stay out of it* much longer. Very soon YOU will have to choose sides as there will not be ANY middle ground. THAT... is what they are preparing. At some point everyone will be able to see where you are. That way they can identify you/us. Love those who *love you*. Turn away from those who only want to *use* you. Love is wisdom.

Look, hardship IS coming your way and the only reason you don't know about it yet is because they have *successfully* distracted you with 'everything's going to be okay'- just keep having fun! Hardship *is* coming your way. This tribulation is the only way people change. We need to stop thinking of only ourselves. 'Everything you think you have will be taken.' That is biblical. They want you unprepared, uninformed and unaware. *And you are!*

The Federal Reserve (not a federal institution but a private bank) is currently printing money on a scale not seen in history. They are doing this to supposedly help bring us out of the recession. What this does is steal your money! This causes inflation of all goods like gas, groceries and clothing. As of May 2011 THEY HAVE STOLEN 20 PERCENT OF YOUR MONEY BY DOING THIS. That's right, every dollar you have is now worth 80 cents! It will soon be worth much less. A bag of rice will cost everything you have.

Melrose Avenue in Los Angeles has always been one of the trendy streets. In the seventies it was a hub of used clothing, book and record stores and had many punk rock clubs. In the eighties and nineties major outlets like Urban Outfitters started coming in, the clubs closed and it became a shopping area for the trendiest clothes and had many outdoor restaurants. On any weekend the avenue was packed. Venice CA has always had homeless people (I know, I was one) but has always been the funky place for street vendors and even clothing sales. There have always been street artists painting people or pantomime artists and guys juggling chainsaws. The muscle pit has always been an attraction and the basketball courts are famous. The Bolivian music store and rasta shops were fun not to mention the beach which is huge and the surfing is great. People come to see Venice beach from all over the world (and pay guys like I was to pose for pictures with them).

One recent weekend my wife and I decided to go out to Venice and needed to pass through Melrose to get there. This was one of many times I have been on Melrose in recent times and we both noticed that most all the stores had 'for lease' signs on the front. The avenue was desolate. Restaurants and shops were closed and the street was empty. We were puzzled. We continued on to Venice and when we arrived we immediately noticed all the homeless people. I mean, I always saw them out there but I hadn't been in a couple of years and the sheer volume was astounding! There were police on every corner and most of them had someone in cuffs. There were booths set up for donations to feed the homeless, there were young girls sleeping together under single sleeping bags and most of the vendor booths were taken over by panhandlers. I looked at my wife and noticed she was crying. "What's wrong?" I asked... "Cliff...they're winning," she replied.

In the book of Revelation, it says, "All your riches, your gold and silver will come to nothing in but a day." If you open your eyes you will see the beginning of this in the price of gasoline. This is *only* the beginning. Very soon it will be food, cotton, everything that is delivered by trucks (which is everything). All this is happening while you are following celebrities' lives and watching reality TV, like stupid bumbling idiots.

"But know this that in the last day's perilous times will come: For men will be lovers of themselves, lovers of money, boasters, proud, blasphemers, disobedient to parents, unthankful, unholy, unloving, unforgiving, slanderers, without self control, brutal, despisers of good, traitors, headstrong, haughty, lovers of pleasure rather than lovers of God."

2 Timothy 1-4

On April 6, 2011, a 42-year-old San Francisco Giants fan was brutally beaten outside Dodger stadium in Los Angeles and suffered severe trauma to the frontal lobe of his brain. As of two weeks after the fact, he remains in a coma. He has 2 children.

My dear friends,...what has happened to us?.......

Look at the scriptures I have given you in this book (even in just this afterword) and tell me if every one of them doesn't reflect the time we are living in right now to a tee. These scriptures were written centuries ago! I want it to dawn on you that this, of *all times*, is the dumbest time to be an atheist or someone that just can't bring themselves to see that Jesus is the one that came to save you from yourself! It is simply *unintelligent* not to believe in Jesus as savior anymore!

"The fool hath said in his heart 'there is no God'."

As I've mentioned in this book many times in different ways, Israel and the Jewish people are here partly to give US an image of WHO we are. From the people that looked to foreign gods in the wilderness to apostates and revolutionaries, we are to look to them to see where we are both in our hearts and in the world. As Israel goes we go. *Get it? They are a mirror image of us!*

Remember, God said about Israel in Genesis 12:3 "I will bless those that bless you and curse those that curse you." They are his chosen.

Right now Israel is being surrounded by her enemies and it is because the forces of Islam are regrouping now and they are being helped by our president. President Obama has just said that he feels that Israel needs to return to the Palestinian/Israeli division of 1967 which was before the six day war which gave Israel her current borders and was a great victory. To return to the borders before the six day war would mean giving up the Golan Heights which would make Israel indefensible and reduce all of their land to an eight mile stretch. They are surrounded right now by Nations that want their extermination!

What do you think about the fact that Christians are being killed en-masse in Muslim nations but never the other way around? Do you also know that Israel never asks the US for help defending themselves? They stand on their own. This is in contrast to these Islamic countries that whine and snivel and beg the US to help them supplant their dictators. F**king pussies!

Do you think that if Israel went ahead and ceded their borders to the 1967 situation that Hamas and the Palestinian people would be satisfied? Or do you think they would then want to bring it back to the 1948 situation (no existing Israel at all).

Do you know that there have never existed a people, culture, language or history as the Palestinian people? They ARE an invented people. Prior to 1967 the residents of the West Bank were Jordanians, the Golan Heights were Syrian and in Gaza they were Egyptian. After '67 they rewrote history and the Arabs there were not given permission to return to their homeland and were refugees by their own countries purposefully to use for the eventual destruction of Israel. They claimed to be under Israeli occupation but if you actually go to most of the Palestinians that DO want peace, THEY *like* living under Israeli law. They have a much better life there than they would under Islamic law in Arabia. Hamas thinks otherwise. The Muslim Brotherhood thinks otherwise.

How about this, in 2005 under pressure from the US, Israel withdrew from Gaza turning governance over to the citizens who promptly (in their hatred) burned working farms and businesses that would have helped *them*. Then they worked on electing Hamas for leadership! What does this tell you? Do these people even *want* to prosper? They *live* for their hatred of Israel and the west. Anyone that lives free. I mean, if you were enslaved, wouldn't you resent anyone free? Not if you are a mature, rational person, but....

Mohammed in 622 made a treaty for 10 yrs with the Qurayish people in Mecca and later when he had gained sufficient strength and numbers in 630 went back on his promise, conquered Mecca and cut the heads off the remaining Qurayish. Again...Mohammed IS the model for Muslim men. LIARS!

Do you also know that a Palestinian authority Hamas official has updated from 72 to 2.5 million the number of virgins given a martyr? Now why would god suddenly do that? Tell me something else (shhh... we won't tell anyone!) do you agree with me that Islam is the STUPIDEST religion ever invented!!! The followers of this belief system that want the destruction of others have to be cowards or *retards!* There's just no other excuse! These are people that *do not want* to live in a civilized society. Hateful bastards! How can I love these people Jesus! How can you ask me to? Why do you love us? Are you crazy?!! You know how hateful we can be!

All this is as much to illustrate to you what is happening in our hearts. As Israel goes in the flesh- we go in our hearts and minds. The people doing this want to isolate us and eventually exterminate us as well. They want to eliminate countries borders to prepare for a one world leader. President Obama is now fast tracking us toward this goal and if he is re-elected (which I believe he will be, I just think most of you are too unaware) I predict he will become crazy, almost maniacal in his grandiosity and will do *everything* he can, knowing it's his last term as US president, unless he can (or needs to) manipulate that too. He wants to rule the world. Whether or not he is *the one* remains to be seen. The look of hatred on his face when confronted with an irate Benjamin Netanyahu (the Israeli Prime Minister) after announcing his plans told me he has very big aspirations.

Here's how far this Jew hatred has gone even in the US. In San Francisco they are trying to get a bill passed outlawing male circumcision! Wow! The same thing has been discussed in Santa Monica. Hey now, that's MY turf!! I don't know about you but I don't miss my foreskin and have had absolutely no health problems (the excuse they are using to implement this) related to it's removal. Look for more similar things to come. These monsters want the entire world to hate the Jews. They really want to drag as many down into the pit of suffering they're going into with them they can. Please, my loved ones, DO NOT buy into this stupidity. Glenn Beck brought light to this story.

Well here's another one from him (can you tell, I really like this guy?). There is now a revitalized NAZI party in Egypt along with a new party (that really is just the Muslim Brotherhood) called the 'Freedom & Justice Party.' Hmmm,... freedom & justice...NAZI...remember what I said in chapter 11 (the long one) about their names for organizations...the LIES! The misinformation!

Side note; Islamic law removes the possibility for repentance (cutting off hands for thievery, stoning to death for adultery). By the way...this is exactly what we all need to do...repent. This makes way for the most beautiful thing, which is... forgiveness.

Another side note; the US has already gotten involved in Syria and their conflict and now President Obama is waging a 'covert' war in Yemen helping the revolutionaries there. So first Egypt, Algeria, the Ivory Coast, then Libya and now in Yemen. Even Hillary Clinton said that the Egyptians are not doing what we thought they would with their newfound freedom (example: killing Christians, burning churches, welcoming in the Muslim Brotherhood to form a more perfect union). Duh!! They're MUSLIM stupid! OUR YOUNG MEN AND WOMEN ARE OVER IN THE MIDDLE EAST HELPING THEM BUILD THEIR CALIPHATE SO THEY CAN THEN BE POWERFUL ENOUGH TO COME OVER HERE AND DESTROY US!!! They are led to believe they are helping these people gain freedoms they really are not at all interested in. Just like the communists, they want to be rulers! LIARS!!!

YOU ARE BEING LIED TO! And most of you don't care because you can't see beyond your immediate wants! Again...*you will deserve everything that happens to you.*

Our scriptures tell us that in THIS time they will soon be saying "Peace and safety" and there will be a treaty made that will be broken after three and a half years and then there will *be no* peace or security.

Dietrich Bonhoeffer said at the time of the dress rehearsal for *this time* (WWII and Hitler), "Silence in the face of evil, *is evil.* Not to speak, *is* to speak, not to stand *is* to stand."

My dear loved ones, it is the time of the end of all things and you *must* make up your minds and stand *firm* on your decision.

Satan is tricky. Recently a Harold Camping, the head of the Family Radio Broadcasting Network has predicted that the world will end and judgment day will be upon us on May 21, 2011. This braindeath is being publicized to trivialize the truth. It will probably accomplish just that. Remember the scripture I gave you at the beginning of this Afterword "But of that day and hour no one knows, not even the angels of heaven, nor the Son, but the Father alone?" Well here's another one for you. "Man looks on the outward appearance of things but God searches the hearts." Think about this please. "False prophets shall rise from among you," our scriptures tell us.

Right now every country that can be, is becoming destabilized. This is being brought on by organized rioting and the reasons for this protesting varies but its main goal is to create a vacuum in every country to be filled at some point by a world leader who will make a peace treaty for seven years that will be broken halfway through (3,1/2 yrs). The people doing the rioting will have no idea what they are REALLY doing, they will be just like the protestors in Greece or Libya and think they are trying to keep their entitlements or win democracy because they will be responding to propaganda fed them. This destabilizing of the nations is for a massive restructuring that will be taking place. Our scriptures tells us of ten kings in the end time that will be in power so look for a ten 'zone' structure of our entire world to come to pass. And then a charismatic leader that seems to have the solution to all the worlds' problems. Know he is doomed even though he seems to 'have everything under control.' This is the 'man of lawlessness' that will take all the people who have not seen love and have not seen their own sin with him and this is the great winepress where the good wine is strained from the grapes. The evil in their hearts will follow him (into eternal torment) and the truly repentant will know they are loved and will endure whatever they have to- to secure their eternal bliss with their savior.

Most of us are not old enough to remember when the United States was just like Japan. I am. But in my youth, things were already beginning to change and I've told you why. Now I'm telling you, you don't even have the foundation for true maturity, which is love. I'm also telling you that neither did I. I'm not saying that I am the most mature person around or that all of my intentions are pure, because this would be lying to you-and I'm not willing to do that. I love you. I have been where you are. Remember that... I would say that what changed me was finding Christ and reading my Bible, but I'm not quite sure that was the whole of it either. Maybe the humiliating nature of my particular sins led to a repentance that made me find out how to truly love you, when before I had nothing but disdain for you. The reason I say this is because I'm certain that even Christians I have known are not fully up to the task of loving you as I do. And, yes, this even goes for all the guys I've addressed: why do you think I'm so hard on you? I just think women are beautiful and special and should be treated as such. They are truly God's gift to us men.

Actually, there are two America's living side by side as evidenced in Joplin, Missouri. After 75% of the town was destroyed by tornadoes there were people that began to loot the ravaged houses. And then there were people that came from Alabama and Texas and all around the neighboring states to help with anything they could. Most of these were churchgoers (yes there ARE great churches you just have to find them!). These are the people that made America exceptional! They took the time away from their own needs to provide for others. Beautiful. These were NOT the people that stand by when girls are fighting and kicking each other in the face and take video's with their cell phones. These are the people that would try to stop the fighting and make peace. These are not the people that try to sue one another but instead, try to help each other. These are the people that will inherit eternal life.

One part of why these disasters are happening is to show the disparity between good and evil. To make it clear what good people do and what evil people do. The dark is getting darker and the light...brighter. Love IS going to win in the end my dear friends. You're not here to observe- but to participate. The people in Joplin were helped by other PEOPLE, not FEMA. Not the government.

I know people have their needs, as do I. People are taught by their churches that fornication (much maligned in the New Testament) means pre or extramarital sex. Extramarital sex is lying and is a terrible thing to do. Look fornication up in the original Greek (that the New Testament was written in) and you will find that it meant prostitution. To sell your intimacy for money is shameful. I have done this with men and women. In today's world people are often single and still have a need for intimacy. I'm just addressing the fact that people ARE GOING TO HAVE SEX with people they are not married to, and that most of them are *not going* to marry someone they don't want to spend the rest of their lives with just for the intimacy. This backs up the Biblical fact that "all have sinned and fallen short of the glory of God."

Many are driven away from coming to know their Lord for this very reason, and this breaks my heart. Jesus did not condemn the Samaritan woman at the well, although he acknowledged that her current man was not her husband and that she had been married five times. He befriended Mary Magdalene WHO EVEN WAS A PROSTITUTE! David had concubines. Look that up and tell me what they're for. David married Bathsheba after he was already married and had Solomon with her.

I'm not encouraging you to be promiscuous, but not to feel tormented for having sexual urges and having acted on them. Some people are not ready for monogamy; there are just not enough quality people around these days. If you lie about it, this is a problem. It is very important that we be honest in ALL things. Many modern churches have gotten so prideful that they actually drive people away for things that even *they* do. This is shameful. They expect people to be pure that haven't even come to know Jesus yet. Nobody comes in this way; we all are sinful. Please--do not knowingly pass an STD on to someone that does not know it. Be pure in your heart- and in your body- if you can. Do not let the church drive you away from Jesus. They do not always know what they are talking about. There is no scripture in the Holy Bible that says 'do not have sex until you are married.' Yet church people have insisted this is true for centuries! Christians are sinners like everyone else and the sinful nature of people likes to elevate themselves above the rest of their brothers and sisters. We are not all going to be as perfect or pure as we want to be. Jesus knows we are all sinful, and he loves us still.

We just must continue to be brutally honest with Him- and ourselves. Monogamy in marriage is truly the only loving and decent way of living life and is the way we should all choose. We must all be obedient to Jesus when we are spiritually developed enough to do so. This simply cannot be expected of a newcomer and it is not my calling to elicit obedience from you. I am after your hearts and minds. I love you.

So, in closing, I'm giving you a choice here. Whoever you are, I do not think you are someone who would like to be somebody else's servant. I have told you what is happening all over the world and in your own country. So you have a choice. You can continue to bury your head in the sand and party, or whatever it is that you do, or you can do something to become a servant of Christ and help others. Thanks to the internet, you can find anything you want about whatever you need and this will empower you to act. That is- while we still have a free internet. There are many organizations who are currently out there making a difference and standing up to this oppressive force trying to enslave you. Find them...go to Glenn Beck's website, at least. If you are a man, BE A MAN. If you are a woman, you too can act. Women are really leading the way in the "Tea Party" movement now thanks to Sarah Palin, Michelle Bachman and many others...do something.

Start by purchasing a Bible (I suggest the New Living Translation Version). I find its wording to be easy to understand. If you want to challenge yourself, read the New King James Version; I find it to be the most accurate. Then begin reading it the way I suggested in the last chapter.

The next thing I ask you to consider is exactly the same thing that the communists (and even to a degree, Islam) are using against us. They use this method because it truly is the most 'results' based of any approach. This is community organizing. Reach out to one person and get them on board with you. Then the two of you reach out to a third, and so forth. Before you know it you have a small movement in your community. Then a larger one. *This is the only way we will change anything!*

Not all the people that believe in entitlement societies or are democrats are necessarily evil. Most of them are not, and are good people, but have just bought the lies told them by the ones that *are* evil and want dependents for themselves to use. The sad fact is that even *these* people would say disparaging things about someone like Sarah Palin who really represents *them.* Do you know why everyone dislikes her so? They're afraid of her. It is because she represents everything the communists are trying to eradicate. She loves God and gives Him credit for everything good, she loves her family and her country and she is willing to speak out against evil. She would defiantly be my first pick for president of the United States. She is more politically savvy than Herman Cain; I just wish she would run! If she doesn't, Cain it is. He's a wise man. In any event, you're going to decide your future by who you vote for. And you will deserve whatever happens. I wish you well.

Actually, there ARE some other candidates to consider. Michelle Bachman is pretty much as good as Palin and has congressional experience. She has been at the forefront of the Tea Party movement from its inception. She is VERY aware of what is going on and what to do about it. Texas governor Rick Perry is another one that would do the right thing. And, if he runs, former NYC Mayor Rudy Giuliani would be a great president.

Okay,... one last forewarning: Just in case I haven't been convincing enough—I need to inform you about something called Agenda 21. This is the SCARIEST thing to come out of Washington EVER!! (Actually the United Nations). This comes from George H.W. Bush and 177 other world leaders. In 1995 Bill Clinton signed Executive order #12858, creating a Presidential Council on 'Sustainable Development.' This is nothing more than cloaked plans to impose the desires of the uber-rich that want to control the world upon American citizens. The Agenda 21 plan openly targets private property. Remember what I told you in chapter 11? The powers want you all to live in little eco-apartments that are live/work spaces to serve them. Agenda 21 will target Private Property ownership, Single Family homes (THINK ABOUT THE IMPLICATIONS HERE!! You would be FORCED to cohabitate with people you don't know), Private car ownership (You ride a bicycle) and individual travel choices (No, you can't go visit your friends in Delaware this month!) and privately owned farms (You MAY NOT grow your own food!). This UN plan was forced through without congressional approval or the knowledge of the American people. They are saying that private property ownership is an instrument of the accumulation of wealth and, if unchecked, an obstacle to 'social justice' and that land needs to be used in the interest of society as a whole (Which means confiscated by the wealthy elites). The source for this information is the United Nations Conference on Human Settlements (Habitat I) Vancouver, BC, May 31-June 11, 1976.

This has all been brought about by a George Soros funded Open Society project called the Council of Local Environmental Initiatives (ICLEI). Currently in California, Agenda 21 is trying to implement plans to create sustainable management of 'open spaces,' the definition of which has sparked some understandable debates. Agenda 21 is no lover of the free market as evidenced by its desire for PPP's (Private Public Partnerships) where the government decides what businesses get tax breaks. This was recently seen in the way GE (General Electric) was exempted from paying ANY taxes at all for the year 2010! And the White House efforts to tell Boeing what state they can open their plant in (mentioned earlier).

ICLIE was launched in 1995 and now has a network of over 600 cities actively trying to make tangible reductions in greenhouse gas emissions. ICLEI USA is the nation's leader on climate protection and 'sustainable development' at the local level. Well, do you agree with your local government agreeing to regulations set up by a UN based organization that wants private property transferred to government control? As I've been telling you, environmentalism is nothing but a tool to control all the people of the world and establish a global government! My friends this was all laid out in George Orwell's book 1984 and Aldous Huxley's Brave New World. If you are someone that has the ability to think independently at all then start getting involved in your local Tea Party events, sign up at gbtv.com, Glenn Beck's new place as he is leaving Fox News (there is a fee as he IS a capitalist-but it is sooo worth it!) and start getting involved in your future.

I'm telling you right now that all the people I talk about in this book, the communists, homosexuals, the Islamics and the sociopaths are trying to do but one thing, and that is to rid the world of God and create a world after their own fantasies. And that in the present time, they will call anybody who differs with them 'racist,' as this is the tool they use because of their 'divide and conquer' scheme. This is so that dialogue will cease- because they need it to. This is because they have no legitimate foundation for their beliefs, because their desires are evil. That is why they so viciously attack any dissenting views. Ironic that they want to kill off the Jews. I mean isn't *that* racist? They don't care; they're not really against racism, that's just the tool they use. They just want power. They want to be rulers.

Y'know, watching the 'end of the end' really *is* fascinating. The only thing that surprises me is *how* it is happening. I really expected it to be more deep and insidious. I mean, it IS insidious but I just expected it to be, I guess, more intelligent. It is coming down *dumber* than I expected. I guess I forget just how stupid people really are. I guess it has to happen in a way they can understand. I guess if Islam is a part of this than....

I'm seeing our politicians and even individuals arguing and bantering and trying to find either common ground with or trying to convince communists and Islamics that we are right. What this tells me is that I've been right all along and there really are NOT any men left. Please, please tell me that Glenn Beck and myself are not the only men left! Shit, I'm a guy that wanted to be a GIRL!! Look people.....YOU DO NOT NEGOTIATE WITH OUTRIGHT EVIL!!! They're EVIL!! They KNOW IT!! YOU'RE stupid if you argue with them. Don't be so weak! Stand your ground and do not listen to them. *They have nothing to say!* THIS...is how to be a man. And a Christian.

Do you remember what I told you about what the high school kids in Tucson are being taught? So the Jews are the occupiers of Palestinian lands and white Americans (who have always in the past been Christian) are the occupiers of Indian and Mexican lands? So Israeli's and Christian Americans are colonialists and occupiers! Why does it just happen to be these two groups of people? Think about it. Jews and Christians.... Jews and Christians must go. They're in the way. The real 'haters' are giving God his eviction notice. I'm telling you now-this is all spelled out in the bible and I'm also telling you that they will win! And *then*,... it is taken from them and they are cast into eternal torment. This, my friends *must* happen because it is the cleaning out of the chaff. That is how our Lord knows who is his! *You are not going to gain eternal bliss comfortably!* Then we who can love are rewarded with eternal life. Because that's what this is all about...love. God wants people that can love him. This time we are living in *right now* is what this whole project called Earth and humanity has been about for all along. Please my beloved...see that Jesus is love and be on the right side of this when it all comes down, because it will, and very soon. You can see the faces of evil because you can see their anger. And you can see the ones capable of love for their compassion. Be lovers of God even if it becomes very uncomfortable to do so. I want eternal bliss for you, not eternal torment, I love you.

What I am saying is that if I can come out from my darkness and find the light, so can you. You just have to want to. I can't make you want it, you have to need it, and some of you do. Come away from your distractions, and learn to show the qualities the Japanese people displayed after their terrible earthquake. I want to help you do this... because I care. Because the time of the end is *perilously* near. And because...

I love you,... more than words can say.

Bio: Clifford James is a musical composer and an ex-competitive bodybuilder. He went to psychiatric nursing school in 1980 and competed in bodybuilding contests through the eighties. Cliff played in rock bands in the seventies and eighties and studied classical music during the nineties. In the late nineties, Cliff found Christ and began writing music that echoed his new worldview. He studied politics from 2008 to 2011, which had been a passion since grade school. He went to broadcasting school in 2010 and began writing a series of monologues which, upon becoming numerous enough to form a book, became *this* book. Its goal is to reach the uninitiated in Christianity. Cliff wants to be convincing enough to reach people like himself, who grew up listening to rock music and unwittingly succumbed to communist propaganda. He feels that he's been called to teach them about Christianity and how to avoid being used to promote a dependent society.

Email   cliffordjames77@gmail.com

Buisiness Email   mccarrell333@yahoo.com

www.ingramcontent.com/pod-product-compliance
Lightning Source LLC
Chambersburg PA
CBHW071321310526
45789CB00015B/78